REPUBLICAN
THEOLOGY

REPUBLICAN THEOLOGY

The Civil Religion of American Evangelicals

BENJAMIN T. LYNERD

OXFORD
UNIVERSITY PRESS

OXFORD

UNIVERSITY PRESS

Oxford University Press is a department of the University of Oxford.
It furthers the University's objective of excellence in research, scholarship,
and education by publishing worldwide.

Oxford   New York

Auckland   Cape Town   Dar es Salaam   Hong Kong   Karachi
Kuala Lumpur   Madrid   Melbourne   Mexico City   Nairobi
New Delhi   Shanghai   Taipei   Toronto

With offices in

Argentina   Austria   Brazil   Chile   Czech Republic   France   Greece
Guatemala   Hungary   Italy   Japan   Poland   Portugal   Singapore
South Korea   Switzerland   Thailand   Turkey   Ukraine   Vietnam

Oxford is a registered trade mark of Oxford University Press
in the UK and certain other countries.

Published in the United States of America by
Oxford University Press
198 Madison Avenue, New York, NY 10016

Library of Congress Cataloging-in-Publication Data
Lynerd, Benjamin T.
Republican theology : the civil religion of American evangelicals / Benjamin T. Lynerd.
p.   cm.
Includes bibliographical references and index.
ISBN 978-0-19-936355-1 (hardcover : alk. paper) — ISBN 978-0-19-936356-8 (pbk. : alk.
paper) 1. Evangelicalism—United States—History. 2. Church and state—United States—
History. 3. Christianity and politics—United States—History. 4. Liberty—Religious aspects—
Christianity. 5. Second Great Awakening. 6. Religious right—United States. 7. Republican
Party (U.S. : 1854–) I. Title.
BR1642.U5L96 2014
322'.10973—dc23
2014005412

1 3 5 7 9 8 6 4 2

Printed in the United States of America on acid-free paper

TO HELEN-JOY

ACKNOWLEDGMENTS

Every author's first monograph should get as much coaching and cheerleading as has been lavished on this one over the past two years. I completed the book in the course of a postdoctoral fellowship with the Benjamin Franklin Project at the Illinois Institute of Technology, a fellowship that afforded not only time and resources for research, but extensive scholarly support as well, culminating in a symposium on the newly completed manuscript in April 2013. The eminent political scientists, philosophers, historians, and theologians at that symposium served as the book's first readers, and many revisions owe to their incisive feedback on the first draft. Any book that attempts a multidisciplinary argument, as this one does, must lean heavily on the critical input from scholars across several different fields, making this symposium, and the informative discussions that ensued, all the more vital. Thus my sincere gratitude goes out to Mark Noll, Robert Gooding-Williams, William Howell, Clare Rothschild, Andrew Murphy, Bryan McGraw, Daniel Strand, Marc LiVecche, and Daniel Bliss.

The Director of the Benjamin Franklin Project, Christena Nippert-Eng, has provided counsel and encouragement throughout the book's many phases. The Franklin Project is sponsored by the Jack Miller Center, which has done so much to advance the study of American Political Thought over the past decade; Pamela Edwards, its Director of Academic Programs, serves as a valued mentor to many Miller Center postdocs, including me.

Several other trusted colleagues have offered guidance on the book, including Kevin Schultz, Sultan Tepe, Dick Simpson, and Stephen Engelmann at the University of Illinois, as well as Jill White, Gerad Gentry, John Mulholland, and David George, who read through the manuscript in its later stages. The Moody Bible Institute in Chicago and its Public Services Librarian, Amy Koehler, provided me much-needed access to its Archives. From start to finish, the composition of this book has relied most profoundly on the clear-eyed wisdom of Helen-Joy Lynerd, who not only edited numerous drafts, but also inspired and enabled my work on it day after day.

Benjamin T. Lynerd
March 2014

CONTENTS

REPUBLICAN
THEOLOGY

INTRODUCTION

PROLOGUE

On October 11, 2012, less than four weeks before Barack Obama's election to a second presidential term, his Republican opponent Mitt Romney paid a visit to the Montreat, North Carolina, home of Billy Graham. The point of the visit was to win a measure of acceptance among evangelicals for the devoutly Mormon candidate. The genial photograph of Romney chatting with the world's most famous Christian in his living room would probably have sufficed, but Graham (or at least his representatives) went a step further, issuing a caption for the snapshot that praised Romney's character and urged Christians to "vote for candidates who will support a biblical definition of marriage, protect the sanctity of life, and defend our religious freedoms." No sooner did this near endorsement reach the press, however, when various news organizations drew attention to the fact that Billy Graham's website lists Romney's faith as an anti-Christian "religious cult." In a move that only amplified attention to the matter, the Billy Graham Evangelical Association scrubbed the offending "cult" reference off the website the next morning, sending bloggers in search of Google web caches of the old page.[1]

In the space of day, the aging evangelist found himself engulfed in a minor scandal. Religious conservatives accused him of compromising his theology for "political expediency," while liberals took in the spectacle of his inconsistency and backpedaling. More than anything,

critics from all sides were shocked that this icon of nonpartisan salvation, whose image as a spiritual counselor to *all* presidents "set him
above the ebb and flow of history," would inject his voice so candidly
into a presidential contest.[2]

Leaving aside the ham-fisted revision of the website, the criticisms
directed at Graham overlook much of his record as a public figure.
They fail to recall his role in recruiting Dwight Eisenhower to the
Republican Party in 1952 and his active campaigning for Richard
Nixon in 1968; and they forget that Graham's courtly style of evangelism nevertheless always drew plain lines in the sand as to what he
counted as true Christianity. Billy Graham in his younger years would
not have avoided the swamp of party politics if he felt his voice was
needed, nor hesitated to support a candidate while also marking their
religious differences. These were all compatible elements of his calling
as an American evangelist.[3]

Graham's mission was always twofold: from the late 1940s onward
Graham stood at the headwaters of two distinct revivals in American
religion. One was a revival of evangelicalism in the style of the First
Great Awakening (*ca.* 1735–1750), a revival that saw millions of individuals commit themselves to personal faith in Jesus Christ, hundreds
of thousands alone at Billy Graham's rallies over the decades. The other
was a revival of American *civil* religion, a nonsectarian recovery of
private morality as a public concern, more in line with the Second
Great Awakening (*ca.* 1810–1835). There are deep, even oppositional,
differences between these two types of revival. Nonetheless, Graham's
unique approach was to treat them as twins of almost equal importance, mutually dependent for support. And although the old-school
Southern Baptist maintained his party registration as a Democrat,
Graham tended to find the Republicans more willing to serve as the
standard-bearers of American civil religion. Indeed, he played a strong
hand in winning Republicans over to the cause.

EVANGELICAL CIVIL RELIGION IN AMERICA

American civil religion—the attempt to spiritualize the nation's shared
political values—forms the broad subject of this book. Civil religion,
broadly construed, needn't find its moorings in Christianity, or in any

other traditional faith for that matter. It refers only to a consensus of deeply held commitments among diverse citizens. Indeed, Jean-Jacques Rousseau, who first articulated the concept of a *religion civile* in his *Du Contrat Social* (1762), intended it as a departure from Christian dogma, believing that citizens of a free republic should hold only to the general existence of a "provident Divinity, the life to come, the happiness of the just, the punishment of the wicked, the sanctity of the social contract and the laws."[4] Thomas Jefferson promoted an American civil religion that elevates the freedom of conscience itself as the preeminent value of public life, a value supported not just by a constitutional framework but also by a tolerant frame of mind among citizens.[5] Kick-starting the discourse on civil religion in the late-modern age, Robert Bellah (1967) latched onto Jefferson's words in the Declaration of Independence— that people's rights are "endowed by their Creator"—as the central creed of American civil religion and the reason why the republic has survived so many crises.[6] Nevertheless, people from different religious backgrounds, even within the same republic, are bound to conceptualize the nation's civil religion in different ways. This book considers the approach to civil religion undertaken by American evangelicals.

Even this narrower subject matter, of course, is much larger than Billy Graham. Evangelical civil religion originated with the American Founding, in churches and at rallies during the Revolutionary War; its theological roots stretch even earlier. Its formative influence on American culture and politics over the decades has drawn the attention of European sociologists like Alexis de Tocqueville and Max Weber.[7] In substance, evangelical civil religion in America has historically supported two broad agendas, the first being the aforementioned emphasis on private morality as a public matter, which as Andrew Murphy notes in *Prodigal Nation: Moral Decline and Divine Punishment from New England to 9/11* (2009), stems from a belief in America's status as a "chosen nation," a belief espoused by Christian settlers in the New World long before the Revolution.[8] The second agenda, which took pride of place during and after the Revolution, is a pronounced affinity for republican liberty and limited government. This attachment to a quasi-libertarian sensibility carries implications for a wide range of policy issues. While American evangelicals have long promoted moral causes, from temperance and anti-obscenity in the nineteenth century to abstinence education in the twentieth, they have also aligned themselves on many other seemingly unrelated agendas—in support of the Revolution in the 1770s, on antislavery in the 1820s, against labor unionism in the 1880s, against the New Deal in the 1930s, on assertive anticommunism in the 1950s (a major theme in Billy Graham's early sermons), and in favor of deregulation and lower taxes in the 1980s.

Indeed, the rise of the "New Right" movement at the end of the twentieth century had as much to do with small-government ideology as with a recovery of traditional morality. In this light, Mitt Romney never really needed Graham's backing to win the evangelical vote: his platform, with commitments to traditional marriage *and* to lowering income taxes, was already tailored to their priorities. Accordingly, he finished the 2012 race with 78 percent of the evangelical vote, a proportion comparable to Ronald Reagan's share in 1980. Had Romney carried Roman Catholics by a similar margin he would have won the election.[9]

If the ideology of American evangelicals—a libertarian ethos combined with restrictive public moralism—seems conflicted, that is because it *is* conflicted, a point not lost on critics of evangelical politics. Evangelicals are routinely called out for "loving small government, except when it comes to people's personal lives."[10] A few minutes browsing the Huffington Post yields abundant critiques of this variety: "The faithful are more intent on fighting evolution than fighting poverty," writes one contributor.[11] "Do you see the political hypocrisy?" writes another. "The Christian Right votes for candidates who are antiabortion and antigay because it believes we must pass laws to protect marriage and protect life (at least embryonic life), but it is unwilling to apply the same principle to 'Obamacare.' Infants in the womb have a right to life, but apparently adults do not have a right to life-saving medical care."[12] This cognitive dissonance, furthermore, creates practical strain both within the New Right alliance—true libertarians deplore the moral agenda—and within the church, particularly among evangelicals interested in social justice. "How did the faith of Jesus come to be known as pro-rich?" demands Jim Wallis, a lonely voice on the "evangelical left."[13]

Its detractors notwithstanding, this dual commitment runs deep among American evangelicals. For evidence of this one needs to look no further than the Faith and Freedom Coalition, the leading Christian Right organization of the 2010s. Ralph Reed, a veteran of New Right politics, launched the coalition in the early months of the Obama presidency, just in time to lend his experience in grassroots campaigning to the insurgent Tea Party movement. Within a year of its founding, the coalition had 500,000 contributing members (60 percent evangelical) with 350 local chapters nationwide; its volunteers made 15.3 million phone calls for Republicans in the 2010 midterm elections. Every single contender for the Republican presidential nomination made appearances at Faith and Freedom Forums in 2011 and 2012.[14]

Its very name, "Faith and Freedom," reveals the civil dogma to which the Coalition adheres, namely a belief that religious faith and individual freedom are vital elements of American life. The "common sense values" which bind its members include "respect for the sanctity and dignity of life, family, and marriage as the foundations of a free society," "limited government, lower taxes and fiscal responsibility to unleash the creative energy of entrepreneurs," and "free markets and free minds to create opportunity for all."[15] The fusion of free-market values with traditional morality, in other words, occupies the center of gravity for evangelical civil religion in America.

REPUBLICAN THEOLOGY

Explanations as to *how* evangelicals manage to straddle two seemingly different value systems tend to focus on the dynamics of social movements. It is accepted wisdom in political science that rational political actors seek to maximize their power, an assumption that applies to both grassroots social activism and coalition-building in electoral systems. On this logic, evangelicals and free-market libertarians see their way clear to join forces, overcoming whatever differences they have, in order to advance their own respective agendas. Sara Diamond's *Roads to Dominion* (1995), Daniel K. Williams' *God's Own Party: The Making of the Christian Right* (2010), and Darren Dochuk's *From Bible Belt to Sunbelt: Plain-Folk Religion, Grassroots Politics, and the Rise of Evangelical Conservatism* (2011) all fill in the intricate historical record of how the alliance between evangelicals and political conservatives took shape in the late twentieth century.

American evangelicals, however, exhibit an affinity for free-market values that extends beyond tactical motivations. They actually believe—and have long believed—in the value of limited government as a spiritual matter and do not consider it hypocritical to make an exception for public moral standards. "To elevate society," said one preacher in 1820s, "and to bring out the human energies in a well-ordered state of things, the mass of mankind must be enlightened and qualified for self-government."[16] Thus the duality engrained in evangelical civil religion has a life quite apart from (and prior to) whatever political alliances were forged in the late twentieth century. An explanation beyond party politics, in other words, is needed to make sense of this tradition.[17] This book ventures a theological explanation, or, more precisely, an explanation that examines the *political theology* of American evangelicals.

Political theology is the doctrinal substance that conveys a particular faith tradition into the public square. It is that which informs political values from within the sacred tradition itself; it marks the distance between private faith and civil religion. This book argues that the civil religion of American evangelicals originates in a political theology that sees limited government as a condition for a thriving church, but also predicates the health of the republic on the church's capacity to elevate civic virtue, an impulse that cuts against the libertarian grain. How evangelicals navigate this logic, which I call "republican theology," forms the entire subtext of their participation in American politics, from the 1770s into the twenty-first century.

The logic of republican theology, at least on its face, resolves the tension between limited government and moralism by subjecting them both to a higher purpose. Republican theology holds that God confers the right to liberty on humanity for the purpose of its sanctification: only in free societies can citizens cultivate Christian virtue, and only a virtuous citizenry can sustain a free society. "Liberty is the parent," went a sermon of the Revolutionary era, "of truth, justice, virtue, patriotism, benevolence, and every generous and noble purpose of the soul. Under the influence of liberty, the arts and sciences, trade, commerce, and husbandry flourish and the wilderness blossoms like the rose."[18] Exponents of republican theology, including John Witherspoon (1723–1794), Abraham Keteltas (1732–1798), Benjamin Rush (1746–1813), Timothy Dwight (1752–1817), Lyman Beecher (1775–1863), Charles Grandison Finney (1792–1875), Henry Ward Beecher (1813–1887), Newman Smyth (1843–1925), Whittaker Chambers (1901–1961), Harold Ockenga (1905–1985), Francis Schaeffer (1912–1984), Billy Graham (1919–), Jerry Falwell (1933–2007),

Os Guinness (1941–), Ralph Reed (1961–), and countless of their disciples, deal in two-sided coins, on one side celebrating America's dual advantages in its faith traditions and freedom, and on the other warning against the moral lapses that could squander those blessings and make the country vulnerable to both internal and external threats. While their sermons do not form an obvious "canon"—in the sense of later preachers citing earlier preachers by name (they are all more prone to cite Washington, Madison, and Jesus)—the figures above nevertheless converge on definite commitments beyond the traditional evangelical gospel. To examine the political theology of these figures is to expose a distinct school of thought, one that predicates republican liberty, private virtue, and the Christian faith upon each other. Os Guinness calls it "the golden triangle of freedom" in *A Free People's Suicide: Sustainable Freedom and the American Future* (2012), a recent polemic in the tradition of republican theology. "Freedom requires virtue," writes Guinness, "which requires faith, which requires freedom, and so on, like the recycling triangle, ad infinitum."[19]

PRÉCIS

This book offers an account of republican theology as the driving force of evangelical civil religion in America. It begins, in **Chapter 1**, by locating evangelicals on the ideological map in American politics, a task that at the outset involves delineating the doctrinal and sociological contours of the evangelical community in America, as well as the ideological contours of the American right wing. This chapter also gives attention to the pragmatic tensions in the New Right alliance and surveys the historical accounts of this coalition before suggesting the need for a theological account.

Chapter 2 defines and examines republican theology, the political theology that informs evangelical civil religion and thereby seeks to unite republican liberty and Christian morality in a common cause. Conceptual tensions remain, however—between the imperatives of limited government and the promotion of common standards in private morality, between moralism and the evangelical gospel of grace, and between the Bible and the belief that life, liberty, and property make up the essence of universal human rights.

Chapter 3 documents the origins of republican theology in covenant theology, the radical model for politics of the Protestant reformation. Covenant theology holds to a collectivist and teleological view of society, a belief that God exerts redemptive influence on a sinful world through the church. Ironically, it was the seventeenth-century experiments in covenantal politics—in Puritan New England and during the English Civil War—that inspired the social contract theories of Thomas Hobbes and John Locke as antidotes to the problems that arise in a covenantal society. The chapter offers an interpretation of the early Scottish Enlightenment as an attempt at a post-covenantal theology, reconciling the social contract theory of Locke with the moral imperatives of reformed Christianity. The "moral sense" philosophy of Scottish Presbyterians like Francis Hutcheson, and later John Witherspoon, envisions a society committed to high moral standards with the aid of the church, albeit within a system of limited government that protects individual liberty.

It is the Scottish tradition that gets transposed into republican theology during the Revolutionary era in America, largely on Witherspoon's influence. **Chapter 4** shows the early development of republican theology in the teachings of John Witherspoon, who moved to America from Scotland in 1768 to serve as president of the College of New Jersey, and in the writings of Benjamin Rush, a doctor and social reformer in the early republic. Republican theology, the chapter emphasizes, had to overcome the evangelical gospel of the First Great Awakening, which took a dim view of human perfectibility. Jonathan Edwards, the leading theologian of that revival, strongly resisted the Scottish Enlightenment and the philosophy of commonsense. How Witherspoon and Rush each manage their transitions from traditional evangelical faith to republican theology reveals much about the birth of evangelical civil religion in America.

At no point did republican theology dominate the American psyche more pervasively, however, than during the Second Great Awakening. During the early nineteenth century a growing catalogue of sins—hard drinking, Sabbath breaking, dueling, and an ever more depraved system of chattel slavery in the South—shook the conscience of American clergy, raising their anxieties over the fate of the republic. Republican theology took root as a source of apprehension and as an incentive for reform: if Americans failed to achieve godly virtue, went the rationale, God would withdraw his blessing from the nation, and

Americans would cease to be free. **Chapter 5** documents the influence of republican theology on the diverse revival movements of this period. Even as these movements gathered steam, however, the tensions embedded in republican theology manifested in conflicts within American Christianity over the priorities of moral reform, over the theology of sin, and over the question of whether slaveholding constitutes a violation of God's law—a debate that pit the Bible itself against republican theology and would ultimately form the theological subtext of the Civil War.

The final chapters trace the journey of republican theology in the century and a half following the war, from its late nineteenth-century adaptation to free-market ideology in **Chapter 6** to its role in shaping late twentieth-century New Right politics in **Chapter 7**. These chapters unfold a surprising twist in the narrative: Republican theology remained the dominant political theology of American evangelicals throughout this entire period, but it did so by successfully migrating from a liberal to a more conservative brand of evangelicalism. The free-market theologians of the 1880s—Henry Ward Beecher and Newman Smyth, for example—were also the leading liberals of day, opposed on economic philosophy by the equally liberal Social Gospel theologians, and on Bible doctrine by the Christian fundamentalists. The quadrant that stood virtually empty at the turn of the twentieth century was the box for fundamentalists who also loved the free market (Social Gospel types could count William Jennings Bryan among their fundamentalist supporters). The story of how this empty quadrant got filled, told in Chapter 7, is also the story of how Christian fundamentalism overtook the evangelical moniker and gained mainstream status. In short, as religious conservatives embraced republican theology they found their way back into American culture and politics.

This final chapter takes a brief but telling detour to consider the Civil Rights movement and its relationship to evangelicalism. The limitations of republican theology for this particular issue come to light in an exchange between eight white Birmingham ministers and Martin Luther King in the spring of 1963, an exchange that culminated in King's *Letter from Birmingham Jail*. The letter highlights not only a moment of drift for evangelical politics in America (an intermission in the dramatic rise of the New Right) but also the relative silence of republican theology in the face of structural injustice, a silence that has proved a vexing source of tension throughout its history.

PREVIEWING THE ARCHIVE: WHO SPEAKS
FOR AMERICAN EVANGELICALS?

Political theology is the discipline of extrapolating political values from religious beliefs and finds expression in literatures as diverse as papal encyclicals and Islamic fatwa. One comes across Protestant expressions in large works of systematic theology (Calvin's *Institutes of the Christian Religion*, for instance) and political philosophy (Johannes Althusius's *Politica*, 1603, is one of the earliest; Nicholas Wolterstorff's *Justice: Rights and Wrongs* appeared in 2008) as well as in small-form sermons, devotionals, pamphlets, and even political speeches and newspaper columns. This diversity yields an archive of rich and varied ideas on politics. For the intellectual historian venturing a substantive description of Protestant political theology, or even that of a subgroup (like American evangelicals), this range presents a challenge: *Who speaks for the tradition at large? Which voices are authoritative on political theology?*

These questions are neither trivial nor easily answered. As the sociologist Christian Smith notes, the "most common error that observers of evangelicals make is to presume that evangelical leaders speak as representatives of ordinary evangelicals . . . The relationship between evangelical elites and common believers is much more complex than that."[20] What makes it complex is not just the fact that the evangelical community is geographically, economically, ideologically and even theologically diverse, but also the fact that the leadership within this community is quite stratified. Local pastors represent perhaps the most influential and representative group of leaders within the evangelical community, although they are rarely studied by social scientists as a group. Nevertheless, local ministers also form the pool from which *national* elites generally surface. Lacking an institutional framework that would provide an intellectual core, American evangelicals tend to find their national leaders through what Andrew Murphy calls "a lively religious marketplace," in which individuals gain stature not by ascending a church hierarchy, but by attracting large audiences to their churches, tent meetings, radio shows, or television broadcasts or by selling a lot of books.[21] Many of the figures addressed in this study, from Charles Grandison Finney in the nineteenth century to Billy Graham in the twentieth, attained elite standing through these means.

In addition to elites *within* the religious community, some evangelicals also achieve elite status in American society at large, working their way into influential positions in politics, academics, business, the arts, athletics, and the news media. Indeed, D. Michael Lindsay's *Faith in the Halls of Power: How Evangelicals Joined the American Elite* (2007) suggests that the cultural influence of evangelicals in the twenty-first century has reached historic proportions. Evangelicals "are prominent in virtually every aspect of American life today," he marvels.[22] In fact, evangelicals have jockeyed for influence over culture and public discourse throughout American history; the elevation of Timothy Dwight to the presidency of Yale in 1795, the many runs for the U.S. presidency by William Jennings Bryan, and Billy Graham's access to various U.S. presidents offer just a few examples that attest to this pattern. The pattern, however, only accentuates the methodological problem that Smith raises: these elites, though affecting to bring evangelicalism to bear on their spheres of influence, cannot fully represent the views of American evangelicals. They should never be taken to speak for evangelicals, even though they often are.

The aggregate views of ordinary evangelicals, of course, can be measured through survey data, provided the survey accurately defines the boundaries of the evangelical community. Chapter 1 of this book examines a wide range of survey data on the political attitudes of American evangelicals. This information largely confirms the premise of *Republican Theology*—that evangelicals favor "free-market" values more highly than other religious groups in the United States. This kind of information, however, reveals only surface-level opinions, not the reasoning (much less the theology) behind those opinions. For a deeper perspective, we might conduct interviews of survey respondents with questions that probe their positions on political theology. While such a study could certainly generate interesting results, its explanatory force would still be limited to present-day believers.

For both historical breadth and intellectual depth, we can only turn to the vast archive of published works on evangelical political theology—the "elites." Hence, a few words in defense of the archive consulted in this book are in order. First, it should be stated plainly that *Republican Theology* does *not* set out to depict evangelical political theology as homogeneous or to prove that republican theology consistently operates as the dominant tradition within it. It does not, in other words, presume that any of the authors cited below "speak for" the evangelicals of their era. On the contrary, the evidence presented in this book suggests that evangelicals have long made their political theology a matter of contention. Instead, the book sets out to document the influence of republican theology on evangelical attitudes toward civil religion. To show this, the book locates the premises of republican theology operating in a *variety* of texts over the course of American history. It observes, for instance, John Witherspoon incorporating the logic of republican theology into his *Lectures on Moral Philosophy* at Princeton in the 1760s and then observes the resurfacing of these arguments in the reform pamphlets of Benjamin Rush in the 1780s, in the pro-temperance sermons of Lyman Beecher in the 1820s, in the anti-New Deal editorials in *Moody Monthly* in the 1930s, in Frances Schaeffer's *How Then Should We Live?* in 1976, and in dozens of other texts. The key to this book's archive is its attention to the full bandwidth of evangelical literature, which stretches from countryside sermons to bestselling books.

Secondly, *Republican Theology* takes pains to provide historical context for the pieces it analyzes. It does so in order to identify the audience and to suggest the possible reach of the work. If it is a fallacy to assume that an elite voice can speak for all evangelicals, it is also a fallacy to assume that elite voices emerge only by fluke, revealing nothing about the broader evangelical culture. As Michael Lienesch notes in the introduction to *Redeeming America: Piety and Politics in the New Christian Right* (1993), "the differences between those who write [evangelical] books and those who read them may be considerably smaller than in other comparable groups."[23] The responsible approach to analyzing the force of popular texts within evangelical culture is to incorporate its readers or listeners into the story. Thus, the fact that Witherspoon's students at Princeton included scores of Presbyterian ministers who would serve in pulpits across Pennsylvania and New Jersey during the Revolutionary War raises the likelihood that his sudden endorsement of Scottish moral sense reverberated well beyond Princeton. The fact that Beecher and Finney preached to hundreds and circulated their sermons to thousands more suggests a level of currency for their ideas in the religious marketplace of the time. And the fact that Billy Graham began his 1949 Los Angeles rally right after the discovery of Russia's new atomic bomb helps to explain why his explicit connections between Christian morality and the blessings of living in a free society drew so many Americans into the tent for weeks on end. As it examines the political content of theological texts, then, *Republican Theology* seeks to make an historical case for the texts' significance.

A CROSSROAD OF INQUIRIES

Although this book sets out to answer a single question—why American evangelicals preach limited government—this one question places it at the crossroads of other important conversations in the social sciences, history, philosophy, and theology. The limited-government ethos of evangelicals, for instance, provides a subtext for certain sociological mysteries, such as why evangelical churches in America maintain such entrenched racial divisions in the twenty-first century, as well as certain mysteries in political science, like why some Roman Catholic politicians perform so well among evangelical voters.[24] The book also interacts with many figures and events of American religious history and offers a new explanatory framework for understanding certain developments, like the denominational schisms of the 1830s and 1840s, the positive reception of Darwinism in the late nineteenth century, and the rise of the National Association of Evangelicals in the 1940s. Students of history who read this book will almost certainly bring to mind other historical phenomena on which republican theology might shed some light (or vice versa). Rather than a work of history, however, *Republican Theology* serves as an introduction to a genre, submitting to the reader the existence of a rich and problematic tradition in American religious history, a tradition worthy of further exploration and critique.

The book's principal contributions are to the fields of political philosophy and theology. *Republican Theology*, first of all, helps to explain American founding philosophy, the role of Christianity in its formation, and the broader comingling of individualism and religious piety in American thought. Inquiry into these matters could be said to originate with Alexis de Tocqueville, who made frequent observations about American religion and its simultaneous promotion and restraint of individualism.[25] Contemporary philosophers still puzzle over this duality, particularly in light of religion's enduring influence on American culture. James E. Block, whose *A Nation of Agents* (2002) reads like an American variation on Charles Taylor's epic *Sources of the Self: The Making of Modern Identity*

(1989), argues that the "the foundational importance of Anglo-American Protestantism" stems from both its covenantal collectivism and its "new understanding of the individual."[26] James Morone, in *Hellfire Nation: The Politics of Sin in American History* (2003), frames the puzzle as an artifact of the Puritan legacy: "The Puritans bequeathed America two different answers to that moral bottom line—Who do we blame for trouble, the sinner or the society? The Puritans believed in blaming both. Salvation and perdition fell on individual souls; however, the Puritan covenants held the entire community responsible. In time, the two halves of the equation—the individual and the community—split."[27]

The perplexing development is that *both* halves of the Puritan legacy appear to live on. George McKenna, in *The Puritan Origins of American Patriotism* (2007), argues that the communitarian side of Puritanism quietly endures in Americans' moral activism and in their "pious attachment" to the founding narrative.[28] Sounding a more alarmist note, David Sehat, in *The Myth of American Religious Freedom* (2011), suggests that the Puritan ethos of religious manipulation prevailed *against* the imperatives of individual liberty from the start—and continues to do so. "Protestant Christian influence in U.S. history," he writes, is "long-standing, widespread, and, from the perspective of dissenters, coercive." Sehat, moreover, characterizes the social justice activists of American history, including abolitionists, women's rights advocates, and socialists, as religious "dissenters" at their core.[29]

Republican Theology certainly casts a skeptical light on this characterization, noting the involvement of serious evangelicals in a variety of reform movements, including abolitionism, temperance, labor, and even socialism. More importantly, however, the book offers a clear narrative that explains *how* many American Christians bundled the concepts of individual liberty and religious morality into a unified ideology. Founding-era evangelicals, it argues, self-consciously rejected the covenantal ethics of Puritan theology in favor of a new paradigm that embraced republican liberty as that which best guarantees that individual citizens will take responsibility for the spiritual health of the nation. The book spells out in concrete historical detail—without demystifying—the new fusion of moral and libertarian imperatives that gripped the evangelical conscience at the founding and long thereafter. It documents a continual endeavor among evangelicals to embrace a civil religion that is morally robust while also affirming the essential liberty of the individual. The approach may well be precarious and contradictory, but it nevertheless represents an observable tradition within American political thought. In effect, this book is an American *evangelical* version of Taylor's *Sources*, telling the story of their particular ontological evolution.

Finally, *Republican Theology* offers something to the discipline of evangelical political theology, assigning a name, for starters, to a tradition that has until now marched to a subconscious drumbeat.[30] More than this, by showcasing this tradition in a wide variety of literatures, the book shines an interesting set of footlights on the political theology emerging from the academy. It is far from accidental that the era of New Right ideology in America has also witnessed a vigorous debate among Christian philosophers around the world on the compatibility of natural rights with theology. Prominent voices in the academy, including MacIntyre, Stanley Hauerwas, Oliver O'Donovan, and Joan Lockwood O'Donovan, have contended against the modern liberal framework and, by extension, against the very idea of rights, arguing for alternative ways of conceiving justice that elevate the Christian's identity within the church—and elevate the redemptive role of the church in society. Hauerwas, in *The Peaceable Kingdom: A Primer in Christian Ethics* (1983), gives it to Christians, not to celebrate the bourgeois virtues and rights of a free republic, but rather to be "peaceable among themselves and with the world, so that the world sees what it means to hope for God's kingdom. Such a people do not believe that everyone is free to do whatever they will, but that we are each called upon to develop our particular gifts to serve the community of faith."[31]

The idea of natural rights, however, also has its defenders among contemporary Christian philosophers. Nicholas Wolterstorff, in *Justice: Rights and Wrongs* (2008), maintains that universal human rights do indeed have their basis in the Hebrew and Christian scriptures and that human rights offer the only reliable mechanism for securing the "good life" that God wants for all of humanity.[32] Yet Wolterstorff also insists that the good life, as described in the scriptures, consists in a great deal more than being left alone by the state. The simple protections of life, liberty, and property that define the liberal framework, in other words, do not even begin to approximate "what God desires for [a] person's life and history." Thus the assumptions of republican theology come in for regular criticism across a wide spectrum of contemporary Christian philosophy, by both critics *and* defenders of human rights.

To these philosophers *Republican Theology* poses a unique challenge, one that highlights an apparent wedge between the academy and the pulpit in the American evangelical world. In one sense, Christian philosophy has moved past the raw tenets of republican theology and has brought into play richer theories of justice from within the Christian scriptures. In another sense, it hasn't, at least in any way that brings ordinary believers into a paradigm-shifting conversation. Republican theology, this book argues, maintains a conspicuous grip on the evangelical conscience in America. It has a long history and continues to find reiteration in the popular Christian press. Whenever political pundits, moreover, predict the demise of the evangelical–libertarian alliance, as they did at the end of the Cold War and again at the conclusion of the second Bush presidency, the alliance reasserts itself in the electoral arena. To change the way American evangelicals think about politics requires philosophers to confront not only the limitations of republican theology, but also its appeal.

Accordingly, the basic contribution this book makes—in each of these various disciplines—is to expose political theology as a factor of influence in politics. Political theology comprises a vast and influential literature, and yet its impact on electoral behavior, constitutional design, political rhetoric, social activism, and a range of other phenomena is not well documented, which means that one major key to understanding the relationship between religion and politics remains mysterious within the social sciences. This book attempts, with some risk, two projects in one with respect to evangelical political theology. First, it documents the presence of a particular school of thought within the American church, as a nearly constant fixture for more than two centuries. Second, it proposes a way to critique this school of thought. This book sees republican theology as an intellectual tradition that may be evaluated both on the terms of its own source theology *and* on the terms of the political system in which it operates. As such, this book invites political scientists to the discipline of political theology. If the secular scholar is (rightly) reluctant to critique a private faith tradition, this study suggests a way to at least critique *how* that tradition finds its way to the public square.

AMERICAN
EVANGELICALS
AS LOCKEANS

As the American political spectrum took form in the twenti-eth century, white evangelical Protestants gradually aligned with the right wing, forging an ideological bond that many journalists, politicians, and clergy now take for granted, and justly so. As an electoral bloc, the evangelical community maintains a level of conformity unmatched by Roman Catholics and Mainline Protestants, rivaled only by the attachment of African American Protestants to the Democrats.[1] The "evangelical left," while vocal, operates mostly as a protest on the fringes of the church.

The "New Right" coalition has a complicated biography. Daniel K. Williams, in *God's Own Party: The Making of the Christian Right* (2010), credits the march of Soviet communism, the mounting intrusiveness of the federal government, and the sexual revolution in the 1960s with creating conditions for a broad conservative reaction, the full extent of which astute politicians like Ronald Reagan understood and exploited. Williams also details the gradual development of a national evangelical identity and the strategic decisions of evangelical leaders in the late 1970s to work across denominational boundaries and into the fray of electoral politics.[2] Darren Dochuk's *From Bible Belt to Sunbelt: Plain-Folk Religion, Grassroots Politics, and the Rise of Evangelical Conservatism*

(2011) covers the same decades and trends as Williams does, but within the microcosm of Southern California, which saw an influx of some three million white Southerners in the wake of the Great Depression. Enriched by entrepreneurial success, Dochuk argues, these migrants blended their conservative religion with the "democratic promises of pristine capitalism," planting churches, private grade schools, and universities to promote these values, and becoming an early bastion of support for Reagan and the New Right ideal in the 1960s.[3]

Underlying the circumstances that gave rise to the New Right, however, is something more elemental—an intellectual affinity between the American brand of evangelicalism and the American brand of right-wing politics. Both traditions, on their own terms, embrace the Lockean philosophy of limited government, a principle with deep roots in American culture, and one that turns out to be a powerful common denominator. For American evangelicals, this book will argue, the commitment to limited government is an article of "republican theology," a tradition that has permeated their worldview since the American founding, long before libertarianism took its place as the North Star of the American right. The alignment that took shape in the twentieth century, in other words, was not accidental: evangelicals showed up to the philosophical battle between liberty and equality with their loyalties to the former well in place (if momentarily shaken by the Great Depression); their version of American civil religion had already sanctified individual liberty as a practical extension of the gospel.

Not that republican theology matches the libertarian credo line by line: American evangelicals have constructed their own rendering of the Lockean social contract, one that predicates the health of the republic upon the virtue of its citizens. This presents a dilemma—how to promote virtue without undermining individual liberty—that hovers in the background of evangelical politics and generates tensions within the right wing. Nevertheless, evangelicals regularly fuse these values, fighting for the rights of liberty and property even as they seek to reform American culture through moral activism.

Before unfolding republican theology and its story, some preliminary discussions will need to set the stage. In particular, the project needs to situate the evangelical community as a stable but autonomous constituent of the American right wing, a task that demands a clear description of these various species. This opening chapter offers a portrait of American evangelicals as a religious community, one of the New Right flank in America, evidence of their alignment; an overview of the moral activism that would appear to undercut evangelicals' alliance with libertarians; and finally, a consideration of the variables that withstand this tension, all of which point to the unique political theology of American evangelicals.

I. AMERICAN EVANGELICALS AS A RELIGIOUS COMMUNITY

Protestant evangelicals form a group whose identity—grounded in a gospel of individual conversion—involves a tacit rather than formal membership. The community can be difficult to demarcate within a given society. There is no official church; instead, evangelicalism forms a spray of subcultures within various denominations and nondenominational congregations. David Bebbington calls it a "wine that has been poured into many bottles."[4] Theologically, the evangelical tradition has long straddled one of the deepest divides within Protestant Christianity—between Calvinist believers in the doctrine of divine election and Arminian believers in the human capacity for free will. The staunchly Calvinist George Whitefield and the even more staunchly Arminian John Wesley, evangelists during the First Great Awakening, never allowed their doctrinal disputes, however publicly aired, to interfere with their shared goal of converting people to faith in Jesus. The best-known evangelical of the twentieth century, Billy Graham, made it a point never to lure his listeners—even his Roman Catholic listeners—away from their home churches. Nevertheless, self-classifying evangelicals do periodically articulate a common set of beliefs, as they did in Lausanne, Switzerland, in 1974, at the first International Congress on World Evangelism. The "Lausanne Covenant," which retains millions of signatories, stresses the historical Jesus as "the only mediator between God and people" and places a premium upon the imperative "to spread the good news that Jesus Christ died for our sins."[5]

Most historians today follow Bebbington's fourfold definition of evangelicalism, which emphasizes (1) a deferential reading of the Old and New Testaments ("biblicism"), (2) the cosmic significance of Jesus' death and resurrection ("crucicentrism"), (3) the transformative importance of adopting a personal faith in Jesus ("conversionism"), and (4) the impetus to share the gospel of conversion with others ("activism") as the unifying features.[6] Bebbington's definition has not only enough latitude to situate evangelicalism as a tradition with long historical roots (St. Augustine would qualify, for instance) but also enough teeth to cut lines of distinction within contemporary Christianity. However, such a checklist can prove vexing when figures of history espouse some but not all of these commitments, as with many late-nineteenth-century evangelicals who embraced more liberal views of scripture. Indeed, as George Marsden notes, *fundamentalism,* which insists on a verbatim understanding of the Bible, emerged in twentieth-century America as a counterweight to an evangelicalism that had abandoned its scriptural moorings.[7]

The challenges with Bebbington's definition multiply when studying religious laity. Respondents in a national survey, for instance, who affirm all four commitments on Bebbington's list, might not necessarily represent the true evangelical community within the survey sample. The subset could not only fail to absorb many who belong to evangelical churches but also *over*-absorb some respondents, such as African American Protestants, who neither consider themselves to be evangelical nor affiliate with those who do. For this reason social scientists tend to define the evangelical community differently than do historians—as an associational group rather than as a cognitive category. As Corwin Smidt explains, "members of a religious tradition are linked together socially."[8] It makes far more sense for a political scientist or a sociologist to observe the behavior of an interactive group than of isolated individuals who merely conform to some stipulated criteria. Thus, in constructing its massive *Religious Landscape Survey* of 2007 (which drew from over 35,000 subject interviews), the Pew Forum presorted some 225 American denominations into the broad headings of "evangelical," "mainline Protestant," "Roman Catholic," and "Black Protestant" and then counted anyone who reported his or her affiliation with the denomination as a member of the larger community. Southern Baptists, for instance, count as evangelical, American Baptists as mainline, and National Baptists as Black Protestants. Only if the respondent reported no denominational affiliation did he or she get sorted on the basis of stated beliefs. The result is a portrait of American evangelicals that admits to considerable variations on matters of theology.[9]

Because of this book's primary focus on text (sermons, pamphlets, and so forth) rather than on mass survey data, it will favor a theological (Bebbingtonian) definition of evangelicalism. However, in view of its broad historical and geographical ambit, the project cannot but recognize a degree of theological variation within the evangelical world. Indeed, doctrinal tensions—not just with respect to ordinary theology but also *political* theology—form a major part of evangelical history in America. This project tries to tell that story more than it tries to delineate a category of believers. Thus while it envisions, as most historians do, the New Light Calvinists of the First Great Awakening (Whitefield, Jonathan Edwards, Samuel Finley, and the like) as the conceptual founders of American evangelicalism, this book also allows each successive generation of evangelicals to define itself, refusing to exclude from the tradition those (such as Charles Grandison Finney or Henry Ward Beecher) from whom Edwards might have distanced himself on the basis of doctrinal differences. For the purposes of this book, "evangelical" will refer to any Protestant who actively promotes a "conversion narrative" to faith in Jesus Christ.[10]

Defined in this way, evangelicalism is today a global phenomenon. Missionary activity has resulted in the growth of evangelical churches in Latin America, Africa, China, and the Pacific Rim. Indeed, over the course of the twentieth century, evangelicalism's center of gravity shifted from its North Atlantic strongholds (Great Britain, Canada, and America) to the Southern Hemisphere. The third Congress on World Evangelicalism, held in 2010, took place in Cape Town, South Africa. Behind the United States, Brazil contains the largest evangelical population in the world, with nearly 23 million followers.[11]

Evangelicalism retains a firm footing in the North America, however. In Canada, for instance, while evangelicals account for only about 10 percent of the overall population, they also constitute the fastest-growing and most active sect.[12] In the United States, the religious map looks something like this: the Roman Catholic Church claims 69 million members, or one quarter of the U.S. population, concentrated in urban centers. Mainline Protestants account for another 18 percent, scattered evenly, but representing a massive decline since the 1960s. Practicing Jews have long maintained a presence of 2 percent of the American public, centered mainly in the Northeast. The adherents of other world religions like Islam, Hinduism, and Buddhism combine to about 4 percent of the U.S. population, favoring the two coasts and certain Midwestern cities like Detroit. Roughly 16 percent of Americans claim no religious affiliation at all (a steep rise since the 1960s), which leaves 34 percent of the population with potential ties to Protestant evangelicalism.[13]

That number, however, requires further scrutiny: African American Protestants, many of whom affirm evangelical commitments but gravitate toward race-specific denominations (and rarely adopt the evangelical moniker), make up 7 percent of the U.S. population, whereas white evangelicals are estimated to make up the other 27 percent.[14] Accounting for black churches within the broader evangelical community remains a puzzle for religious sociologists—not to mention evangelicals themselves. As Robert Putnam and David Campbell emphasize, "Black Protestants are not simply evangelical Protestants who happen to be black. Although they have a common origin, the two traditions evolved along very different paths."[15] The persistence of this segregation into the twenty-first century—even in the face of common theological values—can be traced to a variety of related factors, including neighborhood demographics, a preference for racial (rather than interracial) community on the weekend, cultural trends in music and worship style, and lingering strains of racial suspicion. The most divisive factor, however, remains on the frontier of research: the *political* theology of black evangelicals diverges markedly from that of white evangelicals in the United States, as we will observe at length below. This book primarily analyzes the political theology of white evangelicals, but the African American church provides an important counterpoint, given the striking overlap on theology in general.

The white evangelical population in the United States is concentrated in the South and generally favors small, rural towns—with notable exceptions in Orange County, California, and in the suburban outskirts of big cities like Atlanta and Chicago. On the conventional socioeconomic measurements—income, education, and marital status—evangelicals do not differ markedly from other Americans, but they do exhibit distinct theological commitments, largely (though not rigidly) bearing out Bebbington's historical definition of an evangelical. In a 2008 poll conducted by the Henry Institute for the Study of Christianity and Politics, 86 percent of evangelicals agreed with the statement that the Bible is "the true Word of God," compared with 55 percent each of

Mainline Protestants and Roman Catholics. Only Black Protestants, with 76 percent agreeing, came close to white evangelicals in their commitment to biblicism. On crucicentrism, evangelicals and Black Protestants again joined in distinction from other Christian groups, with nearly 90 percent agreement each on the statement, "Jesus is the only way to salvation," compared with 65 percent agreement among Mainlines and Catholics. Similarly, 79 percent of evangelicals and 85 percent of Black Protestants described their faith as "very important" to their daily lives, highlighting the conversionist ethos that pervades those traditions; by contrast, fewer than 60 percent of both Mainline Protestants and Catholics agreed with this position. In his analysis of the data, Smidt further observes that, unlike with other religious groups, a college education tends to strengthen, rather than weaken, crucicentric and conversionist sentiments among evangelicals, suggesting that the theological features of evangelicalism remain an empirically durable feature of the tradition.[16]

II. THE AMERICAN RIGHT

Like evangelicalism, right-wing politics in America has both a philosophical core and a somewhat elastic membership. It has, however, a much briefer history, at least in its current form. That is because the ideological spectrum as it appears today did not emerge in American politics until the early twentieth century, when the concept of a planned, egalitarian economy took shape as a left-wing ideal, and the quest for national purity and capitalistic hegemony became touchstones of right-wing politics around the world. While rarely embracing these extremities, Americans began to draw their longstanding debates on federalism (states' rights vs. the national government) into broader, economic concepts of justice. Only in the late twentieth century did the two major political parties, Republicans and Democrats, begin to reflect this ideological divide, and even then not perfectly.

Before proceeding with a rich description of right-wing ideology in America, it serves to note the appeal of simpler definitions, particularly those that reduce ideological differences to direct struggles for social power. The most eloquent of these in recent years comes in Corey Robin's *The Reactionary Mind: Conservatism from Edmund Burke to Sarah*

Palin (2011), which depicts the spirit of conservative thought as "a med-itation on . . . the felt experience of having power, seeing it threatened, and trying to win it back." On the left wing of any political spectrum, Robin explains, are those "subordinates of this world" who decide to "contest their fates." On the right wing are those actuated by "animus against the agency of the subordinate classes."[17] Robin does not mean to imply that right- and left-wing thought lack intellectual nuance, only that at the core of their conflict is a struggle for power.

This book pushes back on Robin's intuition, suggesting, first of all, that the content of ideology concerns a great many things in addi-tion to social power and, second, that "the felt experience of having power" (or of *not* having power) cannot adequately explain people's attachments to certain ideas and values. Human beings may well be self-interested creatures, but they are more complex than that. Indeed, if conservatism germinated only among those who have enjoyed "the felt experience of having power," it would represent a much narrower band of Americans than it currently does. Rather than assuming the one-dimensionality of ideological commitment, this study takes ide-ology, including right-wing ideology, as a set of ideas concerning justice—ideas detachable from the private interests of their adherents, even if those adherents have a variety of reasons for embracing them.

A portrait of an ideology should cover not only how it defines jus-tice, but also how it envisions the government's role in promoting justice. As it turns out, the preeminent value of right-wing justice in America *is* limited government, which is to say that many on the right collapse their answers to both questions into a single position. It is an ethos captured on the cover of the popular Jackson-era periodical, *The United States Magazine and Democratic Review*: "The best government is that which governs least." Today this sensibility is called "libertarian-ism," and contemporary forms of it invoke the economics of Milton Friedman and the possessive individualism of Ayn Rand. Its root and essence, however, trace to the republican values of the American founding.[18] To identify as a "conservative," after all, is to signal a desire to *conserve* something, and for many on the right, the object of conser-vation is the American founding ethos.

For the conservers of this ethos, the political philosophy of John Locke serves as the canonical fountainhead. In his *Two Treatises on Government* (1690), Locke developed a portrait of human nature as inherently self-governing and therefore born "with a title to perfect freedom." With this stance came an argument for limiting the function of government to protecting the "life, liberty, and estate" of the governed from those criminals who would violate the law of nature, and grounding the legitimacy of government in the "consent" of the governed.[19] By no means does Locke stand as the singular origin of American founding philosophy; his own theory emerged within the "Commonwealth" tradition in England, and it filtered to the American founders through the Scottish Enlightenment. However, the debts of a document like the U.S. Declaration of Independence to Locke's formulation should seem fairly prosaic.[20] It will hopefully suffice here to assert that the founding generation of Americans espoused a limited-government ideology that was "Lockean" (or "republican") in nature—that is, based on a belief in the common virtue and inherent liberty of the individual. To the extent that American traditionalists of the twenty-first century hearken back to first principles, Locke furnishes those salient principles.[21]

The *New* Right, however, encompasses a wider array of traditionalists than just the proponents of limited government. It serves to remember that many social arrangements in America—white supremacy, male supremacy, Protestant hegemony, and Victorian sexuality, to name just a few—faced progressive challenges in the twentieth century, and the right wing can be said to absorb all of their defenders. Recall the satirical jingle, "Those Were the Days," which opened each episode of "All in the Family" (CBS, 1971–1979) and wove together multiple layers of nostalgia in 40 seconds: Archie Bunker, the archetype reactionary of the post-60s era, pines for his prewar youth, when "guys like us, we had it made," when "girls were girls, and men were men," and when America "didn't need no welfare state" because "everybody pulled his weight."[22] The show's creator, Norman Lear, loads a range of conservative attitudes, social and political, in Archie's character, resonating with Robin's thesis that conservative ideology is mainly about a longing for lost social power. But the reality of American politics often sees conflict between the defense of social and moral traditions on the one hand and the imperative of limited government on the other. Policy discussions on gay marriage, recreational drugs, state support for faith-based initiatives, and even abortion reveal conflicts among American conservatives over not only the government's role in promoting justice but also the conception of justice itself. Social conservatives reject, at least on certain issues, the moral reductionism of libertarians that equates justice with limited government. Many who identify as conservatives define a just society in more expansive terms and show a willingness to empower government with specific tools of enforcement.

It also bears noting that Lockean political philosophy does not offer monophonic answers to every policy question and that, quite apart from the tensions with moral conservatives, contemporary limited-government types disagree even among themselves on immigration policy, on foreign aid, and on military spending, among other issues. The modern right wing in America thus covers a wide range of ideologues and interest groups—business advocates opposed to commercial regulations; critics of the welfare state and of income redistribution; libertarian purists; "originalist" interpreters of the U.S. Constitution; both military hawks and isolationists; defenders of "traditional family values"; foes of abortion; certain religious cohorts like conservative Roman Catholics and Protestant evangelicals; and, farther from the orbit of national politics, white supremacists and members of antigovernment militias like the Montana Freemen.

What is surprising, given this diversity, is the level of philosophical homogeneity right-wing activists have been able to achieve in recent decades, and in particular the religious conservatives who, on *most* policy questions (other than specific moral issues), actually adopt a libertarian sensibility—who accommodate, in other words, competing strains of conservatism in their own thinking. This book looks at evangelical Christians who reside on the right wing of American politics not simply on account of their moral traditionalism but also because of their real philosophical commitment to Lockean liberty, a commitment that is far from a foregone conclusion but nevertheless follows a certain train of logic.

III. EVANGELICALS ON THE RIGHT

Evidence of this commitment comes in two different forms: in the polling data of evangelical laity and in the rhetoric of evangelical leaders. This book mainly concerns itself with the latter, as it helps to unfold the train of logic behind the commitment. But empirical surveys of "non-elite" members of the tradition also support the claim that American evangelicals favor a limited-government ideology, in comparison both to other religious groups in the United States and to evangelicals around the world.

In its *National Survey of Religion and Public Life* (2008), the Henry Institute asked its respondents whether "government is responsible for taking care of those who can't care for themselves." It was found that evangelicals affirmed the statement to a far lesser degree (53 percent) than Mainline Protestants (62 percent), Roman Catholics (75 percent), and Black Protestants (83 percent).[23] The 30-point difference between evangelicals and Black Protestants is especially striking in light of their close alignment on matters of theology like biblicism and crucicentrism. Michael O. Emerson and Christian Smith, in their study of racial segregation in the American church, highlight the Lockean ethos among white evangelicals. Comparing how evangelicals and Black Protestants account for racial inequality, Emerson and Smith find that evangelicals are far likelier to embrace individualistic rather than structural explanations. Only 27 percent of evangelicals blame racial discrimination, with 62 percent believing that blacks are poor because they lack sufficient motivation to succeed professionally. Black Protestants exhibit nearly the opposite views, with 70 percent blaming racial discrimination and 30 percent blaming a deficit of motivation. Mainline Protestants fall roughly in the middle, with 43 percent citing discrimination and 40 percent citing motivation.[24] The belief in limited government is often predicated on a social ethic of individual responsibility; the domestic survey data support the contention that American evangelicals have a stronger attachment to that ethic than do other religious groups in the United States.

Comparisons to evangelical groups outside of the United States also find American evangelicals in a unique political category. In a comparison of Canadian and American evangelicals, Sam Reimer observes that "American evangelicals support their conservative party at twice the rate of Canadian evangelicals" and that there are appreciable differences in the political values of Canadian and American evangelicals. Analyzing responses to statements like, "the less government the better," "the free market can handle economic problems," and "government should not spend more money on fighting poverty" in the *God and Society Poll* (1996), Reimer finds that Canadian evangelicals affirm and deny the statements in almost identical proportion to other, non-evangelical

Canadians, while American evangelicals affirm these statements at a much higher rate than both Canadian evangelicals *and* non-evangelical Americans. On questions regarding social welfare and economic policy, Reimer concludes, "Canadian evangelicals seem to take their political cues from their national context, not from their evangelical subculture," while American evangelicals have distinct political ideas.[25]

Studies of Latin American evangelicals, particularly the millions of evangelicals living in Brazil, likewise reveal dissimilarities with those in the United States. Certain cultural markers, for instance, indicate a generally more empathetic attitude among Brazilian evangelicals toward the poor, such as with the popular hymn "Barnabé," which reminds its singers that "It isn't right for us to do well and another to suffer / Even more so when one knows what to do and does not do it," sentiments one would be hard pressed to find in American hymnals.[26] This is not to say that Brazilian evangelicals embrace the Social Gospel as a matter of course; there is conspicuous variation among Brazilian evangelicals on matters of social and political philosophy. The *Jornal Evangelico*, the widely read newsletter of evangelical Lutherans, regularly denounces the effects of global capitalism on the local economy and ecology and supports land redistribution to help poor farmers, while Pentecostals generally adopt a quieter role in national politics, emphasizing individual salvation and sanctification as the basis for good citizenship. Evangelicals in Brazil, furthermore, have never shown any inclination toward forming a national political coalition.[27]

American evangelicals, therefore, are a singular political breed. In pronounced contrast to other American Christians and to evangelicals abroad, American evangelicals exhibit a high level of electoral unity behind the conservative party and an ideological conformity around the values of limited government. Familiar or not with John Locke's *Second Treatise*, white evangelicals in America embrace a Lockean disposition toward government, placing a high premium on individual liberty.

IV. EVANGELICAL MORAL ACTIVISM

This popular disposition, however, comes with a major caveat. One aspect of evangelical politics—its moral activism—does *not* square with the libertarian ethos, and this impetus has been embedded in American

Protestantism from its earliest days in the Puritan colonies. Andrew Murphy, in *Prodigal Nation: Moral Decline and Divine Punishment from New England to 9/11* (2009), describes the "American jeremiad," a genre of striking continuity from the seventeenth into the twenty-first century that ties the private morality of Americans into a "cosmological" narrative and supports aggressive agendas of reform.[28] A Puritan preacher might point to drunkenness, sensuality, swearing, and disregard for the Sabbath when calling for "a sincere reformation of those evils which have provoked the eyes of God's glory."[29] Alexis de Tocqueville, traveling through the United States a century and a half later, still marveled at the spirit of moral reform among Americans, and particularly the temperance movement, "which keeps American legislatures in a state of continual agitation."[30] The historian David Sehat, in *The Myth of American Religious Freedom* (2011), contends that American society has long been shaped by religious coercion. The United States, Sehat argues, is "a Christian nation in that Christians [have] had significant control over law and governance and used it to enforce morality."[31]

What has evolved among evangelicals over the years are the specific targets of reform, and these vary not just *between* generations of activists but *within* them as well; indeed, competition over which public vice to tackle often proves as contentious as doctrinal disagreements among Christians. Temperance advocates and slavery abolitionists, for instance, feuded relentlessly in the 1820s. The moral reform project at large, moreover, toys with something of a theological trap: evangelicals believe in the moral accountability of individuals before God, but they also believe in the necessity of spiritual regeneration to achieve moral obedience, in that order. An agenda that puts moral reform ahead of individual conversion risks undermining the gospel. Nevertheless, moral activism has remained central to evangelical politics for most of its American history.

Moral activism among American evangelicals has always straddled the private and public spheres, balancing the reluctance to legislate against a sense of moral urgency. The late nineteenth century, for instance, saw the creation of the Young Women's and Young Men's Christian Associations, private institutions designed to save the working class from unwholesome recreations. It also saw (thanks to YMCA lobbying) the 1873 passage of the Act for the Suppression of Trade in and Circulation of Obscene Literature and Articles of Immoral Use, which gave broad authority to the U.S. Post Office to confiscate any mail deemed hazardous to the nation's morals.[32] In 1919 came the long-awaited triumph of the temperance movement, with the ratification of the Eighteenth Amendment (though repealed in 1933).

The most significant wave of moral activism among evangelicals came in the late 1970s, at precisely the moment when they converged on an electoral strategy to scale back the size and role of government. Among other distinctions, what sets this phase apart from earlier initiatives is its holism. Instead of fighting each other over the priorities of reform, evangelicals pooled their resources to establish national organizations like Christian Voice and Moral Majority (both established in 1979), which adopted a full array of initiatives, from curbing abortion rights to fighting obscenity on television. What made the difference this time, in the wake of so many cultural shifts in America, was a sense that the various moral crises were connected under the larger banner of "secular humanism"—a pervasive epistemic movement that denied the authority of God.[33] Evangelicals no longer found themselves fighting behavioral patterns that were commonly recognized as sinful; they were engaged in a comprehensive "culture war" to restore their religion to a place of influence.

Conservative Christians of the late twentieth and early twenty-first centuries have fought this culture war on two primary fronts, focusing on sexual and family ethics and on respect for God in the public square. Among the specific issues that have actuated this coalition are premarital sex, abortion, homosexuality, obscenity on television and the Internet, recreational drug use, antireligious bias in public schools and private universities, and the disappearance of Christianity from discourse on the American founding. The strategies the Christian Right has employed to counteract these moral trends range from the separatist homeschooling movement to activism in electoral politics, including get-out-the-vote efforts for conservative Republican candidates and ballot initiatives at the state and local levels.[34] Between 1998 and 2011, for example, organizations like the American Family Association and the Traditional Values Coalition successfully lobbied more than 40 states to enact bans on same-sex marriage (a growing number of which have since been overturned). Filling the continuum between home and politics are a vast array of civil initiatives like the Promise

Keepers rallies of the 1990s and values-oriented programming on radio and television, like the juggernauts Focus on the Family and Big Ideas Entertainment, which turns out "Veggie Tales" (didactic Bible stories featuring animated produce). Moral activism among evangelicals has reached a new and apparently sustainable peak.

The moral agenda of the Christian Right, however, makes for a constant source of friction with libertarians within the ideological coalition. The tension is felt on both sides. At a May 2011 debate for the Republican presidential nomination, Congressman Ron Paul defended his well-known support for legalizing cannabis: "It's amazing that we want freedom to pick our future in a spiritual way, but not when it comes to our personal habits."[35] Michael Gerson, a conservative Christian columnist for *The Washington Post*, responded to Paul's comments with a broad defense of the Christian Right's moral agenda: "Responsible, self-governing citizens do not grow wild like blackberries. They are cultivated in institutions—families, religious communities, and decent, orderly neighborhoods. And government has a limited but important role in reinforcing social norms and expectations."[36] The activism of the Christian Right generates a second line of friction—with the "evangelical left," those theological conservatives who nevertheless see blights like poverty and pollution as structural rather than individual pathologies. Jim Wallis, the founder of Sojourners, is probably the most prominent spokesperson for this point of view. Among his many critiques of the Christian Right, Wallis accuses its members of ignorance, even callousness, toward the systemic realities of poverty, resulting in part from a lack of contact with the poor: "The critical difference between Jesus' disciples and a middle-class church [in the United States] is precisely this: our lack of proximity to the poor. The continuing relationship to the poor that Jesus assumes will be natural for his disciples is unnatural to an affluent church. The 'social location' of the affluent Christians has changed; we are no longer 'with' the poor, and they are no longer with us."[37]

V. TOWARD A THEOLOGICAL ACCOUNT

Wallis's sociological claim, to the extent supported by demographic data, might shed light on the antipathy of affluent evangelicals toward redistributive policies, but such antipathy runs across socioeconomic

strata within the evangelical community. Even poorer evangelicals—
likelier beneficiaries than benefactors—look upon the welfare state
with suspicion. Data also show that American evangelicals rank among
the most generous supporters, both in volunteer work and in financial
contributions, of private charity to the poor.[38] Their objection, in other
words, does not so much concern whether to sacrifice their money to
help the less fortunate but rather the method of doing so, and in particular whether it is appropriate for the government to oversee a redistribution of private property. Their ideological penchant toward limiting
the role of government requires more than just a demographic analysis.

Historical explanations such as Williams' and Dochuk's work well enough to show why evangelicals converged around a limited-government
electoral agenda in the late 1970s, but that landscape has since changed.
The Reagan Revolution of the 1980s achieved far more in the way of
deregulation, tax relief, and Cold War victories than it did on behalf of
evangelical morals. In the 2010s, partisans of small government (such as
the various "Tea Party" organizations) have made far less effort to court
evangelicals—sometimes openly opposing them—on issues of moral concern, such as gay marriage. Lockean commitments nevertheless remain
strong among evangelicals. Indeed, some opinion surveys indicate a comparable, even greater, level of identification with the Tea Party movement than with the Christian Right agenda among contemporary evangelicals.[39] The ideology's resilience suggests that American evangelicals
might, in fact, have a deep attraction to the philosophy of small government. Did the New Right fashion something novel in the 1970s or did it
tap into a permanent facet of American evangelicalism that had perhaps
grown quiet for a few decades of the twentieth century?

A long view suggests the latter scenario: the rhetoric of American
evangelicalism—its sermons, devotional literature, as well as political
speeches and pamphlets—bears a theological trope, permeating almost
its entire history, that elevates limited government and individual liberty as practical extensions of its gospel. American evangelicals have
embraced a political theology that reconciles the Lockean social contract to the ideals of their faith, from biblicism to conversionism. This
political theology, called "republican theology," not only guides evangelicals as they navigate electoral politics but also provides the rationale for their moral activism and more broadly, has helped to secure
their commitment to the American experiment. Only an intellectual

connection of this depth could so durably bind a faith community to such a narrow (and quixotic) set of political values. Uncovering the logic of this tradition, then, would expose a framework for understanding evangelical politics in America, on a behavioral as well as a conceptual level. It would help to explain not only why evangelicals act as they do, and form the alliances they form, but also why their fixed position on the ideological spectrum generates such distinctive and inexorable friction, both within and beyond the religious community.

REPUBLICAN
THEOLOGY

Republican theology—the doctrine behind the civil religion of American evangelicals—is a specimen of political theology, the practice of extracting political values from religious beliefs. Some distinctions are in order: Political theology and civil religion, for starters, are not simply two terms that mean the same thing. Civil religion, on the one hand, sanctifies existing political values into a common creed for all of society. Political theology, on the other hand, derives political values from an existing faith tradition. Indeed, some religions have their own comprehensive ethical systems of which political theology is just a small part—Roman Catholics have Catholic Social Thought, for instance, and various Muslim sects observe Shari'a. Republican theology, a tradition among evangelical Protestants in America, does not flow out of a comprehensive ethical system (Protestants lack such a system) but instead weds the gospel of individual conversion to the Lockean social contract, yielding a spiritual rationale for limited government and the free market. Republican theology asserts the mutual dependence of individual liberty, moral virtue, and Christian faith to support a civil religion that values all three.

I. CIVIL RELIGION

Often overlooked by social scientists, yet pervasive in modern politics, civil religion and political theology are species of discourse that swim in the gulf between politics and religious faith, albeit in opposite directions. Civil religion, a term that originated with Rousseau but describes a much older phenomenon, refers to foundational beliefs that bind a society together, the kind of unquestioned commitments among citizens that such far-flung (and theologically heterodox) thinkers as Plato, Machiavelli, Rousseau, Jefferson, and Dewey all believe are necessary for sustaining a free republic.[1] Political theology, a term coined by Carl Schmitt in 1922 but also covering a much longer history, involves the extrapolation of political ideals from a specific religious tradition.[2] Thus, while civil religion serves the imperatives of politics, political theology has sectarian moorings. This is not to say that the two cannot inform each other or even overlap in content. A theocracy, for instance, might make little to no distinction between civil religion and political theology. Even in pluralistic societies, civil religion may well draw upon the resources of existing political theologies. Robert Bellah, for instance, depicts what he calls "American civil religion" as rooted both in reformed Christianity and in modern republicanism. "Both patterns," he notes, "see society resting on the deep inner commitment of its members, the former through conversion, the latter through republican virtue."[3]

Bellah's seminal 1967 essay on the subject, "Civil Religion in America," ignited a debate among American philosophers as to whether a free society actually needs, or can even sustain, a civil religion. Bellah insists that American civil religion not only is viable but has proved essential to the survival and identity of the nation at moments of crisis, from the Revolution and Civil War to the fight against communism. Citing the invocation of the "Creator" in the Declaration of Independence, along with John F. Kennedy's similar declaration that "the rights of man come not from the generosity of the state but from the hand of God," Bellah insists that certain articles of faith continue to be "deeply established in the American outlook" and ought to inform "responsible action in a revolutionary world."[4] Bellah's claim, however, invites a libertarian rejoinder: if a free society is grounded on the sanctity of private conscience, then public faith commitments of any kind are anathema to individual liberty. "The idea that liberal societies are bound together by philosophical beliefs seems to me ludicrous," writes Richard

Rorty. "Philosophy is not that important for politics."[5] It might, of course, be noted in response that respect for the sanctity of private conscience itself involves a shared moral position among members of society, making it difficult for even the most committed individualists to completely escape the realm of public morality.

This circular trap has sent many philosophers in search of middle ground, a kind of moral foundationalism for a secular, liberal democracy. Some theorists point to the law of nature as that which confers rights on humans, without the aid of divine revelation.[6] Others suggest that citizens with different (as John Rawls would put it) "comprehensive conceptions of the good" can, through a kind of negotiation, arrive at an "overlapping consensus" of common political values—a common vision "of society as a fair system of cooperation and of citizens as reasonable and rational, free and equal."[7] Such approaches might avoid the term "civil religion," but the foundations they describe have all the relevant qualities.[8]

Hovering in the background of this philosophical debate, however, is a stubborn sociological reality. With or without the approval of liberals and postmodernists, Americans remain a highly religious people. As their religious commitments have diversified, *civil* religion has sometimes taken a more localized valence. Even as the national moral consensus dwindles, social and religious groups in America espouse value systems that have some of the qualities of civil religion. Andrew Greeley, for example, writes of the "civil religion of ethnic Americans," an arrangement of values that emerge from the immigrant experience and that prize both individual freedom and social justice.[9] However, to the extent civil religion can belong to sub-communities within society at large, the entity begins to look and act more like political theology, serving the aims of a particular tradition. This book explores one of those corners, studying the civil religion that Bellah calls "American" but that has always found its most stable habitat among American evangelicals—on account of their political theology.

II. POLITICAL THEOLOGY

For its part, political theology in late modernity reflects a variety of responses to liberal pluralism, from Rawlsian gestures toward an "overlapping consensus" to defiant stands *against* pluralism. As an

example of the first type, many of the ethnic communities referred to
by Greeley have at their disposal the extensive tradition of Catholic
Social Thought, a political theology with origins in the philosophy
of St. Thomas Aquinas and an ever-growing discourse on justice.
Since the 1930s, when Pope Pius XI declared it "impossible to care
for the social organism [unless] each individual member is supplied
with all that is necessary for the exercise of his social functions,"
Catholic Social Thought has embraced universal human rights as its
central cause, finding common ground with other religious groups
and secular entities like the United Nations.[10] For Catholic social
thinkers, a vast array of human rights have the status of natural law,
given by God.

If Catholic Social Thought represents a political theology aimed
at civic consensus, Shari'a, the medieval legal code of Islam, has re-
surged mainly as a reaction against the liberal pluralism of the modern
West. Shari'a is the closest thing twenty-first-century politics has to
an actual scripture-system, explicit decrees about governance flow-
ing out of sacred texts. Derived from the Sunna, Muhammad's recorded advice on everyday life, and from a variegated tradition of
jurisprudence across the Islamic world in the ninth and tenth centuries, Shari'a lays out a code of living that encompasses topics from
worship and prayer to sexuality, family, dress, manners, inheritance,
and commerce.[11] Not that twenty-first-century Muslims all unite
around a common understanding of (or commitment to) these decrees: on the contrary, Sunni and Shiite Muslims each have their
own separate traditions of jurisprudence going back a millennium;
Muslim-majority states today vary widely in their legal systems.[12]
And the Muslim world certainly has its political theologians, such as
Abdolkarim Soroush and Mohsen Kadivar, with distinct inclinations
toward liberal democracy.

The subtlest and most diffuse political theologies in the late modern
era trickle out of Protestant Christianity. The secularization of Protestant societies in the nineteenth century convinced many scholars, even
early observers like Schmitt and Max Weber, that Protestantism itself
had entered a post-theological stage. Weber credits Protestantism with
suicidally ushering Western culture toward a "rationalized image of
the world."[13] However, significant pockets of the faithful, particularly
in America, continue to organize politically around issues specifically

motivated by their religious beliefs. This is not to say, however, that Protestants have a political theology equivalent to Thomism or Shari'a: the decentralized character of Protestantism works against that. And the secularist thesis does have some truth in it: if the Reformation did not exactly create the liberal tradition, it did promote a kind of epistemic individualism that undercuts holistic and legalistic visions of society, making it difficult to sustain a political dogma among Protestants, minimizing the church's power over the state, and ultimately opening the door to intellectual pluralism.[14] The Puritan experiments of the seventeenth century bear that out vividly, as we will see in the next chapter. The modern, nonsectarian republic is at least the partial handiwork of Protestant religion.

As a result, Protestant political theologies generally seek to affirm modernity—but on their own terms and with their own twists. Tocqueville ventured an observation to this effect in his second volume of *Democracy in America* (1840), in which he noted the ability of American Christianity to adapt to a liberal sensibility, upholding individual freedom and property rights and even affirming "the progress of industry" and "the honest pursuit of prosperity." By "respecting all democratic instincts which are not against it and making use of many favorable ones, [American] religion succeeds in struggling with that spirit of individual independence which is its most dangerous enemy."[15]

Broadly speaking, three different Protestant political theologies claim affinity with the ideals of American democracy. One styles itself as "liberation" theology; another as the "Social Gospel" or social justice theology; the third, and by far the most dominant, Protestant tradition is what I call "republican theology" in this book. Liberation theology, with mid-twentieth-century roots across the African Diaspora in the Western Hemisphere, asserts the identification of the Christian God with the plight of the oppressed, and particularly with victims of economic exploitation.[16] Drawing upon the New Testament promise that Jesus came "to preach deliverance to the captives" (Luke 4:18), this political theology interprets the Christian gospel as a call for human equality, a summons, for instance, "to all blacks to affirm their full dignity as persons and [to] all whites to surrender their presumptions of superiority and abuses of power."[17]

Another leftist political theology within Protestantism is the Social Gospel, proposed in the early 1900s by the New York Baptist Walter

Rauschenbusch and carried into the twenty-first-century church by groups like the Sojourners. Less revolutionary and more holistic than that of liberation theology, the premise is that the gospel of Jesus Christ has a transformative social dimension. "Jesus worked on individuals and through individuals," writes Rauschenbusch, "but his real end was not individualistic but social . . . It is not a matter of getting individuals to heaven, but of transforming the life on earth into the harmony of heaven."[18]

The transformation in mind for Rauschenbusch, who had ministered to a working-class congregation in Hell's Kitchen at the height of the Industrial Revolution, concerned economic justice: "As soon as religion will set the kingdom of God before it as the all-inclusive aim, the awakened conscience will begin to turn its searchlight on the industrial and commercial life in detail."[19] The upshot of the Social Gospel for early twentieth-century politics was a disposition toward egalitarian values—dissatisfaction with industrial capitalism, support for unionism, and openness to poverty relief and social welfare programs run by government, not just by churches. While such ideas integrate easily into Catholic Social Thought, American evangelicals have tended to push social justice theology to the fringe. The Sojourners movement represents a lonely (and often exasperated) exception.[20]

III. REPUBLICAN THEOLOGY

Thought it would decline the title, republican theology is a type of liberation theology in that it regards worldly freedom as a component of its gospel. What sets it apart from leftist liberation is how it defines the essential threat to liberty: more in step with secular libertarianism, republican theology identifies unrestrained government as the cardinal enemy of the human spirit. Although the sins of exploitation, greed, sloth, and cheating certainly violate the ethic of republican theology, material inequality as such does not constitute a moral problem. To the extent disparities of fortune reflect moral failures, republican theologians are as likely (if not likelier) to implicate the losers as the winners. The real institutional menace to human liberty—the only relevant source of *systemic* injustice—resides in an overbearing public sphere. In short, republican theology presents a Christian rationale for limited government and free market capitalism, one that has found a wide embrace among white evangelicals in America. The argument of this book, in fact, is that republican theology has supplied the content for civil religion among American evangelicals from the time of the American founding. Indeed, Mark Noll suggests that during America's first century, this fusion, which he calls "Christian republicanism," formed "not only the most powerful value system in the nation, but also the most powerful value system defining the nation."[21]

Here is how the theology works: Wedding the gospel to a Lockean rationale for limited government, republican theology encompasses the belief that (1) God endows humanity with the rights to life, liberty, and property; (2) he makes this endowment on account of the potential each human has to attain Christian virtue; and (3) he ordains these rights for the ultimate purpose of advancing the Christian faith. The Dutch Calvinist Abraham Kuyper, writing about American political culture in 1873, observed in it a "threefold constellation of unlimited personal freedom, strict morality, and the faithful confession of Christianity."[22] All three members of this trinity count equally—republican theology asserts their mutual dependence—and each has its own implications for politics.

As to the first of these legs, republican theologians believe that only in free societies, whose governments are limited to protecting life, liberty, and private property, can citizens flourish in the Christian faith. Whereas John Locke presents these rights as absolutes within the law of nature, republican theologians see them as a vital means to a greater end, namely the authentic worship of God. Authoritarian government, even when geared toward Christianity, undermines the faith of its people by affecting to coerce it. In fact, any governmental intrusion upon personal liberty—even upon the rights of private property—is seen as corrupting the soul. Lyman Beecher, a nineteenth-century preacher, said, "We might as well band with iron the trees of the forest, and expect their expansion" as to ration the liberties of humans and expect them to grow into virtuous Christians. Republican theology maintains that God created the human for *self*-government, which implies not just the right to elect one's governors, but also the right to discern and follow, for oneself, God's individual calling in life. "The source of our strength in the quest for human freedom," Ronald Reagan preached to the National Association of Evangelicals in 1983, "is not material, but spiritual. And because it knows no limitation, it must terrify and ultimately triumph over those who would enslave their fellow man."[23]

The second leg of the doctrine concerns virtue. Republican theology asserts that, just as freedom is essential to virtue and faith, the reverse also holds: only those societies marked by moral virtue can sustain a free republic. George Washington, in his "Farewell" presidential address, suggested that "of all the dispositions and habits which lead to political prosperity, religion and morality are indispensable supports."[24] "Freedom demands—depends upon—self-discipline from both the governed and the governing," wrote an early leader of the Christian Right movement in 1976.[25] "America is good," said Reagan in the same speech quoted above, "and if America ever ceases to be good, America will cease to be great." Thus adherents of republican theology, even as they embrace the value of limited government, seek the purity of the nation's moral culture; any exceptions they make to the libertarian posture are aimed at protecting the public from vices that would undermine the republic.

The third leg raises the stakes: republican theology invests republicanism with eschatological possibility, asserting that God is implementing a redemptive plan for all humanity through free and virtuous nations. Not only do such nations progress in the maturity of Christian faith, they effectuate its spread around the world through their example. In other words, republican theologians transpose the evangelical conversion narrative to the national level and envision the spread of democracy as linked to the spread of the gospel. The poem *Greenfield Hill*, Timothy Dwight's 1794 ode to the still-infant American experiment, lauds the simple virtues of freemen, exhorts the nation to keep its faith, and concludes that America will thereby give light to the world:

> New light, new glory, fire the general mind,
> And peace, and freedom, re-illumine mankind.[26]

In the twentieth century, Whittaker Chambers, an ex-Soviet spy, fed American evangelicals spoonfuls of eschatological hope by depicting the Cold War as an epic spiritual battle, with Jesus and Jefferson co-leading the offensive against Moscow: "Faith is the central problem of this age. The Western world does not know it, but it already possesses the answer to this problem—but only provided that its faith in God and the freedom He enjoins is as great as Communism's faith in Man."[27]

Loosely woven into the literature of American Christianity, republican theology now and then finds itself neatly laid out in a single work, as it does in a well-known sermon of Lyman Beecher, the leading itinerant of the Second Great Awakening and father of the abolitionists Harriet Beecher Stowe and Henry Ward Beecher. Beecher first preached "The Memory of Our Fathers" to the Connecticut State Legislature on Election Day in 1826 (when it was still common for legislators to sit and listen to sermons together) and then preached it again in Plymouth, Massachusetts, in December 1827 to commemorate the Mayflower landing.

Beecher's sermon begins with a prophecy that comes in the closing verses of the Bible: "And he that sat upon the throne said, 'Behold I will make all things new,'" a cherished promise among Calvinists who believe, as Beecher puts it, that "the history of the world [thus far] is the history of human nature in ruins."[28] The promise to make all things new, Beecher explains, refers not just to the physical world, but also to the human soul, encompassing "a moral renovation which shall change the character and condition of men." Beecher's thesis, however, is even bolder: "I shall submit to your consideration, at this time, some of the reasons which justify the hope that *this nation* has been raised up by providence to exert an efficient instrumentality in this work of moral renovation."[29] The history of human nature has turned a corner in America, in other words, and Beecher sets out to explain the reasons why.

His line of reasoning points to republicanism and its civil rights as the principal conditions for moral progress. "Great changes are required," Beecher argues, to reform the character and condition of humanity. First, "the monopoly of the soil"—the feudal institutions of slavery and tenancy—"must be abolished"; that is, individuals must fulfill the Lockean ideal of stewarding their own property. Ownership is not just a natural right but also a means of developing moral character; indeed, it is a natural right *because* it is necessary for developing moral character. "Man must be unshackled and stimulated . . . The earth must be owned by those who till it. This will give action to industry, vigor to the body, and tone to the mind; and by the attendant blessing of heaven, religion to the heart."[30]

The second condition for human renovation, Beecher argues, is republican government itself, the "monopoly of power . . . superseded by the suffrages of freemen." Authoritarianism not only "depresses the multitude" to the advantage of the few, it stunts moral development in much the same manner as vassalage: "To elevate society, and to bring out the human energies in a well-ordered state of things, the mass of mankind must be enlightened and qualified for self-government."[31] The "rights of conscience," finally, "must also be restored to man"— that is, individuals must exercise moral virtue on their own volition. God designed the human soul to worship him without the coercion of law, Beecher insists, and a truly Christian civilization will more likely flourish in the absence of force. In America, he argues, "at the very time when the civil law had become impotent for the support of religion and the prevention of immoralities, God began to pour out his Spirit upon the churches, and voluntary associations of Christians were raised up to apply and extend that influence, which the law could no longer apply."[32]

With this, Beecher's political lecture finally turns into a sermon, a solemn plea to Americans to accept "the duties to which we are called by our high providential destiny." These duties include the promotion of religious institutions and the maintenance of "moral purity," exhortations to which Beecher would devote hundreds of other sermons, scores on the topic of hard liquor alone.[33] Thus, while individual liberty supplies a vital condition for the world's reformation and redemption, it is only that which *enables* the promotion of moral virtue; moral virtue must still get promoted, a task that falls to the church, both its leaders and its members: "The universal extension of our religious institutions is the only means of reconciling our unparalleled prosperity with national purity and immortality," Beecher warns. "Without the preserving power of religious and moral influence, our rapid increase in wealth will be the occasion of our swift destruction."[34]

Beecher's sermon is exemplary. Preachers of republican theology, which include both clergy and politicians, celebrate America's advantages of faith and freedom, while also warning against moral lapses that could squander them. This duality encapsulates the logic of the doctrine: the entitlement to liberty is at once salutary toward *and* conditional upon the moral virtue of those who enjoy it. People cannot attain virtue without liberty, but nor will they enjoy their liberty for long if they fail to attain the virtue. And lest we forget, the eternal fate of all humanity hangs in the balance.

IV. AMBIGUITIES

This book traces the path taken by evangelical civil religion in America with the development, early on, of republican theology as its basis. On one level, it is a story of astonishing success: a faith community manages to preserve its relevance for almost two and a half centuries within a political system designed to minimize religion's impact on lawmaking. The success owes, this work will show, to the compelling way in which conservative Christians have fused the themes of republican liberty, traditional morality, and the faith experience into a single ideology that can attract a broad alliance of Americans, including many not-so-religious types.

The doctrines that make up republican theology, however, also set the stage for certain conflicts that sometimes overtake its influence. Two kinds of conflict dominate the history of republican theology and its followers: first, libertarians and evangelicals, in spite of their ideological alliance in national elections, maintain a mutual suspicion over the public relevance of private morality and over the moral authority of the Bible. Second, evangelicals struggle among themselves to define morality and its precise relationship to the gospel. They have long engaged in fights, for instance, over the priorities of moral reform—rivalries between different vice squads as well as between the anti-vice and social justice wings of the faith. And they wrestle over the question of how to preach morality in the first place—whether, in fact, moralistic jeremiads make any sense at all to a public ambivalent to the Christian gospel. Gospel purists maintain that moralism in any way detached from the preaching of grace does a spiritual disservice to the wider world, while others insist that immorality and injustice within society must serve as the point of departure in any conversion narrative.[35]

These historical conflicts will unfold throughout the book; this section lays out the philosophical tensions that underlie them. As tight as its logic appears, and as attractive a set of commitments it might seem to bring together, republican theology involves several points of ambiguity. We will consider here three such points: (1) the tension between the imperatives of moral reform and of personal liberty, wherein expanding the sphere of public morality cannot but undermine the Lockean ideals of limited government; (2) the discrepancy republican theology has with the typical evangelical conception of sin, placing confidence in human virtue and visualizing sin as external rather than internal to the human soul; and (3) biblical ambivalence on Lockean rights—to life, liberty, and property—as the cornerstone of justice.

Moral Virtue and Personal Liberty

The most palpable tension within republican theology concerns the ways in which it links individual liberty to moral virtue. The theology both sets individual liberty—and government limited to protecting that liberty—as a condition of moral virtue and posits moral virtue as a condition of a flourishing republic. This creed has an appealing logic: virtue and freedom, both desirable things, succeed as mutually sustaining conditions. It offers, moreover, a nuanced account of virtue that encompasses both its private and public dimensions, neatly reconciling the libertarian and communitarian instincts within the American sensibility. The theory breaks down, however, when a free society inevitably fails to meet the standards of moral virtue imagined by evangelical Christians, a fact that Locke seems to have anticipated when he constructed his own case for liberty. Locke establishes the social contract, along with its circumscribed enforcer, upon the narrowest possible set of public virtues, virtues he assumes belong inherently (even if not perfectly) to human nature. Whenever Locke's followers seek to expand the catalogue of virtues necessary to a free society or suggest that these virtues may require centralized cultivation, they undermine Locke's main argument for constraining the power of government.

In the *Second Treatise*, Locke describes a state of nature governed by a simple law of nature: "And Reason, which is that Law, teaches all Mankind, who will but consult it, that being all equal and independent, no one ought to harm another in his Life, Health, Liberty, or Possessions."[36] Even in the state of "perfect freedom" Locke expects people to recognize their obligation to obey that law and to defend others against violators. Individuals eventually leave the state of nature and form a social contract *not* in order to establish moral standards but rather to escape the uncertainty that attends the vigilante enforcement of standards that already exist.[37] Thus Locke charges government only with enforcing a well-recognized law of nature against those foolish enough to violate it: the "great and chief end," he argues, "of Mens [sic] uniting into Commonwealths, and putting themselves under Government, is the preservation of their Property, to which in the state of Nature there are many things wanting."[38] Locke brands any coercive power beyond that role as injurious to the very rights government is supposed to protect.

It is not that Locke subscribes to an exceptionally sanguine view of human nature; nor is he indifferent toward the benefits of cultivating certain virtues through education and even Christian preaching. He draws a bold line, however, between the private and public spheres, confining the education of children, for instance, to parents within the home and insisting that any moral standards particular to private associations (like churches) remain so.[39] Locke maintains, furthermore, a minimalistic concept of public morality, one that requires little more of citizens than to leave each other—and each other's property—alone. This minimalism in public morality is what allows Locke to propose a minimalistic government. If public morality entails more than simple respect for these basic rights, Locke's small government thesis falls apart. And yet as much as republican theologians value life, liberty, and property as human rights, they define the moral obligations of citizens much more broadly, emphasizing the necessity of virtues like sobriety, sexual modesty, and general reverence for God for the maintenance of freedom.

To assert that free citizens must be privately virtuous in order to maintain their republic undermines the Lockean logic, but it does not present a logical contradiction in and of itself. Nor is it a contradiction to suggest, more generally, that virtue and liberty are co-conditional, a claim supported even by nonreligious writers like Aristotle and Kant. What does defy logic is the idea that *moral coercion*, whether in the form of social pressures or moral legislation, is somehow necessary to maintain freedom. Christians before Lockeans, and believers in robust moral standards, republican theologians readily acknowledge that sinful humans do require prodding from their moral guardians to meet the standards of virtue to which the entire republic is accountable; these guardians, moreover, must work to curtail the vicious obstacles—like alcohol, drugs, public obscenity, and a heap of others—that impede the cultivation of individual virtue. An expansive concept of virtue must necessarily give way, then, to an expansive role for the leaders within a community. Once on this path, the only way to avert damage to the Lockean limits on government is to confine the moral guardianship of society to persons who lack formally coercive power, a practical impossibility in a republican system that allows virtually anyone to attain legislative authority through the electoral process.

Moral Virtue and Sin Nature

Not only does republican theology undermine Locke's argument for limited government, it also departs from the evangelical gospel on essential doctrines concerning sin and grace, refashioning American evangelicalism into a works-based moralism that would have been disparaged as "Arminianism" by the New Lights of the First Great Awakening. Awakening-era evangelicals tended to stress the Augustinian view of human nature, which holds that "no man is clean of sin, not even the infant who has lived but a day upon the earth,"[40] or as Calvin put it: "Man is so held captive by the yoke of sin that he can of his own nature neither aspire to good through resolve nor struggle after it through effort."[41] Samuel Finley, an Irish American iterant of the 1730s, puts the doctrine into personal terms: "If you would just make a due estimate of your own heart, you must look on it as containing the seeds of all the wickedness any mortal has ever been guilty of; for, though the inborn corruptions of some are several ways restrained from breaking out into action, yet [the soul] is still under the power of sin."[42] The gospel of grace is necessary, evangelicals argue, because all humans are born into an otherwise inescapable condition of depravity—a continuous rebellion against God's law that attends their separation from God's presence and turns them into "children of wrath," in George Whitefield's frequent terminology.[43] Attempts to behave better are futile and beside the point: what a sinner needs is restoration with God, available only through faith in Jesus as the anointed Son and sacrifice for sins.[44]

Calvinist evangelicals add yet one more complication to the aspirations of human virtue: apart from the particular intervention of the Holy Spirit, they hold, humans are incapable even of putting their faith in Jesus; those who do have experienced particular grace, or divine election, the mysterious exercise of God's sovereign mercy.[45] Such a position does not categorically oppose moral reform as such, but it does resist the hope that the public work of eliminating moral vices can achieve a genuine spiritual transformation within society, much less a nationalized salvation. This would explain why First Great Awakening preachers emphasized the universal need for grace more than they decried this or that sin; it also explains why preachers during the *Second Great Awakening* reconfigured the doctrines of original sin and election to make their reform agendas worthwhile. "It is impossible to advance human happiness," Benjamin Rush wrote after he severed ties with the Presbyterians in 1787, "while we believe the Supreme Being to possess the passions of weak or wicked men and govern our conduct by such opinions."[46]

The Yale theologian Nathaniel W. Taylor cast his entire career in the early nineteenth century to refuting the doctrines of original sin and election—what he called "divine determinism"—efforts that provided the Second Great Awakening with a considerable archive of theological defenses.[47] In an 1828 sermon to students at Yale, for instance, Taylor put an Arminian spin on Whitefield's favorite phrase, "children of wrath." Conceding that this unfortunate distinction refers to all humans, and that the status implies a depraved condition, Taylor nonetheless denies that it refers to a "property of the soul," or to a condition handed down from Adam. When the Bible refers (as it does in Ephesians 2:3) to humans as "children of wrath," Taylor argues, it simply means that everybody sins: "It is man's own act, consisting in a free choice of some object rather than God, as his chief good; or a free preference of the world and of worldly good to the will and glory of God."[48] The Bible does not claim, in other words, that human nature *forces* humans to sin, but rather that it simply *allows* them to sin; their freedom in the matter is what Taylor wants his listeners to understand. Taylor's practical agenda—to give theological cover to the reform movement—becomes clear toward the end of his sermon:

> To what purpose do we preach the Gospel to men if we cannot reach the conscience with its charge of guilt and obligations to duty? And how, I ask, can this be done unless sin and duty be shown to consist simply and wholly in the acts and doings which are their own?[49]

To the extent that Calvinism denies complete freedom in human moral agency, it not only undermines the project of moral reform, it also undermines republicanism itself, along with any millennial hopes attached to it. And yet the gospel of Edwards, Whitefield, and the Wesleys does exactly that: sinners stand hopelessly trapped under God's wrath, unable to escape the slavery of sin apart from God's grace. It makes no sense to appeal to unregenerate sinners' "obligations to duty" except in order to point them to their need for Christ.[50]

By reimagining sin nature as an external malady rather than as an internal condition of the soul, republican theologians transfigure evangelical Christianity from a faith movement marked by individual conversion narratives into a works-based moralism that pins its hopes on broad social transformations. "The exposition of public guilt and danger," said Beecher in 1812, "is the appropriate work of gospel ministers. They are watchmen set upon the walls of Zion to descry and announce the approach of danger."[51]

Scriptural Ambivalence on Lockean Rights

One final area of tension within republican theology festers between its Lockean conception of justice and the moral authority of the Bible. "Biblicism," a deferential reading of the Old and New Testaments, marks one of the defining features of evangelical Christianity. Jonathan Edwards calls the Bible "the only rule of our faith and practice."[52] One would therefore expect a marshaling of scripture proof to accompany any ethical framework to which evangelicals subscribe. However, the Lockean framework, with its emphasis on natural rights, relies on an idiosyncratic reading of the Christian scriptures that runs up against significant caveats. While it stands far beyond the task of this project to provide critical accounts of the Bible by which to measure republican theology, it remains feasible to note some ways in which the Hebrew law, as well as the moral teachings of Jesus and Paul, complicate the idea that life, liberty, and property are universal and unalienable rights, or that limited government represents the ideal Christian framework for human politics.[53]

The most glaring rift between Lockean and biblical ethics concerns the apparent absence of universal human rights in the latter. Indeed, almost no other question has occupied Christian philosophers in recent decades more than whether human rights have a basis in the Hebrew and Christian scriptures. Not only Alasdair MacIntyre, who is Roman Catholic, but also well-known Protestants like Stanley Hauerwas, Oliver O'Donovan, and Joan Lockwood O'Donovan have noted the lack of biblical support for the idea of universal rights and have disdained the "possessive individualism" that lies at the heart of modern rights thinking.[54] Nicholas Wolterstorff has made the most concerted effort to counter this trend in Christian philosophy, arguing that the Bible indeed supports the idea of universal human rights on account of the "bestowed worth" retained by all those who "bear the image of God."[55] Even Wolterstorff admits, however, that the Bible does not contain a "theory of rights" as such, but only a "framework of conviction" concerning the needs, and therefore entitlements, with which God has endowed humanity for its flourishing on earth—a state of justice, Wolterstorff adds, that entails far more than simply living undisturbed on one's private property.[56]

For our purposes, it will suffice to observe some of the biblical obstacles to the Lockean argument for human rights. For one, moral teachings in the scriptures often point to obligations and prohibitions,[57] sometimes to promises of reward,[58] but only rarely to rights,[59] and never to universal rights, at least with any explicit language to that effect. If any universal statement on the human condition radiates from the biblical narrative, at least on an evangelical reading, it is that the sinfulness of the human race entitles it to God's judgment and punishment.[60] Still, Locke never claims that *God* owes human beings their life, liberty, and property, but rather that these rights exist *among humans* who stand as equals in the sight of God, and this he derives from the law of nature:

> The state of nature has a Law of Nature to govern it, which obligates every one: And Reason, which is that Law, teaches all Mankind, who will but consult it, that being all equal and independent, no one ought to harm another in his Life, Health, Liberty, or Possessions. (*Second Treatise*, §6)

> Man being born, as has been proved, with a title to perfect freedom, and an uncontrouled enjoyment of all the rights and privileges of the law of nature, equally with any other man, or number of men in the world, hath by nature a power . . . to preserve his property, that is, his life, liberty and estate, against the injuries and attempts of other men. (*Second Treatise*, §87)[61]

Just as Locke parlays duties into rights, the commandments in Exodus 20, "Thou shalt not murder" and "Thou shalt not steal," might well imply the universal rights to life and to private property. This is precisely the thinking of early Protestants like Calvin, Beza, and Althusius, to whom the legal historian John Witte Jr. traces the modern human rights tradition. "Calvin argued," writes Witte, "that God imposes various duties . . . on all persons in the earthly kingdom," including the moral duties, laid out in the Decalogue, "to respect the person, property, reputation, and relationships of their neighbors." A person's "duty to this neighbor," Witte continues, "could be easily cast as the neighbor's right to have that duty discharged."[62]

However, one must remember that there are eight other commandments in the Decalogue, four of which deal with human relations—"Honor thy father and mother," "Thou shalt not commit adultery," "Thou shalt not bear false witness against thy neighbor," and "Thou shalt not covet"—not to mention the far more inward vision of human morality, one that emphasizes the purity of motive and intention, that Jesus preaches in the Sermon on the Mount.[63] Other imperatives, in other words, share a moral status with human life and private property in the Bible.

The Hebrew law, furthermore, details a long list of ways in which an individual may actually lose his right to life, a list that far exceeds that of Locke, who marks for a just death only those who threaten the lives of others.[64] Under Hebrew law, one can get himself executed by striking or even cursing his parents, by kidnapping another human being, by having sex with an animal, by working on the Sabbath, by engaging in homosexuality, by practicing necromancy, by entering the tabernacle as a non-priest, by committing blasphemy, or by simply belonging—man, woman, or child—to an enemy nation that God has designated for elimination.[65] The right to life, in other words, enjoys neither a universal nor an unalienable status on the pages of scripture.

Private property rights encounter an equally long list of biblical riders, some of which make American tax rates look comparatively low and American contract law rather rigid. The Israelites, for instance, were called upon to regularly sacrifice their most precious livestock in public offerings;[66] landowners were instructed to leave the edges of their property open and untouched for the "poor and sojourner" to harvest for themselves;[67] sales of land could be revoked if the seller or his family acquired the means to purchase it back;[68] and, in what today would seem a radical policy of redistribution, every fiftieth year in Ancient Israel marked a "jubilee" in which private debts were alleviated, slaves manumitted, and all the poor returned to their old property.[69]

In further contrast to Locke, the scriptures present an ambiguous portrait of material self-sufficiency, which Locke makes the nub of his rationale for private property, and indeed the mark of a flourishing human.[70] While many passages of scripture venerate the prosperous,[71] others, particularly in the New Testament, stress the blessedness of the poor and the precariousness of the wealthy.[72] "It is easier," Jesus warned of the wealthy young man who couldn't part with his riches, "for a camel to go through the eye of a needle than for someone who is rich to enter the kingdom of God."[73] The scriptures project at least two themes that overshadow the sanctity of property rights as Locke would construct them. One is a realism concerning the inequality of wealth, which often attends the charge to help the needy. "The land is mine," God reminds the Israelites before outlining a policy of leniency toward those who fall on hard times.[74] This is, in fact, the very theme that pervades Governor John Winthrop's sermon to the seaboard settlers of Massachusetts in 1630: God permits material inequality, Winthrop argues, "that every man might have need of other, and from hence they might be all knit more nearly together in the bond of brotherly affection."[75] Another, even more sobering, theme concerns the Bible's continual mindfulness of material transience. "As they came from their mother's womb," sighs the writer of Ecclesiastes, "so they shall go again, naked as they came; they shall take nothing for their toil."[76] And Jesus warns, "Do not store up for yourselves treasures on earth, where moth and rust consume and where thieves break in and steal; but store up for yourselves treasures in heaven."[77] Even as the Eighth Commandment (against stealing) might recognize the right to private property as an organizing principle for society, much of the Bible points to the futility of material possessions in matters of ultimate concern.

Civil liberty, as a universal right, stands on by far the shakiest ground within biblical ethics, as American abolitionists discovered to their endless frustration. The scriptures offer no categorical injunction against slavery, and the New Testament letters of Paul repeatedly exhort slaves to remain loyal to their masters.[78] In their own ways, the Old and New Testaments do recognize slavery as a degraded status: Hebrew history,

for instance, revolves around the Israelites' deliverance from slavery in
Egypt, their privilege of enslaving other nations, and their humiliating
return to slavery (or at least civil subjugation) in Babylon as a punishment for abandoning God.[79] For its part, the New Testament transposes
the slavery/freedom trope into a spiritual analogy, most famously in
Paul's letter to the Romans. In Chapter 6, Paul describes sin and death
as the true enslavers of humanity; freedom, purchased by the death
of Christ, entails both the attainment of eternal life and the ability to
obey God in the present life: "We know that our old self was crucified
with him in order that the body of sin might be brought to nothing,
so that we would no longer be enslaved to sin. For one who has died
has been set free from sin." The passage highlights a dilemma for the
evangelical Lockean: while the New Testament places a premium upon
freedom, it points to a spiritual rather than social meaning and entitles
it only to those who "have died with Christ."[80] In the context of society, the scriptures offer no clear-cut justification of slaveholding—but
neither do they suggest, explicitly or implicitly, that people, by mere
virtue of their humanity, possess a basic right to liberty, from the grip
of slaveholders, feudal lords, governments, or anyone else. Republican
theologians, in other words, must argue for natural liberty by way of
Locke (and other moderns), not by way of the scriptures.

Of all the planks of republican theology, the one that finds the most
explicit support in the Bible is republicanism itself, the belief that decentralized self-rule offers the ideal framework for human politics. For
some 400 years following their capture of the Canaanite territory (the
"Promised Land"), the Israelites enjoyed an arrangement akin to republican government, albeit one that coexisted with a religious hierarchy.
While this era of Hebrew politics, known as the "time of the judges,"
was marred by brutal intertribal warfare, the model represents an ideal
polity for republican theologians—a nation that manages its affairs of
state without a monarch because its only king is God.[81] When the Israelites finally demanded the appointment of a king in I Samuel 8, they were
castigated by God, who told the Samuel, the last of the judges, "they have
not rejected you, but they have rejected me from being king over them."
Thenceforth the Israelites' standing before God tended to rise or fall on
the virtue of its kings, who became moral proxies (and largely nega-
tive ones) for their subjects. Eric Nelson credits an explosion of Hebrew
and Talmudic scholarship in the sixteenth century with reawakening

an interest in the *respublica Hebraeorum* and with introducing European Christians to the idea that the Bible takes an anti-monarchical stance. On the view of some medieval rabbinic writings, widely disseminated during the Puritan era, "monarchy itself is a sin; it is everywhere and always the act of bowing down to flesh and blood instead of God."[82] In the midst of the ratification debate in 1788, American preachers frequently pointed to the Israelite "republic" as a scriptural paradigm for the new constitution.[83]

If the Old Testament suggests a theological rationale for self-rule over monarchy, however, the New Testament takes, of necessity, a more ambivalent approach. The gospel came earliest to subjects living in a pagan empire, and neither Jesus nor Paul (nor any of the gospel writers or other apostles) ever encouraged converts to seize upon the rights of self-government or to break away into autonomous republics. On the contrary, as he does to converted slaves, Paul advises the church at Rome to "be subject to the governing authorities; for there is no authority except from God, and those that exist have been instituted by God." Indeed, Paul explicitly undermines the virtue rationale central to republican theology—that Christian virtue increases as human government decreases: "For rulers are not a terror to good conduct, but to bad . . . [The governor] is God's servant for your good."[84] This from a man who had done hard time in Roman prisons! To advance such a claim about the governing authority in late first-century Rome—the Emperor Nero, for instance—suggests a political theology of radical acquiescence. Whatever the arguments for republicanism over monarchy that flow from elsewhere in the Bible, they do not accrue to much on behalf of the Christian gospel: God can work through any framework of human politics, Paul asserts, to strengthen the faith of his people. "My kingdom is not from this world," Jesus reassured the prefect of Judea at his trial.[85]

In sum, republican theology supports significant ambiguities within its doctrines, around the very fault lines it seeks to bridge: its emphasis on private virtue as a public good undermines the Lockean rationale for limited government and obscures the evangelical conversion narrative. The spiritual gravity it lends to natural rights, furthermore, rings hollow within the scriptures that supposedly have final authority among evangelicals. Individual liberty, in the Lockean sense of the term, has no protection whatsoever as a universal right on the pages of scripture; when the Apostle Paul speaks of freedom as something of eternal value, he refers to freedom from the sin of one's own heart, not freedom from societal or political bondage. Republicanism, of a kind, does find favor in the Old Testament but no comparable status in the New Testament. These philosophical tensions, as we will see in subsequent chapters, underlie the controversies that chase after evangelical politics in America, from the divisions within the abolitionist movement in the nineteenth century to the fractious alliance with libertarians in the twenty-first.

3

COVENANTAL
ORIGINS

Whenn republican theology came to dominate the American pulpit in the late eighteenth century, it displaced covenant theology, a tradition that, in one form or another, had propelled Protestants through most of their revolutionary history. Covenant theology posits a special relationship between God and certain "chosen people." Protestant Christians point to God's covenant with Abraham and the Israelite nation as paradigmatic of a "new covenant" God makes with all believers in Christ. John Calvin emphasized three aspects of the new covenant—its individual character, its redemptive capacity in the here-and-now, and its strict reliance upon divine election—that encouraged but also complicated an application of covenant theology to politics. Indeed, the question of how to put the new covenant to work in the polis may well be the grandmother of modern political philosophy, having spawned the diverse experiments in Puritan governance to which the likes of Thomas Hobbes, Samuel Pufendorf, and, most influentially, John Locke, responded with their various social contracts.

Historians of American civil religion often draw a straight line from its contemporary iteration back to its covenantal origins in New England.[1] Even if the Puritan commonwealth of the seventeenth century vanished as a legal institution, in certain cultural respects, writes George McKenna, "it did not die at all." Even today, McKenna argues,

"American patriotism has its roots in Puritanism, and at some level . . . most Americans recognize that fact."[2] This intuition certainly sheds light on the resilience of American religiosity. From a substantive angle, however, the *departures* American civil religion makes from covenantalism are as telling as what it retains from the tradition, as is the story of how these revisions took hold.

Viewed from the twenty-first century, covenantal political philosophy offers up a strange brew of ideas, mixing communitarian, theocratic, and even totalitarian elements with a forward-reaching commitment to voluntarism and individual rights. In one plausible reading, covenant theology, with its "bottom-up" orientation, presented the first widespread challenge to monarchy in modern Western thought. Telling the "human rights side of the Calvinist story," John Witte Jr. argues that, courtesy of the covenant tradition as led by Calvin, Theodore Beza, Johannes Althusius, and the New England Puritans, "there were many human rights in place before there were democratic revolutions fought in their name."[3] Even so, the *Lockean* argument for rights, which shaped political thought from the 1690s onward, breaks with covenant theology on issues of defining importance—achieving social consensus without theological unity, making individual rights the very essence of the social contract and the reason for government, and, above all, drawing a clearer line between private and public morality.

If Protestant politics introduced human rights and republicanism to the modern world, this bequest was not a matter of simple intellectual genealogy stretching from Calvin to Locke, but rather one of theological clash and compromise between the imperatives of the Christian covenant and the rights of the individual. Republican theology of the American founding represents a latter stage of this dialectic. At the midpoint stands the Scottish moral sense tradition, which attempted (against much resistance from conservative Calvinists) to accommodate covenantal ethics to the rationalism of Locke—or, from the flip side, to infuse Lockean politics with a robust Christian morality. Jonathan Edwards's rebuttal of Scottish moral sense in the 1750s reveals an American evangelical tradition that as yet retained the moral idealism of the new covenant. Seen in the light of these foregoing debates (which form the subject of this chapter), republican theology emerged in America as a final rejection of Edwards in favor of the Scottish position; more comprehensively, republicanism supplanted the idea of a covenant altogether with a new political theology—a contract among free agents who nevertheless work to secure God's blessing for the whole through their individual virtue.

I. COVENANT THEOLOGY

The covenant theology of the Reformation drew upon a distinction, advanced by Paul in his Letter to the Galatians, between two types of covenant that appear in the Old Testament. One type is the covenant of "law," in which God offers blessing to people in exchange for their loyalty, examples of which include the pact with Adam concerning the fruit of the Garden[4] and the Ten Commandments at Mt. Sinai.[5] In the other type, the covenant of "promise," God confers an inheritance upon certain recipients based solely on his own will and mercy. Examples of this type include God's promises to Abraham[6] and to David[7] concerning their salvific lineage and, Paul argues, the promise of salvation to all who have faith in Christ. The difference between these two types of covenant lies in their conditionality: the first rests upon the condition of human obedience; the second rests upon the constancy of divine will—an unconditional promise. That Israel stands under both the Mosaic and the Abrahamic covenants explains why it sustains temporal punishments for its sins, including banishment from Canaan, while never losing the promise of an ultimate savior. Old Testament prophets, acting as God's "covenantal attorneys," appeal to both the law and the promise, castigating Israel for its disloyalty to God but also reassuring them of eternal salvation.[8] Since humanity is categorically unable to fulfill the covenant of law, Paul characterizes this covenant as one that serves only to reveal the essential bondage of the human race to its sinful state. "Now before faith came, we were imprisoned and guarded under the law," he tells the Galatians. "But now that faith has come, we are no longer subject to a disciplinarian, for in Christ Jesus you are all children of God through faith."[9]

Reformers like Zwingli, Bullinger, Luther, and Calvin confronted the sixteenth-century church with essentially this same message, believing that the Roman system disregarded the covenant of promise and trapped its people in a corrupted code of law.[10] The covenant, in fact, had virtually disappeared as a paradigm of faith among the church fathers after receiving only sporadic treatment by Augustine.[11] Under-scoring its non-legal character, reformers presented Christian faith as a "covenant of grace" and labored to emphasize its individuality: people must come to faith in Christ on their own—that is, without the medi-ation of church or law. For Calvin, even God's covenant of law oper-ates on an individual level; human sin does not merely violate a code but rather betrays God's image in and authority over the human soul.[12]

While the promise of eternal salvation pervades the horizon of this covenant of grace, Calvin highlights the immediate foreground as well: faith in Christ not only secures one's place in the covenant of promise but also repairs one's capacity under the covenant of law. The elect are not liberated from the law but only from its power to condemn. In faith the elect can actually obey the law, which serves as the visible mark of their salvation in Christ. The "object of regeneration," Calvin writes, "is to manifest in the life of believers a harmony and agreement between God's righteousness and their obedience, and thus to confirm the adoption they have received as sons. The law of God contains in itself that newness by which his image can be restored in us."[13] This regeneration begins in the heart of the believer,[14] but its redemptive power spreads outward as the believer lives out the ethics of the cove-nant.[15] For Calvin a vast theater of spiritual warfare, with God's forces battling Satan's, forms the subtext of all human life; the covenant of grace, then, represents the gradual triumph of good over evil.[16] Calvin is as sure of the salutary effects of Christian faith for the world at large as he is that faith originates in the intimacy of relationship between God and the elect. How this exactly works—how, in particular, the covenant of grace operates among the elect and beyond—forms the trickier question. A law-based covenant offers a relatively straightfor-ward application to society and its governance; a covenant of grace, however, raises questions as to the sanctifying role of church and state.

Calvin develops a concept of "twofold government" upon his own experience as a church leader *qua* resident alien in the republic of Geneva. While the regenerate soul, he argues, needs no further priestly intercession, it does need all the help it can get in "nourishing" its faith against temptations. Christ instituted the church to strengthen believers through the encouragement of fellowship, the sacraments of baptism and communion, the exposition of scripture, and moral disci-pline.[17] As for "civil government," Calvin believes it exists in order to "to cherish and protect the outward worship of God, to defend sound doctrine of piety and the position of the church, to adjust our life to the society of men, to form our social behavior to civil righteousness, to reconcile us with one another, and to promote general peace and tranquility."[18] Calvin stops short of describing human society in covenantal terms, in other words. Indeed, Witte suggests that Calvin envisions "two tracks of morality—a simple 'morality of duty' demanded of all persons regardless of their faith, and a higher 'morality of aspiration' demanded of believers in reflection of their faith."[19]

Nevertheless, Michael Walzer, in *Revolution of the Saints: A Study in the Origins of Radical Politics* (1965), credits two features of Calvin's theology with pushing modern political thought in a covenantal direction. First, by treating the covenant of grace as a redemptive departure from the course of nature, Calvin orchestrates a decisive break with a "hierarchical and organic" view of human life. Nature no longer encloses the sacred; structures and authorities are no longer taken for granted. Second, by individualizing the covenant, Calvin elevates the priestly status of every member of the faith community. Without ever advocating a revolutionary stance among citizens or promoting political rights like the freedom of conscience or self-governance, Calvin opens these doors by undermining the authority of the "natural order" in politics, by focusing the covenant of grace on individuals, and by stressing the redemptive potential of the covenant in the here-and-now—real power brought to bear in the spiritual warfare against the Devil. While Calvin's politics tended toward a conservative application, writes Walzer, "his dramatic view of Satanic strife suggested something quite different: in time of war, the old Roman maxim went, the laws are silent. Military discipline then replaces legal order; peace and tranquility wait upon victory."[20]

II. COVENANT PHILOSOPHY

It took the succeeding generations of Calvinists to transform covenant theology into a mature political philosophy, positioning the "covenanted community" as vital to God's redemptive work in human history. Theologians like Theodore Beza (1519–1605) and Johannes Althusius (1563–1638) developed the covenant as a paradigm not just

for faith and church but also for society, while at the same time highlighting the tensions inherent in this move. It was Beza, following
the St. Bartholomew's Day Massacre (which took the lives of nearly
100,000 French Calvinists in 1572), who floated the idea that civil government is only properly constituted as a three-way covenant between
the ruler, the ruled, and God, and that the ruled possess the right of
resistance when that covenant is violated. In his ironically titled tract
*Concerning the Rights of Rulers Over Their Subjects and the Duty of Subjects
Toward Their Rulers* (precisely the inverse of what the tract was about),
Beza draws on Paul's Letter to the Romans, in which he exhorts believers to "be subject to the governing authorities. For there is no authority except from God, and those authorities that exist have been
instituted by God."[21] Beza turns the imperative back on rulers to suggest that the ordination of their authority is covenantal in nature and
thus conditional on their performance of God-given duties, in Paul's
words, to act as "God's servant for [the subjects'] good." Indeed, Beza's
argument, coming as it does in response to state violence against his
sect, asserts a fundamental liberty of conscience and a right of rebellion
that come more than a century before Locke published his *Letter Concerning Toleration* (1685).[22]

Althusius, a German immigrant to the Dutch city-state of Emden,
is responsible for constructing the first systematic theory of covenantal politics, which he did in a trilogy of works on ethics (*Civil
Conversations*, 1601), government (*Politics*, 1603), and law (*Theory of
Justice*, 1617). What Althusius came up with was a layered vision of
political society—smaller units like families and parishes within the
larger units of the state—but with this innovative distinction: that
these communities form as *covenants*, based on mutual consent, from
the smallest to the largest. "Human society develops from private
to public association by the definite steps and progressions of small
societies."[23] This is on account of the basic intimacy of the covenant of grace, which begins among individuals before spreading outward. Althusius stresses the intentional and voluntary character of
the arrangement: society must be "initiated by a special covenant
among its members for the purpose of bringing together and holding in common a particular interest."[24] As such, the signatories to
these covenants have the status of autonomous agents enjoying all the
rights of self-government. Moreover, as Witte explains, "not only

do the people retain their fundamental sovereignty and rights; the lower political associations also retain their fundamental identity and sovereignty as parts of these broader political structures."[25] This formulation, which Althusius called "*foedera*" (Latin for "treaties" or "agreements"), eventually took shape in the modern concept of federalism, or layered government.

Protestant affinity for self-government, it should be noted here, did not stem solely from covenant theology. In *The Hebrew Republic: Jewish Sources and the Transformation of European Political Thought* (2010), Eric Nelson credits the broad resurgence of Hebraic scholarship in the late fifteenth century with supplying Protestants with the tools to challenge monarchy on biblical grounds. What they discovered, in an array of ancient texts and rabbinic commentaries, was an argument for the spiritual superiority of republicanism, based on God's anger over the Israelites' request for a human king in I Samuel 8. Though God granted the request, monarchical mischief soon followed, and, according to the rabbinic commentaries, experience bore out the doctrine that "monarchy itself is a sin . . . everywhere and always the act of bowing down to flesh and blood instead of God."[26]

It is vital to stress, moreover, that whether arguing from covenantalism or from Hebrew history, Protestant theologians never promoted self-government for its own sake, but rather for the sake of spreading the Kingdom of God and shoring up the Christian faith. "The final cause of politics," Althusius argues, using the Aristotelian term for purpose or end, "is the conservation of a human society that aims at a life in which you can worship God . . . without error."[27]

When applied to politics, the covenant of grace attains a horizontal dimension—a "social" covenant—while maintaining its vertical orientation toward God. A new political puzzle attends the juncture: Christian theologians now view the individual as prior to society, retaining an ontological integrity before God and as a member of the community. This individual voluntarism, however, does nothing to diminish God's designs on the community as a locus of redemptive activity, making God's covenant of grace visible to the rest of humanity. From the vantage point of divine covenant, these individualist and collectivist aims harmonize perfectly; from the vantage point of politics, however, serious questions of application emerge when members start to find doctrinal disagreements forming among their ranks and (harder yet) non-Calvinists living in their midst, a reality that does not take long to materialize.

III. COVENANTAL POLITICS, 1559–1689

Covenant theology dominated the politics of at least four different theaters in the seventeenth century, including many of the Reformed enclaves of northern Europe, where Althusius developed his theories; Scotland, where Presbyterianism, the first "federal" church of the Reformation, took hold; Massachusetts, where English Separatists launched a covenantal society in a clean break from the Church of England; and England, where Puritans attempted (in the course of an 18-year revolution) to reform the Church on covenantal principles. Each of these movements confronted questions concerning the coercive power of the state, the individual liberties of citizens (particularly with respect to conscience and worship), and the rights of resistance and rebellion; some participants faced these dilemmas both as rebels and later as governors, creating a fluid ideological landscape from which eventually emerged the most influential tradition of modern politics, that of the social contract. The contract, seen against this backdrop, surfaced precisely in order to correct the defects of covenant as a paradigm for society.

While covenant theology came to drive their political thinking, most of these hyper-Calvinist communities arose in the first place because of monarchical pressures in France, Scotland, and England that forced thousands of Protestants into exile in the latter decades of the sixteenth century. The exceptions to this trend could be found in the relatively free city-states of northern Europe to which most of the exiles fled. It is in these exilic enclaves, such as in Geneva, Emden, Strasbourg, Leiden, and Basel, that lay Calvinists found the occasion to contemplate politics as a subfield of theology. The "Marian" exiles of England, for instance, while spending four years with Calvin as their pastor in Geneva, put together an explosive tract on "How Superior Powers Ought to be Obeyed" (1658), which gave themselves permission to disobey rulers who fail to uphold the standards of the new covenant. The persecution of Protestants, in other words, nourished not only their sense of community as a new church but also their belief in the prerogative of the elect to seek the purity of their union in Christ. On precisely how to seek this purity, however, these brethren would never come to complete agreement.

Divisions among the Marian cohort opened up as soon as they returned to England. Elizabeth, the new queen, drove the wedge herself by asserting, in the 1559 "Act of Uniformity," her absolute control over the Church of England while also handing out coveted bishoprics to some of the returning émigrés. Elizabeth's move set off a fierce debate among Puritans over whether to try to reform the Church from within or to maintain a separate fellowship. Eventually the "Separatists" left England altogether, the first wave stopping at Leiden and then making their way to North America. The famous "Mayflower Compact," signed by 41 men off the shore of Plymouth on November 11, 1620, furnishes one of the earliest examples of a Calvinist society constituting itself from scratch on the basis of covenant.[28] When John Winthrop's group joined them 10 years later (and 40 miles to the north in Boston), the covenant of grace again provided a conceptual basis for this settlement: "Thus stands the cause between God and us," Winthrop preached to his flock aboard the *Arbella* in 1631:

> We are entered into covenant with Him for his work. We have taken out a commission. The Lord hath given us leave to draw our own articles . . . [But] we must consider that we shall be as a city upon a hill. The eyes of all people are upon us. So that if we shall deal falsely with our God in this work we have undertaken, and so cause him to withdraw his present help from us, we shall be made a story and a by-word through the world.[29]

It is notable that the earliest societies to embrace voluntary association as their starting point did so within a broader commitment to a religious end. As such their emphasis on mutual consent did not produce anything like a liberal regime; on the contrary, the Puritan covenant favored personal piety and doctrinal conformity over any rights of privacy.[30] It is equally notable, then, just how quickly the social covenant came apart under the stress of theological deviations. Scarcely four years after docking, the Boston settlement formally banished Roger Williams from the colony for his "diverse, new, and dangerous opinions," a move that did little to quell the disputes that Williams had fanned among the settlers, such as over the veiling of women in church services.[31] If the covenant perhaps survived this early trauma through the sheer muscle of its clerics, the religious gaps produced by generational drift made for a much more complicated problem. Those who formed the intimate covenants on the *Mayflower* and the *Arbella* did so upon the basis of their individual conversion to faith in Christ—their personal standing in the covenant of grace. But what would happen to the community if their children did not profess a similar conversion? By the 1660s Puritan leaders faced the necessity of reinventing the social covenant in order to salvage the confluence of church and state within it. The "half-way covenant," as they called it, granted the "unconverted" a status of partial membership in the church—pastors would not serve them Communion but would baptize their children; that way the church could retain a measure of disciplinary authority over all members of the civil community. Gradually the half-way covenant gave way to greater concessions—participation in the Lord's Supper for the unconverted, for instance—but its goal of keeping all of New England under the "Puritan canopy" nonetheless proved ever more difficult to attain.[32]

England undertook its own experiment in covenantal politics—much grander but also much shorter-lived than in North America—in the mid-seventeenth century. The year 1640 handed the non-separatist Puritans an unexpected occasion to reform the Church of England. A decade of aggressive crackdown on Protestant worship by Charles I had produced a backlash, one further empowered by the first convening of Parliament since the 1620s. The new Parliament, composed in part by Puritans, confronted the king with legislation rolling back the restrictions on Protestant worship and asserting its institutional independence. A series of legal jousts in 1641 gradually descended into military brinkmanship, and the king soon found himself locked out of the Royal Army and Navy, raising his own forces among stalwarts in the western countryside. Several waves of an English Civil War would rage for eight years until Oliver Cromwell's victory at Worcester in September 1651. The king (or rather Charles Stuart, the deposed king) was tried and executed for treason in January 1649 by a Parliament by then purged of all non-Calvinists.

In the course of war Parliament set about enacting a religious reformation and convened an assembly of Puritan clergy at Westminster in 1643 to draft a new settlement for the Church. Drawing upon the creeds and structure of the newly established Church of Scotland,[33] the Westminster Confession of Faith laid out a vision for a national covenant on a Presbyterian model. In keeping with the covenant of grace, the Westminster Assembly left it to individual Christians to subject themselves to the authority of a local congregation, and left it to local pastors to preach their own sermons and to discipline their own members. However, the system called for the formation of regional "synods" as well as a permanent national assembly "to determine controversies of faith and cases of conscience; to set down rules and directions for the better ordering of the public worship of God and government of his church; and to receive complaints in cases of maladministration."[34] In the vein of Althusian federalism, representatives from the congregations would constitute these larger bodies, although the Westminster divines also granted the prerogative to convene synods to the civil magistrate, "that unity and peace be preserved in the church, that the truth of God be kept pure and entire, that all blasphemies and heresies be suppressed, all corruptions and abuses in worship and discipline prevented or reformed, and all the ordinances of God duly settled, administered, and observed."[35]

Factional infighting among the Westminster divines brought the individualism of covenant theology into sharper focus. The question of how much autonomy congregations ought to enjoy from each other, both on matters of worship and of preaching, subsumed a broader discourse on the liberty of conscience that subdivided the Puritans until the restoration of the Stuarts in 1660 (at which point they found themselves urgently united in favor of toleration). The case of John Owen, a young and charismatic supporter of the Revolution, serves to highlight this ongoing debate. Preaching to Parliament as they ratified the Westminster Confession, Owen proclaimed it a "day of visitation" from God and cast the English Reformation as a watershed in salvation history, a transformation "more glorious than that of any nation in the world, being carried on neither by might nor power, but by the Spirit of the Lord of hosts."[36] Owen believed in the covenant of grace; he believed in its capacity to draw a nation-full of elected saints into its fold; and he believed in the responsibility of political and religious authorities to "let all parts of the kingdom taste of the sweetness" of the gospel message. Owen did not believe, however, in Presbyterianism.

As soon as he threw his support behind the English Reformation, Owen aligned himself with the Congregational faction, advocates of independent parishes and opponents of a nationalized church. Owen tethered his case for Congregationalism to an outspoken defense of religious toleration, warning Parliament repeatedly against the legal compulsion of faith and warning church leaders against appealing to anything other than "the hammer of the Word and the sword of the Spirit" in their promotion of the gospel.[37] Owen went as far as to revise the Westminster Confession itself, huddling with other Congregationalists in October 1658 in the Savoy Hotel in London to draw up changes concerning the role of the civil magistrate: "Although the magistrate is bound to encourage, promote, and protect the professors and profession of the gospel," wrote Owen, "yet in such differences about the doctrines of the gospel or ways of worship of God as may be befall men exercising a good conscience, [as long as they are] not disturbing others in their ways or worship that differ from them, there is no warrant for the magistrate under the gospel to abridge them of their liberty." The covenant of grace, in other words, permits some differences—even on doctrine—among the elect.

Not that Owen's revision would amount to anything permanent: 18 months after the "Savoy Declaration," a new Parliament reseated the Stuarts, chasing the Puritans out of Westminster and summarily ending the farthest-reaching experiment in covenantal politics to date. For 29 years after the Restoration, Puritans (with John Owen as their main spokesman) were reduced to fighting not for "glorious" reformation, but for humble toleration. They won it in 1689 with an act of Parliament that permitted a measure of nonconformity within the Church of England. By this point, however, political philosophy had moved on to a new paradigm, the social contract, and its main proponent in England would seek to privatize religion to a far greater extent than even Congregationalists would have preferred.

IV. FROM COVENANT TO CONTRACT

Hobbes and Locke propose contract theory as a corrective for covenant theology, though in different ways. The central problem with the covenant, as it played out in seventeenth-century politics, is its convergence of the private and public spheres—its placement of a special relationship with God at the core of society. The personal nature of the covenant of grace makes it an unstable basis for society, particularly as it depends so radically upon the mysterious workings of individual faith. Efforts to codify faith in doctrinal commitment, furthermore, offer little more than a prescription for disorder, an opening to turn every divergence of private persuasion into a matter of public discord, their distaste for which Hobbes and Locke shared in equal measure. Their respective solutions to these problems tend in opposite directions—Hobbes seeks to weaken the *private* dimension of religion while Locke ultimately seeks to weaken its *public* dimension—but they flow from a strikingly unified critique of the Calvinist covenant, as well as from a similar burden to minimize the spiritual dimension of morality.

One gets a foretaste of Hobbes' vision for church and state from his self-designed frontispiece to the *Leviathan* (1651): with an imposing sovereign holding a sword in his right hand and a bishop's crosier in his right, it is pretty clear that Hobbes does not have in mind an intimate community structured around the covenant of grace. In fact, Hobbes devotes more pages (almost the entirety of Part III) to defending the king's absolute prerogative over religion than he does to any other thesis in the book. His argument, moreover, directly attacks the epistemological premises of covenantalism, and in particular the possibility that God communicates with individuals in ways that give them autonomous standing in society. Rather, Hobbes argues, God communicates to humans chiefly through the *state*. Even the scriptures derive their authority from the king: "It is manifest that none can know they are God's word (though all true Christians believe it) but to those whom God himself hath revealed it supernaturally; and therefore, the question is not rightly moved of our knowledge of it . . . The question truly stated is: *By what authority are they made law?*" And the answer: "It is the authority of the commonwealth." The danger in fixing the scriptures upon the realm of private conscience is all too clear to Hobbes: "For if every man should be obliged to take for God's law what particular men, on pretence of private inspiration or revelation, should obtrude upon him . . . it were impossible that any divine law should be acknowledged."[38] Hobbes' larger point, however, is not to defend the status of the divine law but rather to hand it over, in one solid piece, to the king as an instrument reinforcing his own authority:

"The right of judging what doctrines are fit for peace and to be taught the subjects is in all commonwealths inseparably annexed . . . to the sovereign power civil."[39]

The rationale with which Hobbes calls society into existence in the first place does as much to reject covenant theology as his specific policy on state religion. Indeed, by the time he gets around to constructing the church, Hobbes has already deflated the moral universe from which the covenant of grace derives its meaning. Not only does Hobbes deny that God elects certain individuals to fulfill the covenant of law by faith, he denies the existence of the legal covenant itself. The Hobbesian state of nature has but one law, that of self-preservation; only to escape the dangers that attend this state do people form society and submit to a law higher than their own immediate desires. This "higher law," which Hobbes calls the "law of nature," derives only from the rational self-interest of individuals, not from the revelation of God. Hobbes sees no covenant, therefore, prior to that formed among humans for their self-preservation. This agreement, in which people renounce the absolute rights they enjoyed in the state of nature—and which Hobbes calls a "contract" to underscore its perfect mutuality— defines the society and takes precedence over all other agreements and pacts.[40] Indeed, Hobbes specifically forbids any covenant that individuals might consider forming with God on their own: "They that vow anything to God contrary to any law of nature vow in vain, as being a thing unjust to pay such vow. And if it be a thing commanded by the law of nature, it is not the vow, but the law that binds them."[41]

Thus Hobbes circumvents the political volatility of the divine covenant by undercutting its relevance to human morality. If one can accept Hobbes' contention that humans have no moral dimension other than material self-interest until the moment they come together into society, then the Hobbesian social contract offers a level playing field unmatched by the covenant of grace. Everyone enters society on equal footing—no one stands "elected" by God—because there is no such thing as moral status prior to the formation of society.

Locke's account of the social contract strives to achieve this essential equality among the human parties without relying on moral emptiness in the state of nature. That Locke's state of nature has a "law of nature to govern it, which obliges everyone . . . [not] to harm another in his life, health, liberty, or possessions," marks the decisive departure from Hobbes' hedonist assumption. The implications of this difference carry forward to the contract itself: relieved of having to restrain the self-interest of natural man, the Lockean contract seeks only to uphold one's rights to life, liberty, and estate and thereby circumscribes the reach of government in comparison to Hobbes' absolute sovereign.

Locke's pre-social morality also advances a much subtler rejection of covenant theology: far from dismissing the covenant of law out of hand, Locke nevertheless simplifies it radically from the Puritan tradition. To be sure, God stands over this law with unmediated authority over every human soul: "for men being all the workmanship of one omnipotent, and infinitely wise maker; all the servants of one sovereign master . . . they are his property." That the natural law derives from this theological position lends it a covenantal quality; however, Locke's human agent comes to the knowledge of this law by means of "reason," not by means of any didactic communication from God. Moreover, this law of nature bears only the scantest resemblance to the legal covenant of the Old Testament, overlapping with only two of the Ten Commandments ("Thou shalt not murder"; "Thou shalt not steal") and confining human morality to the obligations that exist among humans (not between an individual and God). In de-spiritualizing the law of nature Locke seeks to make it universally accessible.

Indeed, Locke makes the God-given capacity for reason the essence not only of humanity but also of Christianity: the burden of so many of Locke's writings, from the early *Tracts on Government* (1660) to the *Essay Concerning Human Understanding* (1690) and *The Reasonableness of Christianity* (1695), is to undermine the epistemic exclusivity of covenant theology, the idea that certain individuals, by dint of divine transformation, can "adopt themselves children of God."[42] Locke bears as much suspicion toward Puritans as does Hobbes, writing in 1660 that the covenantal politics of the revolution had "turned us loose to the tyranny of religious rage."[43] His misgivings were so great that Locke initially supported the outright suppression of Puritans—and the preeminence of the Church of England—after the Restoration. It has never been established what brought Locke around to Owen-style Congregationalism and to the liberty of conscience as a fundamental right, but it was not likely a sudden affinity for Puritans.[44] Whatever the reasons, by the late 1660s, and most famously in his 1685 *Letter Concerning Toleration*, Locke came to advocate an almost total privatization of religion, the separation of the civil and religious spheres. Locke ended up going much further than Owen (who, incidentally, served as Locke's dean at Christ Church, Oxford, in the 1650s) in promoting congregational independence and religious freedom. For Locke the state should play no role, financial or otherwise, in the support of the church but must confine itself to enforcing everyone's natural rights to life, liberty, and estate. For its part, according to Locke's mature theory, the church must restrict its purview to matters of faith and to those who have voluntarily joined it. If Locke imposes anything on independent congregations, it is to cultivate a toleration of other congregations: "if the law of toleration were once so settled that all churches were obliged to lay down toleration as the foundation of their own liberty, and teach that liberty of conscience is every man's natural right, equally belonging to dissenters as to themselves . . . the establishment of this one thing would take away all ground of complaints and tumults upon account of conscience."[45]

What sets Locke apart from Hobbes on one end and from the Puritans on the other is his moral epistemology: parties to the Lockean social contract are neither lawless automatons nor God's chosen people to fulfill the covenant of law; instead they come to the table as equal subjects to a simple law of nature whose content they have discovered through a common capacity for reason. They form the contract solely to enforce this law; they can form whatever private association or covenant they want thereafter, provided its terms do not infringe upon the mandate of the commonwealth.

V. SCOTTISH MORAL SENSE

The question for the eighteenth century, then, is what Calvinists will do with the Lockean social contract. The surprising answer is that they quickly (though not unanimously) come to accept it, albeit with an important modification. Uneasy with Locke's minimalism in the realm of human morality, eighteenth-century Calvinists reconstruct Lockean ethics upon a richer, and more explicitly Christian, conception of the good life; however, they retain Locke's commitment to the natural operations of the human mind (rather than divine revelation) as the means of understanding this life. Scottish Presbyterians in the eighteenth century took the lead in enticing Christians away from the covenant as the paradigm for the public sphere and toward a more inclusive model that nevertheless cherishes Christian virtue, which they encapsulate in the natural disposition toward "benevolence." They called the innovation they use to bridge this gap "moral sense." The term originated in the 1737 *System of Moral Philosophy* by Francis Hutcheson, the chair of this subject at the University of Glasgow, where he taught the famous economist Adam Smith and where, according an early biographer hoping to shore up Hutcheson's "devout sentiments," he delivered a weekly sermon "on the truth and excellency of Christianity, in which he produced and illustrated, with clearness and strength, all the evidences of its truth and importance."[46]

Hutcheson's ethics move decisively away from the Calvinism dominant in the Church of Scotland while also achieving some distance from Locke. To prove that human morality consists in more than just respect for the privacy of others, Hutcheson ascribes to human reason a "perception of a finer kind."[47] Specifically, the mind takes pleasure in aesthetic values, like symmetry, and imitation of the known. Aesthetics are basic and universal, appealing most obviously to our senses of sight and sound, but also more subtly to taste, touch, and the rest. This aesthetic faculty contributes to benevolence in two ways. The first is that humans take intuitive pleasure in finding their own nature replicated in other humans. Thus there is an aesthetic delight in common society, which humans are therefore inclined to cultivate. Of much greater importance to Hutcheson, however, is the aesthetic delight our consciousness takes in the virtues of the soul. Hutcheson sees the faculty of self-awareness not as a mere register of internal thoughts, but as a nerve capable of its own pain and pleasure: "A certain temper, a set of affections . . . when we are conscious of them in ourselves, raise the most joyful sensations of approbation and inward satisfaction."[48] If our natural inclination toward society educates us on the substance of moral virtue—a state of mind necessary to good society with our fellows—it is the pleasure of consciously beholding that state of mind within ourselves that propels us to realize it. The social impulse is not enough; the greater happiness is looking back in upon oneself and catching a glimpse of a truly benevolent soul. It is a visceral pleasure, akin to hearing the perfect melody, or marveling at a fine structure, though in every way more intense, elevated, and personal.

This "experience of moral distribution" in the soul, which involves both discerning and desiring goodness, is what Hutcheson calls "moral sense." Moral sense, therefore, is what makes humanity a benevolent species. Benevolence cannot derive from material self-interest; that would be a contradiction in terms, not to mention an insufficient source of goodwill.[49] Nor is benevolence mere "sympathy," which Hutcheson dismisses as a "variable disposition," dependent on other passions, senses, and circumstances.[50] Benevolence is not even, at root, obedience to divine law; indeed, only through the experience of pleasure in a well-ordered soul (and pain in its opposite) do we even discern the presence of a "moral government in the world" and thus entertain "notions of a Deity and of providence."[51] Even human reason is "only a subservient power to the ultimate determinations" of moral sense.[52] Benevolence is an ordering of affections possessed of its own raw and immediate beauty.

Hutcheson's theory, while comprehensively argued, was by no means original in the 1730s. A decade earlier, the Anglican Joseph Butler had been preaching to London audiences about "the natural principle of benevolence in man" as well as the "principle of reflection in men, by which they distinguish between, approve and disapprove their own actions." Butler, like many divines in the early eighteenth century, sought to accommodate the Lockean argument for self-government to the full range of Christian obligations and to thereby ground Christian morality upon "the rule of right within."[53]

The moral sense project, furthermore, rolled along for decades following Hutcheson's *System*, consuming the works of Scottish philosophers like Lord Kames and Adam Smith, whose *Theory of Moral Sentiments* (1759) sought those "principles in [man's] nature which interest him in the fortune of others, and render their happiness necessary to him."[54] Smith's account resonates with Hutcheson's—attributing to human nature the capacity to embody an "impartial spectator" and the human need for "self-approbation."[55] However, Smith in the same treatise later observes that even *unbenevolent* behavior can have benign outcomes—that an "invisible hand" guides people acting out of "selfishness and rapacity" to "advance the interest of society."[56] For Christians seeking to salvage the necessity of Christian morals, the invisible hand argument would come as an unwelcome twist in the theory.

Even apart from the invisible hand, traditional Calvinists can find much to protest in moral sense philosophy. While they would not reject the aesthetic appeal of a well-ordered soul, or even the instinctive pleasure of society as a viable motive in human behavior, Calvinist covenantalists would place the desire for society *with God* above both, superseding them in intensity, priority, and importance. Only in society with God can the human hope to find (even discern) beauty in her own soul or sweetness in human fellowship. Thus the traditional Calvinist would also find moral sense theory deaf to the tragic reality of sin, which destroys relationship with God, and everything else along with it. Hutcheson rejects this pessimism unequivocally. Of course, he concedes, there is great malevolence in the world; most people, in fact, are quite susceptible to the influence of "selfish passions." Hence, he grants, "the general tenor of human life is an incoherent mixture of many social, kind, innocent actions, and of many selfish, angry, sensual ones; as one or other of our natural dispositions happens to be raised, and to be prevalent over others."[57] But selfishness is not a deformity within human nature to be solved only through divine intervention; rather, it is a problem of aesthetic cultivation. The moral horizon is simply too limited within the minds of the egocentric; if they could only envision a benevolent society, they would wish to see nothing else within their souls but the virtues that attend it: "As we improve and correct . . . a low taste for beauty, by presenting the finer works, which yield a higher pleasure, so we improve our moral taste by presenting larger systems to our mind."[58]

VI. JONATHAN EDWARDS, THE LAST (PHILOSOPHICAL) COVENANTALIST

Moral sense theory generated its share of opponents among Calvinists in Scotland. By the 1740s, in fact, the Church of Scotland had split into Moderate and Evangelical parties, protracting a durable schism over the heterodoxy of moral sense. Its most prolific critic, however, lived in North America. By the time he took up this fight, Jonathan Edwards had already made a long career promoting and defending the covenant of grace. In the 1730s his youthful congregation in Northampton, Massachusetts, lit the early embers of the Great Awakening that would sweep

New England, the Middle Colonies, and the British Isles; 20 years later that same congregation dismissed Edwards over his refusal to give Communion to "unconverted" parishioners. Edwards stood athwart the common tendency to preserve the inclusiveness of the Puritan covenant at the expense of doctrine and regenerating conversion.

Famous for the severity of his Calvinism—his "Sinners in the Hands of an Angry God" more or less defines the sermonic genre known as "fire and frimstone"—Edwards' relentless commitment to the doctrine of election flows from an equally fervent belief in what lies at the heart of the covenants of law and of grace: God's intense capacity for love. For Edwards, the essence of covenant is mutual friendship, and it begins within the Trinity itself. In a 1738 sermon entitled "Heaven is a World of Love," Edwards suggests that the character of God consists chiefly in love: "Love is in God as light is in the sun, which does not shine by a reflected light as the moon and planets do, but by his own light, and as the fountain of light." This flame burns eternal on account of the love between the Father and the Son, "an infinite and mutual energy . . . a pure and holy act whereby the Deity becomes nothing but an infinite and unchangeable act of love," which then proceeds undiminished outward to the heavens. Edwards depicts even the creation of the world as an expression of love, and the endowment of God's image in the human as an expansion of the sphere of mutual affection: "It seems to be a thing in itself fit and desirable," he writes in *A Dissertation Concerning the End for Which God Created the World* (1755), "that the glorious perfections in God should be known and the operations and expressions of them be seen by beings beside himself . . . It seems equally reasonable it should be esteemed and delighted in, answerable to its dignity."

That God desires the reciprocated (though uncoerced) adoration of those whom he adores, for Edwards, forms the baseline of all covenant theology and, therefore, of all human ethics—if one accepts, as Edwards does, that the covenant of law extends to all created in God's image. As with Calvin, Edwards does not see the fall in the Garden in purely legal terms but rather as an inexplicable rejection of God's love. All sin, therefore, conforms to this tragedy. One cannot understand human morality without first acknowledging that God creates humans to "enjoy him and to worship him forever"; to walk away from this original covenant, then, is to reject one's essence as a human.

Edwards advances this point as a direct challenge to Scottish moral sense theory in his *Dissertation Concerning the Nature of True Virtue* (1756), a sequel to *The End for Which God Created the World*, both of which he wrote after his dismissal from Northampton but before taking the presidency at the College of New Jersey in 1758. Confronting a post-Calvinist tradition that constructs ethics from the aesthetic appeal of benevolence, Edwards suggests that "true virtue consists in benevolence to Being in general"—that is, an unselfish, unconditional pursuit of the happiness of *all* beings, especially "that Being who has most of being, or has the greatest share of existence."[59] To be counted virtuous in Edwards' universe, one must love God and all of his creation as ardently as God himself loves. If contemporary theorists want to build a moral system from the particles of the human condition, he huffs, let them do it: but partial benevolence is at best partial virtue, and the aesthetic appeal of goodwill in one's soul can never attain anything more than "secondary beauty." Indeed, for Edwards, most of what passes for benevolence in the world is nothing other than "self-love." Familial affections, native loyalties, even satisfying one's contractual obligations within a "private system" may appear sublime to the moral sense, but they "will be against general benevolence, or of a contrary tendency; and will set a person against general existence, and make him an enemy to it." In light of true virtue, then, the moral sense approach to ethics sets a vicious trap in that it satisfies the human conscience with an impoverished, even depraved, morality. Nothing less than a total love for God and a delight in his glory counts as virtue for Edwards.

Edwards' larger point in rejecting Hutchesonian (and with it Lockean) ethics is to recover a place for the covenant of grace in moral philosophy. Not bending from his idealist ethics is Edwards' way of underscoring that no human being on earth can attain true virtue. All have failed this covenant, which is why the Christian gospel becomes a necessary means for restoring one's relationship with God as well as one's ability to even comprehend the nature of true virtue let alone pursue it. Indeed, individual restoration with God and the pursuit of true virtue amount to pretty much the same thing in Edwards' view, or at least the two complementary processes—justification and sanctification—that mark one's entry into the covenant of grace. That one enters this covenant only through faith in Christ and that with this conversion comes a significant transformation in one's affections and behavior is what Edwards seeks to emphasize against a philosophical tradition that he perceives as undermining the very rationale for the covenant.

Edwards' reluctance to write about politics deprives his covenant theology of a chance to answer the questions raised in the seventeenth century concerning covenantal governance, the limitations to which Hobbes and Locke responded with the social contract. Edwards offers no further clarity, for instance, on how a covenanted society might handle differences in religious doctrine, or more generally, how it might navigate the distinct burdens of the public and private spheres. The pitch of both Edwards' theological output and his pastoral career exhibits that of a Puritan reactionary, someone who defiantly holds to the covenant as the only true paradigm for society, regardless of the conflicts it might generate in a fallen world. His most recent biographer, George Marsden, suggests that Edwards' social views "reflected seventeenth-century American Puritan ideals of a biblical commonwealth led by authoritarian patriarchs. Edwards was looking forward to a worldwide triumph of Reformed-evangelical culture that would amount to those Puritan ideals writ large."[60]

It invites all kinds of counterfactual musings that Jonathan Edwards died of a smallpox inoculation in 1758, just a few years before the colonies were overtaken by the Revolution. Edwards' final perch as president of the College of New Jersey, the preeminent training ground for evangelical clergy (and later statesmen like James Madison), would be ceded to divines, like John Witherspoon, who were friendlier to Scottish moral philosophy. While Edwards certainly had his posthumous following, his idealistic ethics found almost no voice during the Revolution. Nathaniel Niles, a young graduate of the College, preached one of those rare sermons in which the First Great Awakening broke through the din of revolutionary fervor: "How strangely inconsistent we are," Niles scolded New England rebels in 1774, "in treating that liberty [in Christ] which is of infinite worth with neglect and contempt, when it is most freely offered us, while, at the same time, we are ready to sacrifice, not only our fortunes, but our very lives and friends to purchase and defend that which at best is but imperfect, uncertain, and temporal." The political liberty at the heart of the American rebellion, Niles laments, has at best a degenerative horizon: "We can enjoy no more of it than terminates in the private good of an individual."[61]

AMERICAN
FOUNDATIONS

Republican theology, with its merging of Christian piety to the philosophy of limited government, came to dominate the vernacular of American evangelicals by the 1770s as a point of entry to the revolutionary project.[1] It took many sermons on liberty—one itinerant pronounced it "the parent of truth, justice, patriotism, benevolence, and every generous and noble purpose of the soul"—to convert skeptics into patriots in the pews of colonial churches.[2] In absorbing the tenets of republican theology, evangelicals were able to create for themselves a role in the American founding. That role would consist in the guardianship of national virtue, which their new theology predicated upon Christian faith, and upon which it predicated the health of a republic and the liberty of its citizens.[3]

The new theology entailed, however, a departure from the idealist conception of human virtue advanced by Jonathan Edwards in the 1750s, a task for which no shortage of modernists emerged.[4] The intellectual journeys of two such figures stand out in the development of republican theology. John Witherspoon found a way to make Scottish moral sense palatable to conservatives like him and trained hundreds of pastors and dozens of statesman at the College of New Jersey for over 25 years as president. Benjamin Rush, the Philadelphia doctor and social activist, cultivated a lay-level engagement of republican theology by churning out, over these same decades, a steady stream of proposals—on everything from prison reform to public education—to make American society more just, humane, and, above all, virtuous. An analysis of their writings—this chapter will focus on Witherspoon's *Lectures on Moral Philosophy* (1768) and on Rush's *Of the Mode of Education in a Republic* (1786)—reveals not only the content of republican theology, but also its provenance, its adaptability to various moral and political agendas, its immediate influence on evangelical thought, especially among preachers of the "New Divinity," and its early trials as a political philosophy.

I. WITHERSPOON, RUSH, AND THE AMERICAN FOUNDING

On August 14, 1767, in an act of quiet desperation, John Witherspoon invited Benjamin Rush, then a 22-year-old medical student at the University of Edinburgh and a bare acquaintance, to "make a jaunt" out to his parish home in the village of Paisley, near Glasgow.[5] Rush accepted the invitation and showed up at the Witherspoons' door two days later. He stayed with the couple and their seven children for five days and then returned to Edinburgh, having performed a monumental task on behalf of his host. Somehow—historians may never know for sure—Rush had convinced Witherspoon's wife, Elizabeth, to move to America. John Witherspoon, several weeks prior, had declined the offer from the College of New Jersey to serve as its sixth president. That offer, extended the previous November, had for months riveted the evangelical world, from Philadelphia to Edinburgh, where Rush, a recent graduate of the College and a nephew of its late fifth president (Samuel Finley), saw in Rev. Witherspoon the intellect, charisma, and evangelical zeal needed to reinvigorate the academy: "Your talents have been in some measure buried" in the Scottish lowlands, Rush wrote to Witherspoon in March, "but at Princeton they will all be called into action, and the evening of your life will be much more effulgent than your brightest meridian days have been."[6] Witherspoon, it turns out, never needed convincing: he spent months trying in vain to win over his wife before conveying his regrets to the College in May. The Witherspoons had buried three of their children already, and the prospect of relocating to the American frontier sent Elizabeth into fits of illness whenever her husband brought it up: "My wife continued under such distress on the subject," he wrote to a College trustee who had visited in April, "that for some weeks after you left us she was scarcely ever half a day out of bed at a time." That the College had lost four young presidents (including Jonathan Edwards) to untimely deaths in just eight years cannot have sweetened the deal.[7] Even as Witherspoon hatched his 13th-hour scheme, he warned Rush, "She was excessively struck with the bare mention of [moving to New Jersey] as having believed it to be quite over, and discovered the same, or if possible, a greater aversion at it than ever, plainly saying that such a resolution would be as a sentence of death to her."[8]

Neither correspondence nor diary entries reveal the content of Rush's personal plea to Elizabeth Witherspoon, but the optics of his visit—a vigorous, brilliant youth on adventure from America, an enthusiastic Christian promoting her husband's cause—probably made an impression.[9] In any event, Rush took it upon himself to pass on her change of heart to the College trustees, who reapproved Witherspoon's appointment several months later. The family moved to America in the summer of 1768, and John Witherspoon served as president of the College of New Jersey until his death in 1794.

The alliance forged in Paisley between Witherspoon and Rush only deepened in America, where their common cause for the spread of the Christian gospel merged with a political cause: both men served in the Continental Congress and signed the Declaration of Independence in 1776, and both men gave many subsequent years to shoring up—and shaping—the new republic. For Witherspoon and Rush this embrace of American patriotism followed something of an intellectual journey, one that took each man from provincial religious attachments to a profound commitment to republican government. In each case, the high point of this journey came as a happy epiphany, a confluence of Christian faith with the tide of social progress. What is more, the clarity with which Witherspoon and Rush came to see the American experiment as a divine initiative turned them each into apostles of republican theology. It is easy to forget the angst with which many colonists accepted the morality of defying a sovereign king. Churchgoers relied heavily on their pastors to make sense of the Revolution in light of Christian obligation; their pastors, in turn, relied on the likes of Witherspoon and

Rush to construct the narrative. The personal stories of these two men reveal much about the narrative they would construct.

II. WITHERSPOON ON VIRTUE

By the 1750s John Witherspoon had won fame, even in America, as a piercing voice for the evangelical movement. Coming of age at the height of the Scottish Enlightenment, Witherspoon made his name heckling it, deconstructing its theology with a bit less perspicacity but a great deal more panache than his American contemporary, Jonathan Edwards. Aided by the Great Awakening as it swept the Scottish countryside, Witherspoon succeeded in bringing the debates of the Enlightenment—particularly those surrounding the doctrine of moral sense—back from the universities to where they had originated, in the Church of Scotland. Whereas the Church had once repressed Enlightenment thinkers, the General Assembly Witherspoon joined in 1747 had now flipped over to the cause of "moderation"; indeed, a self-styled Moderate Party dominated the Assembly, taking cues from philosophers at Edinburgh and Glasgow, and, more offensively, imposing heterodox pastors on evangelical congregations.[10]

For Witherspoon, the situation provided the perfect atmosphere to stoke populist reaction. With evangelical masses demanding to choose their own ministers, Witherspoon fired off a defense of their cause in 1753 in a pamphlet doubling as a raucous satire on the Moderate Party. *Ecclesiastical Characteristics: Or, the Arcana of Church Policy* affects to catechize the ways of moderation, offering "a plain and easy way of attaining to the character of a moderate man." The essay instructs churchmen, for instance, to avoid reading the scriptures as much as possible, to celebrate "good humored vices" in their pastors, and above all to steer clear of the Westminster Confession, "which was framed in times of hot religious zeal; and therefore can hardly be supposed to contain anything agreeable to our sentiments in these cool and refreshing days of moderation." Reserving his most mordent mockery for the philosophers of the Scottish Enlightenment, and in particular Francis Hutcheson, Witherspoon reveals the heart of his critique: Moderate Christians, he chides, must supplant the "old" confession with something even older, an "Athenian Creed" that pins one's faith upon "Dame Nature," upon the hope that "there is no ill in the universe," and upon the writ of such divines as Aristotle, Leibniz, and "the late Mr. H---n," notwithstanding "their present tendency to oblivion."[11]

Quite beyond a defense of congregational independence, *Ecclesiastical Characteristics* amounts to an evangelical manifesto, a pocket-sized rant on Scottish moral philosophy: Christians cannot confess faith in the gospel *and* in the doctrine of moral sense, he charges. Moral sense theory stages too many departures from the gospel—on the presence of evil in the world, on its dominion over the human heart, and on the need for divine redemption—for there to be any comfortable degree of compatibility. Moreover, ordinary believers seem to understand this far better than their leaders, intellectual or ecclesiastical. As a defiant affirmation of the Great Awakening, and as a vindication of country religion, *Ecclesiastical Characteristics* struck a nerve in America. One Boston preacher recommended that every American preacher "read it once a month," a blessing that at least boosted sales.[12] A full decade prior to his arrival, Witherspoon was already one of the best-known Calvinists in America, chiefly on the stridency of his Calvinism.

So how, then, did it happen that John Witherspoon would be the man to undo the Edwardsian tradition at the College of New Jersey and to replace it with something much closer to Hutchesonian moral philosophy? Nothing less than this transpired in the course of Witherspoon's tenure, and the shift was felt in pulpits across the colonies. Touching shore to fanfare in the late summer of 1768, Witherspoon moved into his post at Princeton having prepared 16 inaugural *Lectures on Moral Philosophy*, making a serious effort at a genre he had only ever ridiculed as a parish priest. The object of these lectures was to establish an academic direction for the College, particularly in the disciplines of theology, ethics, and politics. He begins with an almost self-conscious defense of the latter two against the first: "I am of opinion that the whole of Scripture is perfectly agreeable to sound philosophy; yet certainly it was never intended to teach us everything"; to make a systematic study of morality one must also understand "the nature of man."[13]

Jonathan Edwards also began moral philosophy with human nature, but, like other evangelicals, he differentiated between human nature before the fall, human nature after the fall, and the regeneration of human nature by faith. Witherspoon forecloses that entire conversation:

what matters to moral philosophy, he states in Lecture #1, is to understand humanity in its original condition—"how his Maker formed him, or, for what He intended him." Edwards might concur with this priority, but when Edwards meditates on the divinely intended virtue of the human, he does so in order to behold the perfection that Adam destroyed. When Witherspoon here rewinds to the Garden of Eden, by contrast, he finds a readily available system of justice. All we need to know about our moral condition, according to Witherspoon, is that it derives from a law "which our Maker has written upon our hearts and both intimates and enforces duty, previous to all reasoning." This law boils down to two straightforward imperatives: to love God and to love others. These imperatives do not even approximate "benevolence to being in general," Witherspoon emphasizes; indeed, his most explicit reference to his predecessor's philosophy is also his most dismissive: "True virtue certainly promotes the general good," he offers, "but to make the good of the whole our immediate principle of action is putting ourselves in God's place, and actually superseding the necessity and use of the particular principles of duty which he hath impressed upon the conscience."[14] For the purposes of moral philosophy, Witherspoon favors an ethic that is comprehensible and achievable. It never comes up in Witherspoon's lectures that human sinfulness undermines virtue in any terminal way.

Nevertheless, virtue is a serious matter for Witherspoon. To love God, he stresses, one must sincerely recognize both God's "natural perfections"—his sovereignty and power—and his "moral perfections"—his holiness, justice, truth, goodness, and mercy—and respond in worship, prayer, and obedience to all of the commandments revealed in the scriptures. Love for others follows a different impulse: rather than starting from Edwards' holistic and self-abnegating "benevolence to being in general," Witherspoon suggests we cultivate a "calm good will to all." We transcend the vices of parochialism, in other words, not by enlarging our affections but rather by dousing them with cold water.[15] In naming the duties that follow from this "calm good will," Witherspoon makes his embrace of Hutcheson official. We love others, he concludes, by respecting their rights—to life, health, liberty, and property: "Justice consists in giving or permitting others to enjoy whatever they have a perfect right to—and making such a use of our own rights as not to encroach upon the rights of others." Human virtue, then, has both an inner and an outer life; but whereas Edwards connects the two with the categorical imperative of benevolence, Witherspoon disentangles them: we are to love God in a very different way than we love each other.

If Francis Hutcheson, back in the 1730s, had struck an implicit deal with Locke to broaden the scope of human virtue,[16] John Witherspoon, in the late 1760s, strikes a deal with Hutcheson, toning down his previous hostility to the moral sense tradition. The compromise goes like this: Witherspoon now accepts the essential capacity of the human to know the way of virtue; he concedes that *public* virtue consists in no more than calm respect for the privacy of others; and he adopts Hutcheson's (not Edwards') approach to affirming that *private* virtue matters. What he holds on to from the evangelical tradition is a reliance on the absolutes of revealed religion—rather than on personal, aesthetic experience—to inform the content of private virtue. Otherwise endorsing Hutcheson (often by name), Witherspoon challenges him on this one point: "It is so far from being true that there is no more in virtuous action than a superior degree of beauty . . . It is not duty because pleasing, but pleasing because duty."[17]

Witherspoon's compromise reconstructs Scottish moral philosophy with an evangelical twist: the Lockean social framework of natural rights and limited government that Hutcheson preserved intact now includes a vigorous religious element, not to dominate public life, but to guide the cultivation of private virtue. Whereas Locke and Hutcheson leave room for the church in a free society, Witherspoon makes it necessary: our duties to God are too vital—and too well defined—to leave to haphazard reflection. Yes, God has written these duties on our hearts; but unlike our obligations to each other, our obligations to God involve an inner discipline that relies on engagement with scriptures, creeds, catechisms, hymn-singing, prayer, and other acts of worship that are more easily practiced in community with others.[18] Here the irony comes out into the open: private virtue inhabits a quasi-public dimension. It is precisely this duality that holds republican theology together, of course; Witherspoon's revision of Hutcheson, then, achieves nothing less than the most scrupulous introduction yet of republican theology to the colonies—a defense of liberty grounded in the cultivation of Christian virtue.

What accounts for Witherspoon's shift on virtue?[19] It may be impossible to know for sure, but in hypothesizing we get a sense of why this shift is so consequential for American Christianity. The most probable explanation involves context: biding one's time as a gadfly parson in the liberal Church of Scotland is a different enterprise than helming a conservative evangelical college in America. In his new job Witherspoon faced the need not only to develop a new academic curriculum but also to establish the College's voice in the midst of political upheaval.[20] If the American colonists were indeed advancing toward a broad assertion of natural rights and republican government (which they were, even by 1768), the evangelical community could either find its way into the story or find itself on the sidelines. Moreover, Witherspoon had always been a populist, and perhaps even a republican: his famous polemic, after all, defended not just evangelical orthodoxy but also the rights of individual congregants to choose their leaders against the whims of church hierarchy.

In any event, Witherspoon's moral philosophy provided an evangelical entry point into the nascent American creed, and did so effectually: while churchgoers probably never read Witherspoon's *Lectures* (published long after his death), their pastors knew the *Lectures* well; Witherspoon delivered them biannually for most of his 25 years in Princeton, and the College of New Jersey trained many of the evangelical clergymen active—particularly in the Middle Colonies—during this period. To supply the Pennsylvania and New Jersey countryside with New Light pastors, in fact, was a substantial motivation for the College's founding in the 1740s. From the 1750s through the 1810s it filled most of the Presbyterian pulpits in, among other places, the Cohansey River region of southern New Jersey. In studying period sermons from this cluster of townships, historian John Fea describes them as a fusion of various "moral languages," including that of evangelical Calvinism, the values of classical republicanism, and "the new moral philosophy" of Scotland, a brew of ideas that turned these villages into "important centers of revolutionary activity in the countryside."[21]

For a window onto how Witherspoon's political ethics translates into revolutionary preaching we need look no further than his own sermon to Princeton Presbyterians in May 1776. Insisting that "this is the first time of my introducing any political subject into the pulpit," Witherspoon places his call to arms within a broader, Calvinistic thesis concerning the "dominion of providence over the passions of men": God's ultimate sovereignty over human events, he argues, is such that even "the wrath of man praises God," that God marshals even the evil schemes of humanity into a redemptive storyline that enhances his own glory. The scriptures teem with examples, from Haman's plot against the Jews in the Book of Esther to the crucifixion of Christ. In this light Britain's injustice against the colonies must give way to an even greater justice, the exalting of God's glory through the righteousness of a liberated people. Witherspoon does not assume this trajectory, however. His sermon comes as a warning: "I do not blame your ardor in preparing for the resolute defense of your temporal rights. But consider, I beseech you, the truly infinite importance of the salvation of your souls. Is it of much moment whether you and your children shall be rich or poor, at liberty or in bonds?"[22] With that caution Witherspoon then blesses the Revolution:

> I willingly embrace this opportunity of declaring my opinion, without any hesitation, that the cause in which America is now in arms is the cause of justice, of liberty, and of human nature. So far as we have hitherto proceeded, I am satisfied that the confederacy of the colonies has not been the effect of pride, resentment, or sedition, but of a deep and general conviction that our civil and religious liberties, and consequently in a great measure the temporal and eternal happiness of us and our posterity, depended on the issue. The knowledge of God and his truths have from the beginning of the world been chiefly, if not entirely, confined to those parts of the earth where some degree of liberty and political justice were to be seen, and great were the difficulties with which they had to struggle from the imperfection of human society, and the unjust decisions of usurped authority. There is not a single instance in history in which civil liberty was lost and religious liberty preserved entire. If therefore we yield up our temporal property, we at the same time deliver the conscience into bondage.[23]

III. RUSH ON VIRTUE

In comparison to Witherspoon, Benjamin Rush came by his transition to republicanism with greater transparency, adopting republican theology at a much younger age and later reflecting on that experience in his *Autobiography*. Indeed, the term "republican theology" appears to have first entered the lexicon in an essay on Rush by the historian Donald D'Elia in the journal *Pennsylvania History*. D'Elia describes Rush's "belief in the unity of truth," and the lengths to which he goes to merge his Christian and republican sympathies – along with his scientific and medical sensibilities. Rush's construction of republican theology is in some ways more delicate than Witherspoon's, involving self-conscious departures from Calvinism (he would eventually leave the Presbyterian Church over theological differences). In other ways his version is more straightforward, lacking the irony and subtlety that courses through Witherspoon's philosophy. Rush adhered, writes D'Elia, to the "divine origin of republicanism in an absolute God, without the mediation of Lockean precepts of nature." He believed that man "had life and other rights only because God gave them to him continuously out of his benevolence."[24] Rush's political theology, in other words, tracked more intently to that of the Declaration of Independence than any of its other signatories.

Born in Philadelphia at the peak of the First Great Awakening and educated at New Light academies, Rush emerged from his youth with a mindset steeped in evangelical reformation and millennial warfare. Following the early death of his Anglican father, Rush's Presbyterian mother reared her children in the congregation of Gilbert Tennent, one of the stars of the revival movement.[25] Rush spent most of his youth at the West Nottingham Academy in Maryland, where he received regular Calvinistic instruction from another leading figure of the Great Awakening, his uncle, Samuel Finley.[26] After Nottingham, Rush enrolled at the College of New Jersey, where Finley would later precede Witherspoon as president, and where the 15-year-old came to the surprising decision in 1760 to pursue medicine instead of ministry or law.[27]

Rush's medical training afforded him exposure to several new intellectual disciplines—not only to science, but also to European literature, and to the philosophy and politics of the Scottish Enlightenment. In the course of a two-year fellowship (1766–68) at the University of Edinburgh, Rush taught himself French, Italian, and Spanish; he came under the influence of the modern psychologist David Hartley; and he even made the acquaintance of the moral philosopher David Hume.[28] In his *Autobiography*, Rush details a concurrent epiphany in his political thinking. A fellow student introduced him to the writings of Algernon Sidney and thereby to the concept of republican government: "Never before had I heard the authority of Kings called into question. I had been taught to consider them nearly essential to political order as the Sun is to the order of our Solar System. For the first moment in my life I now exercised my reason upon the subject of government." Rush follows this reflection with a revealing comment on his own intellectual process: "It has been said that there is no such thing as a solitary error in the human mind. The same may be said of truths. They are all related, and delight in Society."[29] Rush's metaphor personifies the interdisciplinary nature of truth itself, visualizing a mystical fellowship that exists between all claims about the universe, regardless of their particular subject matter. Thus a physicist might have something to learn from a philosopher, a minister from a doctor. To be sure, this could be the epistemic outlook of any polymath, and on this count Rush held his own with the likes of Benjamin Franklin and Thomas Jefferson, earning fame in biomedical research, psychiatry, religious prose, and philosophy, in devising new schemes for law enforcement and public education, and in chartering the first liberal arts college in the United States (Dickinson College, 1783, in Carlisle, Pennsylvania).

More than just a clue into his multiple careers, however, Rush's desire to maintain a "society" of truths in his head explains his inclination toward republican theology: Rush hadn't given up on his belief in the evangelical conversion narrative or in its cosmic implications, only now he had to reconcile these beliefs with a new political insight, a principle of governance that appears more just and reasonable than the prevailing monarchical tradition. Rush makes sense of his new political persuasion with a theology that not only justifies republicanism and complements it with religion (both of which Witherspoon does in his *Lectures*) but also infuses it with cosmic potential; Rush comes to attach a great deal of spiritual promise to a Christian republic, and he marshals every tool in his kit—from medical expertise to programmatic reforms—to advance the moral sanctification of his country.

Rather than lay down his republican theology in one grand treatise, Rush let it trickle out of dozens of essays on social issues that he released over several decades of semipublic life. Between 1773 and 1806 Rush argued in writing for the gradual abolition of slavery, for the end of capital punishment, for vocational training in prisons, for the establishment of a public school system, for the prohibition of liquor, for mass inoculations, and for an interdenominational congress of Christian ministers. The one topic that threads through all of Rush's essays is virtue—what it consists in, how to achieve it, and above all its value to the life of the republic. Rush understood the difference between private and public virtue, but, perhaps even more than Witherspoon, Rush placed a premium on private virtue: not only does private virtue require a collective effort to cultivate, but it also carries public consequences in the eyes of God. A collective vice might well entail sins committed behind closed doors. Rush measures sin from the standpoint of divine judgment: "Remember," he addresses the pastors of slaveholders in 1773, "national crimes require national punishments, and without declaring what punishment awaits this evil, you may venture to assure [your congregations] that it cannot pass with impunity, unless God shall cease to be just or merciful."[30]

Rush's philosophy of human virtue, however, rests as equally upon his commitment to individual liberty and republican government as it does upon the moral standards of God. Indeed, he sees an almost perfect confluence of aims between them. On the one hand, Rush sanctifies individual liberty as essential to a godly society, God having created human beings free to worship him uncoerced. On the other hand, he sets a nation's obedience to the laws of God as a principal factor in its rise or decline; righteousness and liberty, in other words, work hand in hand.

On no other subject did Rush develop this concept of virtue more cogently than on the education of the young. Indeed, Rush was one of the earliest Americans to advocate for a public school and university system, always tying his rationale to the necessity of cultivating republican virtue among the citizenry. In 1786, three years after he chartered his own college in Carlisle, Rush proposed to the Pennsylvania legislature the creation of a single state university, four state colleges, and free grammar schools in every township, all administered in a single system funded by state taxes.[31] Before outlining his plan, Rush preemptively defended the idea of publicly funded education, turning in the first place to its advantages for religion and for a free society. Education, he argues, "is friendly to religion, inasmuch as it assists in removing prejudice, superstition, and enthusiasm, in promoting just notions of the Deity, and in enlarging our knowledge of his works." As for liberty, "Freedom can exist only in the society of knowledge. Without learning, men are incapable of knowing their rights, and where learning is confined to a few people, liberty can be neither equal nor universal."[32] A flourishing church and a flourishing democracy share at least one common link, in other words: they both need well-educated members.

Rush draws a more graphic connection among religion, liberty, and education in a follow-up essay, *Of the Mode of Education Proper in a Republic*, which outlines his thoughts on curriculum. In it Rush prioritizes "religious, political and moral instruction" over the "arts and sciences": "The only foundation for a useful education in a republic is to be laid in Religion. Without this there can be no virtue, and without virtue there can be no liberty, and liberty is the object and life of all republican governments."[33] This syllogism forms the basis of an extensive discussion of public religious education, the potential controversy over which Rush tries to foreclose by framing the argument in purely civic terms: "Such is my veneration for every religion that reveals the attributes of the Deity, or of a future state of rewards and punishments, that I had rather see the opinions of Confucius or Mahomed [*sic*] inculcated upon our youth, than see them grow up wholly void of a system of religious principles." However, Rush immediately qualifies this generality: "The religion I mean to recommend in this place is that of the New Testament . . . All its doctrines and precepts are calculated to promote the happiness of society, and the safety and well being of civil government."

Christian virtue, Rush argues, coincides perfectly with republican virtue. "A Christian cannot fail of being a republican," and this for four reasons. First, a Christian understanding of the creation account reveals "the original and natural equality of all mankind," precluding the reflexive deference to social hierarchy of the feudalists; second, "the Gospel inculcates those degrees of humility, self-denial, and brotherly kindness which are directly opposed to the pride of monarchy and the pageantry of the court"; third, Christianity teaches its followers that no man "liveth to himself," making them capable of seeing past their own interests; and finally, the heart of all Christian virtue is the Golden Rule, which renders its adherents "wholly inoffensive"—that is, suitably self-restrained to live in a free society.[34]

These values, while emanating from the Christian gospel, still require cultivation at every level of society, which is why Rush insists upon bathing children in Christian doctrine even against the libertarian objection that "it is improper to fill the minds of youth with religious prejudices." Impressionable young minds crave "principles" of life as well as knowledge of the "invisible world," Rush explains. Young people may well evolve in their religious views over time, but "knowledge of one system will be the best means of conducting them in free enquiry into other systems of religion." In the meantime, Christianity provides a perspective that expands the horizon of moral obligation all the way to the Creator, making it much easier to inculcate civic duties:

> Our country includes family, friends, and property, and should be preferred to them all. Let our pupil be taught that he does not belong to himself, but that he is public property. Let him be taught to love his family, but let him be taught, at the same time, that he must forsake, and even forget them, when the welfare of his country requires it. He must watch for the state as if its liberties depended upon his vigilance alone . . . [35]

The virtuous individual, on Rush's logic, derives the value of his life from the promotion of something much larger than himself. This principle reveals the essence of both Christianity and republican citizenship, according to Rush. If one learns how to obey God he will also learn how to pursue the godly welfare of his nation; the nation occupies that sphere of consequence just beneath the glory of God itself, a sphere in which every virtuous life plays a small but vital role. Rush sees it as imperative to the sustenance of liberty that *every* member of American society pursue this kind of virtue. Even in his 1773 critique of slavery, for instance, Rush proposes to abolish the institution, but only in a gradual scheme designed to prepare slaves for the responsibilities of free society: "Let the young Negroes be educated in the principles of virtue and religion—let them be taught to read and write—and afterwards instructed in some business, whereby they may be able to maintain themselves." As for older slaves, who have "acquired all the low vices of slavery," such as sloth and diffidence, Rush recommends "for the good of society, that they should continue the property of those with whom they grew old."[36]

A triangular dependence among liberty, virtue, and Christianity emerges as the axiomatic logic for most of Rush's essays. Cripple just one of these legs, the warning goes, and the others will soon fall as well. What usually gets Rush to pick up his pen against this or that deed, in fact, is his sense that the deed undermines both liberty and Christian morality at the same time and thus poses a double threat to the whole nation. His early objection to slavery, for instance, flows not only from his belief that it flouts "the cause of humanity and general Liberty" but also that it brings out the worst character—"covetousness, intemperance, pride, uncleanness, theft, and murder"—in everyone, "both from the master and the slave."[37] His opposition to hard liquor follows a similar instinct. Spirits "beget quarrels, and lead to profane and indecent language; they are the parents of idleness and extravagance, and the forerunners of poverty, and frequently of jails"; in short, the abuse of alcohol renders people unfit for liberty, positioning the republic itself "for misery and slavery."[38]

Like Witherspoon in his *Lectures*, Rush's essays on public morals reveal the philosophical tension within republican theology. Tending to private virtue often requires collective action. Rush is no doctrinaire Lockean; he seeks to surgically remove every impediment to American virtue, and he does not mind handing scalpels to local, state, and federal governments in addition to pastors and other guardians of society. Besides abolishing slavery, banning liquor, and educating the young, Rush sees a role for government in outlawing gambling and cockfighting, and in rehabilitating convicted criminals. However, Rush does not fly to government as a reflex. In fact, Rush qualifies his moralism with a basic commitment to limited government, an agenda he supports by developing a rich concept of civil society, a realm of public life that operates independently of the government. Rush rarely frames his pamphlets in terms of a legislative agenda. He appeals first to the consciences of individuals and second to their pastors. He sees the clergy possessing a moral authority that surpasses that of governors and statesmen; in his 1773 slavery article, for instance, Rush refers much of his case to "ministers of the gospel, whose dominion over the principles and affections of men is so universally acknowledged and felt." In the summer of 1788, as the ratification process for the Constitution came to a close, Rush drafted an address to "The Ministers of the Gospel of Every Denomination in the United States, upon Subjects Interesting to Morals," in which he outlined the duties of ministers—both in and out of the pulpit—toward the upkeep of public morals and in which he proposed an interdenominational "convention" of Christian ministers, modeled after the newly forming U.S. government, in which elected representatives from each denomination would meet to discuss "the advancement of morals." Matters of doctrine and church government would be kept off the table: "the design will be, not to make men zealous members of any one church, but to make them good neighbors, good husbands, good fathers, good masters, good servants, and of course, good rulers and good citizens."[39] The proposal reflects Rush's commitment to a religiously grounded civil society as a vital organ of republican life. Government, for Rush, forms the *last* defense—not the first—against the moral degradation of American society. His many letters to the American people manifest a deep faith in the virtue of the individual, but they also point to his belief that such virtue takes shape in community.

This is how both Witherspoon and Rush make practical sense of republican theology, resolving its tensions as a political philosophy. A healthy church, one that promotes virtue, stands as a ballast against despotic government because it maintains a citizenry capable of exercising their liberty. Far from an incidental benefit, liberty remains a central priority for Witherspoon and Rush, an end unto itself. Rush concludes his 1788 address to ministers with this aspiration: "America has taught the nations of Europe to be free, and it is to be hoped she will soon teach them to govern themselves."

IV. THE PROPAGATION OF REPUBLICAN THEOLOGY IN AMERICA

Republican theology has permeated the pulpits and devotional writings of American preachers from the 1760s onward. It offers so clean a narrative for Christianity in the new republic that its basic lines are easy to reproduce; its doctrines inhabit a couple of syllogisms, flexible enough to adapt to a variety of religious, political, or moral agendas, whether one wants to rally Christians as Americans, or to rally Americans as Christians. Indeed, rather than drawing disciples into a particular school of thought, republican theology found its way not only into most church pulpits, but also into the vernacular of American civil religion.

Statesmen as well as clergy preached republican theology to the founding generation. Writing from Philadelphia in 1776, John Adams warned that "Public *virtue* cannot exist in a Nation without private *Virtue*, and public *Virtue* is the only Foundation of Republics."[40] "Human rights," George Washington later expressed in a letter to Gen. Lafayette, "can only be assured among a virtuous people."[41] And James Madison, a Princeton student during the Witherspoon era, seems to have transmitted Witherspoon's lectures into the *Federalist Papers* when he wrote of the "qualities in human nature which justify a certain portion of esteem and confidence. Republican government presupposes the existence of these qualities in a higher degree than any other form."[42] If the American founding, as Ralph Lerner suggests, flagged a new era of "commercial republicanism" in which political ethics shook off the religious moralism of the past and affirmed "the common passions for private gratification and physical comfort," the rhetoric of the age suggests that the leaders of the republic nevertheless believed in the necessity of private virtue and restraint.[43]

On the religious front, republican theology dominated the sermons of the revolutionary period, by way of both encouragement and warning to the colonial rebels. Not surprisingly, revolutionary preachers drew frequent analogy to the liberation of Israel in the Book of Exodus, but rather than use this analogy to construct a "covenantal" theology—one that emphasizes a singular relationship between God and America—these republicans labored to extract more general principles for human politics. Abraham Keteltas, for example, a Long Island Presbyterian who fled to Newburyport, Massachusetts, during the British occupation of his town in 1777, urged his temporary hosts to maintain faith that "God has [always] pled his own and his people's cause." But, he adds, God's cause concerns that of all humanity, namely their "religion, liberty, and virtue." Indeed, "if the principles on which the present civil war is carried on by the American colonies against the British arms were universally adopted and practiced upon by mankind, they would turn a vale of tears into a paradise of God . . . We cannot doubt that the cause of liberty, united with that of truth and righteousness, is the cause of God."[44]

Samuel Cooper, pastor of the Brattle Street Church in Boston, proclaimed ancient Israel itself a "free republic" in its original (and most righteous) form, "till growing weary of the gift of heaven, they demanded a king," which sealed their moral and political demise: "Impiety, corruption and disorder of every kind afterwards increasing among them, they grew ripe for the judgments of heaven in their desolation and captivity."[45] Henry Cumings, a Congregationalist, echoed these same things at a ceremony in Lexington marking the sixth anniversary of the war's commencement: "We should take courage still to stand fast in the liberties wherewith [God] has made us free," he urged, but not without warning: "Nothing darkens our prospects more, or gives us more reason to be fearful as to the event of the present contest, than the great and general prevalence of unrighteousness among us . . . A good cause often suffers, and is sometimes lost, by means of the sin and folly of those who are engaged in it."[46]

Carrying the banner beyond the American Revolution, the "New Divinity" movement illustrates the appeal of republican theology as an enduring feature of American Christianity. A large cohort of conservative evangelical preachers led by Samuel Hopkins and Joseph Bellamy, the New Divinity claimed the mantle of the Great Awakening during the founding era, styling itself as the next generation of New Lights after the death of Jonathan Edwards in 1758. But the New Divinity preachers also made significant departures from Edwardsian tradition, particularly on the nature of virtue, the human capacity for it, and the role of the church in promoting it. Alterations to the tradition began shortly after Edwards' death, even before Witherspoon and Rush graced the scene. Samuel Hopkins, Edwards' brother-in-law, fellow Congregationalist in western Massachusetts, and his closest friend, worried that Edwards' concept of true virtue was too abstract, that its idealism effectively dampened the rationale for evangelical activism in the realm of social morality.[47] Believing it the only way to preserve Edwards' legacy in a revolutionary context, Hopkins and Bellamy, another longtime Edwards associate, crafted a political theology in the 1760s that elevated social morality beyond the "secondary" status to which Edwards had consigned it and grounded any nation's future (Britain's or America's) upon its obedience to the "moral government" of God.[48] Even Jonathan Edwards Jr., a pupil of both Hopkins and Bellamy, gave voice to this sensibility in his preaching: "Political prosperity," he told his congregation in 1794, "requires the general practice of a strict morality. But this cannot be so well secured by any other means as by a belief in Christianity."[49] If Hopkins, Bellamy, and Edwards Jr. essentially gave evangelicals room to consider "improvements" to Edwardsian ethics—revisions that could give the church a clearer role in revolutionary politics—Witherspoon and Rush made the connection between Christianity and individual liberty more explicit. Republican theology popularized a vocabulary that intertwined the aspirations of Christianity and of human liberty, a language that New Divinity preachers came to weave into their own sermons.

In fact, aside from Benjamin Rush, the most fluent exemplar of this new language by the century's turn was also by then the most powerful member of the New Divinity, Timothy Dwight IV, the president of Yale from 1795 to 1817. A grandson of Jonathan Edwards, Dwight's ascension to the Yale presidency—replacing the moderate Ezra Stiles—was seen as a victory for the New Divinity and for the evangelical church in general. Dwight marked his tenure at Yale, and a long pastoral career before that, with an offensive against the apparent tide of Continental philosophy encroaching upon American schools. He issued blunt warnings to his fellow citizens about the perils of secular thinking to American Christianity (and thereby to the republic itself) but also tried to cultivate an American literary tradition, steeped in Calvinism, that would hold its own in the salons of Paris, an ambition he pursued with several other Connecticut writers who dubbed themselves the "Hartford Wits."[50] Over some 20 years of collaboration, the Wits failed to produce anything that garnered much attention in Europe, but Dwight's literary efforts nevertheless leave behind a poetic expression of their republican theology.[51]

Greenfield Hill (1794), an ode to the Fairfield, Connecticut, church where he served for more than a decade, supplies a colorful example. The 167-page poem pays tribute to Fairfield's expansive, pastoral landscape overlooking the Atlantic and the resilience of its people in the face of British tyranny and offers "advice to the villagers"—a chapter-full from a clergyman, urging persistence along the "strait, and rough, and narrow" and another from a farmer, commending industrious, orderly living.[52] The poem culminates in a "Vision" of European demise and American ascendance, a vision that links the "mischief" and "despotism" of the one and the virtue and freedom on the other:

O happy state! The state, by Heaven design'd
To rein, protect, employ, and bless mankind;
Where competence, in full enjoyment, flows;
Where man least vice, and highest virtue, knows;
Where the mind thrives, strong nerves th' invention string;

And daring Enterprize uplifts his wing;
Where splendour spreads, in vain, his peacock-hues;
Where vagrant sloth, the general hiss pursues;
Where business reigns, the universal queen;
Where none are slaves, or lords; but all are men:
No nuisance drones purloin the earner's food;
But each man's labor swells the common good.[53]
. . .
Thrice wretched lands! Where, thousands slaves to one,
Sires know no child beside the eldest son;
Men know no rights, no justice nobles know;
And kings no pleasure, but from subjects woe.
. . .
O blissful visions of the happy West!
O how unlike the miseries of the East!
There, in sad realms of desolating war,
Fell despotism ascends his iron car;
Printed in blood, o'er all the moving throne,
The motto glows, of—Millions made for One.

The poem brings together the essential elements of republican theology—spiritual prosperity enabled by political freedom. As with Rush, republicanism here does not merely present a more benign system of government: it actually promotes Christian virtue among citizens in a way that other systems of government undermine it. When a government stifles property ownership among laborers, for instance, it stifles the chief inducement to the hard work and creativity for which God made humanity, enabling instead pervasive idleness and sloth. When it coerces men into obedience to a despot, or to any hierarchy of authoritarian lords, it robs them of opportunities to build and obey a system of laws as a matter of conscience—to exercise the God-given faculty of moral sense. And yet republics, on their own, cannot make their citizens virtuous, Dwight concedes: it presents only an opportunity—a moment of decision—for a nation to achieve collective virtue, an opportunity easily squandered by public vices. Like Rush before him, Dwight loads his writings with urgent appeals to the American people and to their pastors: "Two only paths before you spread/And long the way, your feet must tread/This strait, and rough, and narrow lies/The course direct to yonder skies."[54] But Dwight's tone is manifestly optimistic: America enjoys the twin advantages of faith and freedom; this "happy state . . . by heaven designed" could not have been designed in vain. It seems clear to Dwight that America's future holds the promises of a robust Christianity, material prosperity, and a firm political tradition of limited government and personal freedom.

V. RUSH'S LAMENT: A THEOLOGY OF UNFULFILLED PROMISE

It makes for an ironic epilogue to this chapter in the development of republican theology that Benjamin Rush comes to abandon that aspiration just as a younger generation was taking it up. Rush, in fact, spent the last several years of his life nursing doubts about the enterprise to which he had devoted most of his career. Just as New Divinity preachers were sharpening republican theology for the first national revival since the American Revolution, Rush withdrew from public life, despairing over his own failure to inspire moral reform and wondering whether republican theology actually tapped into anything more achievable than Edwards' true virtue. In 1806, after a decade of political rancor between Federalists and Republicans, violent disorder over the whiskey tax in his own Pennsylvania, and an epidemic of yellow fever that brought Philadelphia to its knees for several years, Rush declared the American experiment a failure, concluding that the republic had managed in short order to alienate itself from blessing of God. To John Adams he wrote,

> Never perhaps was there a time in which there was more to fear from the wickedness and folly, and less to hope from the virtue and wisdom, of man . . . All systems of political order and happiness seem of late years to have disappointed their founders and advocates. Civilization, science, and commerce have long ago failed in their attempts to improve the condition of mankind, and even liberty itself, from which more was expected than from all other human means, has lately appeared to be insufficient for that purpose. If we fly from the lion of despotism, the bear of anarchy

meets us, or if we retire from both and lean our hand upon the wall of our domestic sanctuary, the recollection of past or the dread of future evils bites us like a serpent.[55]

And to Thomas Jefferson just before his own death in 1813, "From the present complexion of affairs in our country, are you not disposed at times to repent of your solicitude and labors and sacrifices during our Revolutionary struggle for liberty and independence?"[56]

As observed repeatedly in this book, republican theology deals in two-sided coins, with eschatological optimism shining one on side and the specter of irrevocable failure shading the other. Rush's despair shows how quickly the coin can flip for the true believer in republican theology. Writes the historian Robert Abzug, "Rush had dreamed an implausible dream, the transformation of a diverse and unsettled people into a unified nation whose hallmark would be personal, social, and political virtue. He compounded that folly by seeking such a goal under the banner of Republicanism, which in its practical constitutional form insured the kind of individual freedom that made his task well-nigh impossible."[57] As a new generation of republican theologians took up the cause of American civil religion in the 1810s, they faced not only the broad dilemmas of freedom but also the complex matters of moral reform—when so many different vices, from intemperance to slavery, cast a shadow over the American experiment.

ENTRENCHMENT
IN THE SECOND
GREAT AWAKENING

A religious revival in the early nineteenth century seared republican theology onto the American conscience. From the 1810s through the 1830s, as hundreds of preachers advanced their sundry visions for national renewal, civil and private religion practically operated as one. By midcentury the dogma of republican theology—exalting liberty and moral virtue as the essence of human progress—had become accepted wisdom in American Christianity. Alexis de Tocqueville, traveling through the country in 1831, observed that "for the Americans, the ideas of Christianity and liberty are so completely intermingled that it is almost impossible to get them to conceive of the one without the other; it is not a question with them of sterile beliefs bequeathed by the past and vegetating rather than living in the depths of the soul."[1]

By no means, however, did the consensus on this logic unify American Christians on matters of doctrine or even on the priorities of social reform. On the contrary, the tensions built into republican theology manifested in religious divisions—including denominational ruptures splitting North from South—that anticipated the Civil War itself. Evangelicals loyal to the ideals of the Second Great Awakening engaged each other in turf battles over competing moral reform agendas as well as over two major articles of their faith—the sinful condition of the human soul and the moral authority of the Bible. Paradoxically, perhaps, the entrenchment of a political theology became the unraveling of American Christianity.

I. THE REVIVAL

Two trends mark the Second Great Awakening—religious revival meetings across New England and the Western frontier that recalled those of the 1730s and 40s, and the birth of hundreds of voluntary societies self-tasked with reforming American morals. In search of continuity between the two Great Awakenings, historians generally trace the second wave to the progeny of Jonathan Edwards—his disciples Samuel Hopkins and Joseph Bellamy; his son, Edwards Jr.; and most especially his grandson, Timothy Dwight V, who galvanized a generation of preachers when he took the presidency of Yale in 1795. However, an ocean of social, political, and even religious upheaval stands between the two movements, and theological differences manifest even in the early writings of Hopkins and Bellamy. Changes to the landscape include the American Revolution, its dénouement in the ratification of the Constitution, more remotely (but no less portentously) the French Revolution with its elusive dénouement, and as a final straw, the Jeffersonian sweep of American politics in 1800. The changes brought not just new battlefields for the evangelical gospel, but a new vocabulary with which to preach it, namely the republican theology of Rush and Witherspoon. The departures of the Second Great Awakening from the First—its fixation on public morality and its shifting view of sin—are much better understood in light of republican theology than in tracing a genealogy to Jonathan Edwards. Indeed, the unique expectations that republican theology raised in the minds of founding-era evangelicals are what fostered the very anxieties that fueled the revivals.

Moral laxity in American culture—hard drinking, Sabbath-breaking, and a slavery system that seemed to grow more brutal by the decade—came as a shock to many evangelicals, most of whom had supported the Revolution at the prospect of upward spiritual mobility. Dwight's appointment at Yale, replacing the moderate Ezra Stiles, can be seen as an institutional reaction to the problem. Dwight, as we have seen, had already taken up the cause of arresting the slide toward European morality and theology, and had done so with language that also sanctified the commitment to personal freedom in America, "where competence in full enjoyment flowers; where man least vice, and highest virtue, knows."[2]

The clergy that came out of Dwight's Yale aimed their ministries at the redemption of American liberty: if Americans declined morally, went the motivating logic, they would not be a free people for very long. Moving into parishes across New England, the Mid-Atlantic region, and the newly admitted states of Ohio, Kentucky, Tennessee, and Illinois, these young preachers pushed two initiatives to achieve national redemption. First, they preached revival, changing not only the tone, rhythm, and substance of the evangelical sermon but also its venue—from the Sunday confines of the church to the open air all week long. Second, the preachers lent their stature to the creation of reform societies, local and national organizations that promoted moral virtue.

Lyman Beecher's career, though luminous, offers a microcosm of the sort of path taken by dozens of ministers in this era. Leaving Yale in 1798, Beecher settled for a decade in East Hampton, New York, where he established his first reform society, this one aimed at "restoring to the town, as far as might be its ancient purity of morals."[3] He moved to Litchfield, Connecticut, in 1810, where he launched no fewer than four statewide organizations, including the Connecticut Society for the Suppression of Vice and the Promotion of Good Morals, which enlisted 2,000 members to fight "intemperance, Sabbath-breaking, and profane swearing" through direct pressure on clergy and public officials and through mass mailings.[4] Beecher's Litchfield years also saw the development of his revival sermon style, focused less upon scripture and doctrine than upon application and action. His daughter, the author Harriet Beecher Stowe, wrote, "A sermon that did not induce anybody to do anything [my father] considered a sermon thrown away."[5]

Beecher extended his preaching ministry beyond the Sunday pulpit, calling his own parishioners to midweek meetings and embarking on itinerant schedules to Hartford, Boston, and New Haven. Eventually every meeting Beecher presided over took on the character of a revival, complete with invitations to the unconverted and prayer gatherings for new converts and repentant sinners.[6] An appointment to the prominent Hanover Church in Boston in 1826 gave Beecher a perch from which to take the revival movement national. Not only did he interact with a wider slice of the American public in Boston (William Lloyd Garrison, for instance, came to faith under Beecher's preaching there), but Beecher came into far greater demand as an itinerant. Additionally, Beecher took the lead in proposing, to the American Sunday School Union in 1830, a missionary campaign to the newly settled Mississippi Valley, a commitment that ultimately led to his appointment as the founding president of Lane Theological Seminary in Cincinnati, where he finished out a long career that touched nearly every reform movement of the era, including abolitionism.[7]

Other preaching celebrities of Beecher's generation, often crossing paths (and sometimes swords) with Beecher himself, include Asahel Nettleton, another Yale graduate and a conservative Calvinist itinerant to whom is credited over 30,000 conversions from Connecticut to South Carolina; Charles Grandison Finney, a New York evangelist and abolitionist who eventually moved west to be the president of Oberlin College; James McGready, who spent 17 years planting Presbyterian churches in Kentucky; Peter Cartwright, a Methodist circuit rider in the Western states who baptized over 12,000 converts (and who lost a seat to the U.S. House of Representatives to Abraham Lincoln in 1846); Lorenzo Dow, whose preaching adventures throughout the states regularly attracted crowds of thousands; William Lloyd Garrison, founder of the American Anti-Slavery Society; and Sylvester Graham, a New Jersey Presbyterian who concocted a bran and wheat-germ flatbread in 1829 intended to suppress sexual urges (modern-day Graham crackers now contain honey and refined sugar and are no longer marketed as vice suppressants).[8]

The "meeting mania" achieved tabloid fascination in the 1820s and added significant numbers to church rosters.[9] In the first half of the nineteenth century, the U.S. population quadrupled to 20 million, while the number of clergy increased 20-fold to 40,000. Registered denominations doubled in number, and there was a tenfold rise in church membership, largely fueled by the explosive growth of Baptists and Methodists.[10]

The shift from Presbyterian dominance to the prevalence of Baptist and Methodist congregations (which grew, respectively, from 450 to over 12,000 and from zero to roughly 20,000 between 1780 and 1860) points to two other trends in American religion, the first being its migration from Calvinist to Arminian theology (discussed at length later in the chapter) and the second being its decentralized operation.[11] Though American denominations were never very centralized to begin with, this particular revival followed a republican mindset that downplayed ecclesiastical ties and prized local, independent congregations and preachers. As Andrew Murphy notes, the most influential Christians of the day were "leading players in a lively religious marketplace rather than an elite marked off from the people by distinction of education and [biblical] literacy."[12]

In the spirit of grassroots religion, every state and many towns (even on the frontier) saw the birth of private societies and leagues aimed at moral reform of some sort or another in the decades preceding the Civil War. The appendix of one study of the era lists 159 such organizations, from the Bangor Sabbath School Society in Maine to the New Orleans Temperance Society.[13] The voluntarist movement made a strong enough imprint on American civil life for Tocqueville to take notice: "Americans of all ages, all stations in life, and all types of dispositions," he observed, "are forever forming associations . . . If they want to proclaim a truth or propagate some feeling by the encouragement of a great example, they form an association."[14] As these societies bourgeoned, argues one historian, "evangelicals thought they had found a way to win the nations of the world for Christ, with none of the disadvantages of establishment."[15]

In all of its aspects, from its decentralized ecclesiology and market-generated elites to its voluntarism and works-oriented theology, the Second Great Awakening exemplified what Gordon Wood calls the "democratization of mind" that trailed the American Revolution.[16] In the span between the two awakenings, writes William McLoughlin, "Americans moved 180 degrees from a patriarchal to an egalitarian view of politics, or, as some would put it, from a deferential social order to an essentially individualistic one. In that process they dramatically redefined their understanding of nature, of human nature, and of the locus and operation of God's power."[17] I wish to argue that this "democratization of mind," far from some vague ethos that oozed into the American psyche, actually took its effectual form in the doctrines of republican theology. Revivalists of all stripes made conscious efforts to latch their aims to the aspirations of the new nation, a task for which republican theology, as expounded by founding-era evangelicals, was already uniquely suited.

II. REPUBLICAN THEOLOGY AS THE LANGUAGE OF THE MOVEMENT

The Second Great Awakening covered a vast religious terrain, brooking disparities in doctrine and a variety of reform initiatives. Gradually, pluralism gave way to fissure—and, by midcentury, mass bloodshed. At the outset, however, a common theological impulse, to shake off Calvinism, permeated all of the sects that experienced revival. While Arminian denominations like Methodism reaped most of the benefits, the impetus of the movement captivated Presbyterians and Congregationalists as well. What accounts for this early continuity, I will argue here, is the broad attractiveness of republican theology to American Christians. Not until the 1820s, in fact, did the Arminianism of republican theology become as upsetting to American Calvinists as it had been (in its pilot version, as Scottish moral sense) to Jonathan Edwards in the 1750s. By the early nineteenth century republican theology had settled too deeply into the American conscience to suffer much by way of contestation. Midcentury Calvinists found themselves fighting its implications, not its premises.

A cross-denominational sample of preaching from this period shows a broad commitment to the central themes of republican theology: First, revivalists and reformers affirm the sanctity of liberty as a God-given right and as a condition of vibrant Christian faith. Second, they point to the necessity of moral virtue for the maintenance of liberty. And third, despite the decibel of their alarms, revivalists of this era project optimism toward the ability of Americans to reform their society and to thereby lay claim to a privileged eschatological destiny. Each of these premises found an ample foothold in the sermons of this era.

Liberty as Sacred

The consecration of natural liberty—and of its citadel in the American republic—comes in a grab bag of pronouncements. Beecher's are the most emphatic: "No other portion of the human race ever commenced a national existence as we commenced ours," he exulted to the Connecticut Society in 1812. "Nowhere beside, if you search the world over, will you find so much real liberty, so much equality, so much personal safety and temporal prosperity, so general an extension of useful knowledge, so much religious instruction, so much moral restraint, and so much divine mercy, to make these blessings the power of God and the wisdom of God unto salvation."[18] Beecher posited the organic necessity of liberty to faith repeatedly throughout his ministry. He named "the suffrages of freemen" and "the rights of conscience" as preconditions for the "moral renovation of the world" promised in the final chapter of Revelation.[19] He even hailed the collapse of Puritanism in the eighteenth century as a boon for Christian revival: "At the very time when civil law had become impotent for the support of religion and the prevention of immoralities, God began to pour out his Spirit upon the churches; and voluntary associations of Christians were raised up to apply and extend that influence, which the law could no longer apply."[20] The Holy Spirit, in other words, does his best work in the land of the free.

Moral crusaders of this era took Beecher's line of reasoning for granted, largely assuming the sacred entitlement to liberty as their starting position. Indeed, the rhetorical battles between temperance advocates and abolitionists often revolved around a contest as to which vice—booze or slavery—presented the gravest threat to American liberty. That abolitionists held the upper hand in this contest is even more telling than it would seem. Antislavery rationales had come a long way since the early 1700s: whereas eighteenth-century Christians routinely condemned the chattel regime for its sins—its reliance on kidnapping, its brutality, its spiritual neglect of slaves, and its denigration of families—nineteenth-century abolitionists adopted the categorical (and counter-scriptural) position that slaveholding itself is sinful.[21] In *The Bible against Slavery* (1838), Theodore Weld, a onetime protégé of Beecher's, implicates the generic slaveholder in crimes against humanity: "He does not merely disenfranchise the humanity of one individual, but UNIVERSAL MAN . . . He attacks not only the human race, but universal being, and rushes upon Jehovah. For rights are rights; God's are no more—man's are no less."[22] The Congregationalist Jonathan Blanchard, later the founding president of Wheaton College, defended this viewpoint at a Cincinnati forum in 1845, staking upon it the moral authority of Christianity itself: "The question is, whether humanity can look to Christianity and find protection. Whether the oppressed can flee to the sanctuary of the Gospel of Christ and find a refuge there—or whether the religion affords no protection to human rights. In other words, whether the religion we profess is a humane or an inhumane religion."[23] Whereas Beecher would tout the advantages of liberty for Christian faith, Weld and Blanchard went a step further: it is Christianity that serves the cause of liberty.

Temperance advocates took a somewhat different tack in promoting their cause but nevertheless hung the concept of liberty in the balance. Seeking to co-opt the abolitionist rhetoric, temperance reformers pointed to alcohol as the true enslaver of American society. An Independence Day address by Heman Humphrey, another Congregationalist, and president of Amherst College, is characteristic: "May the fourth of July never dawn," he exhorts, "without exciting in every American bosom the warmest gratitude to Heaven for the blessings of civil and religious liberty." But, he pivots:

> Slavery and not independence will be my theme [today] . . . You
> will naturally suppose I allude to that grievous anomaly in our
> free constitution, which darkens all the southern horizon; but
> I have a more brutifying and afflictive thralldom in view. For,
> however cruel and debasing and portentous African servitude
> may be, beyond the Potomac, there exists, even in New England,
> a far sorer bondage, from which the slaves of the South are
> happily free . . .[24]

This "man-devouring shape," Humphrey explains, is hard drinking: "It chains and scourges the soul, as well as the body. It has a servitude from which death itself has no power to release the captive." Humphrey's contention holds significance in two ways: yes, it further underscores the centrality of liberty to moral reasoning among nineteenth-century Christians, but it also shows the variable definition of liberty within that discourse. In arguing that excessive alcohol robs people of their freedom, Humphrey refers to a different kind of freedom than what slaves are deprived of in the South—not civil liberty, but something far more existential, namely the moral capacity to self-govern, the possession of rationality, the proper rule of the mind over the body. A man is not truly free, goes the principle, if he is morally impaired by alcohol, or worse, addicted to getting drunk.

If the antislavery rhetoric showcases republican theology at its outer edge—subjecting religion to the cause of civil liberty—the temperance movement recalls *why* evangelicals embraced civil liberty in the first place. Following Witherspoon, American evangelicals came to believe in the freedom of the will, in a person's natural ability to discern and obey the law of God, and even to perfect oneself in righteousness; that is, they rejected, however implicitly, the Calvinist tenets of original sin, total depravity, and divine election. Those doctrines had long divided Protestants, but during the First Great Awakening it was the evangelicals like Edwards and Whitefield who held fast to them. Republicanism changed that: Benjamin Rush left the Presbyterians over these very issues in the 1780s, just as he was fusing the reformist agenda to the language of republican theology. By the nineteenth century evangelical Presbyterian clergy took the lead in affirming the essential freedom of the will, none more provocatively than Charles Grandison Finney, the longtime president of Oberlin College. "All men are naturally free," he preached in 1856, "and none the less so for being sinners." Liberty does not mean the license to do as one pleases, Finney explained, but rather a status of "moral sovereignty" in which "every man knows that he has a conscience which tells him how he ought to act, as well as a moral power in the exercise of which he can either heed or repel its monitions."[25] For Finney, natural liberty consists in freedom of the will, which itself consists in what the Scots called "moral sense"—the ability to discern right from wrong and the power to do right. The tragedy of vice, particularly in a society enlightened to this natural state of liberty, is that it subjects sinners to an utterly preventable state of slavery: "Their bondage," Finney laments, "is altogether voluntary."[26]

Moral Virtue as Essential to the Republic

Republican theologians predicate a free republic upon the moral rectitude of its people, and not just because certain vices, like chattel slavery and alcoholism, undermine the image of a free society. The connection between moral virtue and civil liberty is seen as cosmic. Writes Finney:

> God has always providentially given to mankind those forms of government that were suited to the degrees of virtue and intelligence among them. If they have been extremely ignorant and

vicious, He has restrained them by the iron rod of human despotism. If more intelligent and virtuous, He has given them milder
forms of limited monarchies. If still more intelligent and virtuous,
He has given them still more liberty, and providentially established republics for their government. Whenever the general state
of intelligence has permitted it, He has put them to the test of
self-government and self-restraint, by establishing democracies.[27]

Behind this apparently linear relationship between liberty and virtue
stands another one between individual and collective morality. The
moral agendas of nineteenth-century reformers pertained not only
to matters of public justice, like the honoring of contracts and the
peaceful treatment of neighbors, but also to what many might consider to be *private* behavior, like marital fidelity, personal moderation,
and the proper worship of God. Finney lists among national sins such
vices as Sabbath-breaking, vulgarity, intemperance, and the "love of
money."[28] The Christian character of *individual* Americans, in other
words, was very much on the mind of moral reformers in the early
nineteenth century. What is distinctive about republican theology is
that it posits a collective accountability for these private virtues and
vices. "Each nation," Finney suggests, "is regarded by God as a unit."
As a result, national sins must be "publicly confessed and renounced."
Private vice becomes public vice, it seems, not on account of its civic
consequences but rather on account of its cumulative corruption of
individual souls.

Murphy points out that the "jeremiad," a prophetic genre with roots
in the Old Testament, has maintained a nearly constant presence in
American discourse from the Puritan era into the twenty-first century. This type of sermon, moreover, has exhibited several continuous
features, including reference to "a larger, sacred story," a belief in the
"chosen" status of the nation, a "lament" over the nation's moral decline, and a warning to reform. What is unique about the American
jeremiad of the early nineteenth century, Murphy notes, is their consciousness of America as not only a *chosen* nation, but also as a *liberated*
nation: "The notion of an American Israel throwing off oppression
in order to take up its national mission settled ever more deeply into
American public rhetoric."[29] The American jeremiad, in other words,
became inflected with specifically republican stakes.

Second Great Awakening preachers had in common the nagging apprehension that a republic of immoral citizens presents a contradiction in terms and stands doomed to failure. Such a fear provided the impetus for the numerous voluntary societies, like Beecher's Connecticut Society for the Suppression of Vice and the Promotion of Good Morals. He outlined the stakes at its founding summit in 1812: "When the people will not endure the restraint of righteous laws, and suffer them to sin with impunity, and when magistrates will sell their consciences and the public good for a little brief authority, then the public suffrage is of but little value, for the day of liberty is drawing to a close, and the night of despotism is at hand."[30]

This kind of warning reemerged at moments of social crisis, never more urgently than in the months preceding the start of the Civil War, when nearly all of the reform movements in America, including abolitionism, seemed on the verge of collapse with the republic itself. Evangelical preachers on both sides of the slavery question took to pulpits in the winter of 1860–61 to pin the country's troubles upon the eroding morals of its people. The Virginia Presbyterian Robert Dabney declared in November that "The kingdom of Jesus Christ . . . is committed by its Divine Head to human hands, and is partially dependent on the course of human events" as he called Americans to the "humble confessions of our sins, individual and social." Dabney derided "that peculiar sin of the Southern country, the passion for bloody retaliation of personal wrong, which has been so often professed and indulged among us, unwhipped of justice," referring at length, not to slavery (which goes unmentioned in the sermon), but rather to the practice of dueling.[31]

Up North, Henry Ward Beecher (Lyman's son) issued a summons to his Brooklyn church in early January, one identical, in form at least, to Dabney's: "It is well, then, that every one of us make this day the beginning of a solemn review of his own life . . . [for] the sins of a nation are always the sins of certain central passions." Instead of dueling, however, Beecher focused his ire upon the mistreatment of American Indians, Mexicans, and above all African slaves, in which he implicated Northern merchants and consumers as much as Southern plantation owners.[32]

If their conflation of public and private morality strains against the libertarian sensibility, so do the methods to which republican theologians of the nineteenth century willingly turn to reform society.

Their first line of defense against depravity, of course, is the pulpit, and the preaching juggernauts of this era exhibit ample confidence in this mode of reform—appealing directly to the people to alter their behavior. Even this ministry, however, enjoyed government assistance. It was commonplace, for instance, for U.S. presidents, in a relic tradition of the Puritans, to proclaim days of national fasting, which, while not legally binding upon citizens, gave American clergy a public platform upon which to "arouse and quicken the public conscience" and to call upon citizens to repent of their sins.[33] The quotations above from Finney, for instance, date from a fast day proclaimed by President Tyler to commemorate President Harrison's untimely death in 1841; the sermon extracts from Dabney and H. W. Beecher trace to a similar summons from President Buchanan after the secession of South Carolina in 1860.

Far beyond the pulpit, however, evangelical leaders believed in the necessity of law to restrain immoral behavior. As Lyman Beecher reasoned, "In a free government, moral suasion and coercion must be united . . . It is indispensable, not only that new fidelity pervade the family, the school, and the church of God, but that the laws against immorality be restored to their ancient vigor."[34] On temperance, for instance, Beecher believed that "it is in vain to rely alone upon self-government and voluntary abstinence" and instead proposed "the banishment of strong drinks from the list of lawful articles of commerce," a dream that wouldn't come to national fruition until 1919.[35] When Congress ruled in 1820 that the U.S. mail would be delivered on Sundays, there emerged "a spate of societies" lobbying against the law, including, for instance, the General Union for Promoting the Observance of the Christian Sabbath.[36] And abolitionists, of course, endorsed legislation that ranged from the gradual to the immediate emancipation of slaves, with various proposals for compensating plantations, and some advocating the deportment of freed slaves back to Africa.

Eschatological Optimism

The stakes attached to the moral health of the nation reinforce the impetus to promote virtue. The price of degeneracy, according to the prophecy, is nothing less than national obliteration; the reward for righteousness, however, is an eschatological march to glory. While this march is seen as gradual and progressive, republican theology offers no complacent middle ground: either America moves forward in grace or slumps backward into ruin. "The scale is on a poise," warned Finney in 1835, "Things cannot remain as they are."[37] That the United States enjoyed the twin blessings of freedom and Christianity only raised the ante. The urgency of reformist preaching emanates as much from the cosmic triumph that would attend a successful reformation—and optimism over America's potential to achieve it—as from the tragic consequences that would accompany failure. Lyman Beecher predicated much of his preaching ministry on the confidence "that *this* nation has been raised up by providence to exert an efficient instrumentality in the work of moral renovation" for the entire human race.[38]

Abolitionists tethered the nation's progress in righteousness to the emancipation of slaves in the South. Benjamin Lundy, an early associate of William Lloyd Garrison, invested the abolition of slavery with teleological force in their Baltimore journal, *The Genius of Universal Emancipation*:

> The principles and maxims adopted by those sages who laid the foundation for this great and flourishing Empire, are beginning to develop themselves more fully to the view of the American people, and to attract the admiration of millions of the human race. Thousands are daily becoming more and more enlightened, the prejudice of education is vanishing before the luminous orb of truth, and the gloom of superstition is partially dispelled by the effulgent rays of reason and Christian philosophy . . . And seeing it hath often pleased the All Wise to make use of human agency as a means whereby the foulest corruptions have been rooted out, and the most glorious reformations have been effected in the societies of men, it may fairly be presumed that the present generation will have much to do towards eradicating the noxious plant from the soil of Columbia.[39]

In general, American evangelicals of this era, facing not only a tide of socio-ethical quandaries but also the specters of religious pluralism and skepticism, were eager to consolidate Christianity, national greatness, and civic liberty into a unified movement of history, and to invest that movement with a sense of destiny. Finney, celebrating the "great and glorious revival" in American religion, went as far to predict, in 1835, that "if the church will do all her duty, the millennium may come in this country in three years."[40]

Nevertheless, warned the preachers, it is never too late to blow it. Finney noted, "It has always been the case, whenever any of the servants of God do anything in his cause, and there appears to be a probability that they will succeed, that Satan by his agents regularly attempts to diver their minds and nullify their labors." Twenty-five sins make up Finney's list of "hindrances" to the cause of God, ranging from denominational rivalry, Calvinistic naysaying, and clerical sloth to the usual suspects—Sabbath-breaking, intemperance, and slavery, which are subjects "upon which [Christians] cannot be silent without guilt."[41] Despite his underlying optimism for an American millennium, Finney harbored real anxiety that the nation would fall short: "If revivals do cease in this land, the ministers and churches will be guilty of all the blood of all the souls that shall go to hell in consequence of it . . . The curse of God will be on this nation, and that before long."[42] Beecher, too, peppered his progressive vision with dire warnings against failure: "If we do not awake and engage vigorously in the work of reformation, it will soon be too late . . . Our sins will be upon us, and we shall pine away and die in them. To this state of things we are hastening; and if no effort be made to stop our progress, the sun in his course is not more resistless than our doom."[43] In these early expressions of what later thinkers will call "American exceptionalism," the onus falls upon the public to preserve the nation's cosmic status—or lose it in a spectacular show of wrath.

III. THE FRACTURING OF THE AMERICAN CHURCH

In the end, the lofty aspirations and broad canopy of republican theology proved no match against—indeed, they aggravated—an array of conflicts within American Christianity, some of which lay subtext for the Civil War itself, and others of which settled deep into religious life, driving many Christians out of politics and into an antagonistic relationship with American culture. Four kinds of internecine tension merit discussion here: rivalries over the priorities of moral reform, denominational schisms, friction over the theology of sin, and a crisis of identity centering on the moral authority of scripture.

Conflicts over Moral Reform

The most superficial tensions played out as rivalries between different reform movements, none more strident than between abolitionists and temperance advocates. Itinerants with broad followings like Beecher and Finney tried their best to remain above this fray and to reconcile the competing initiatives under the common banner of preserving liberty and Christianity, but even those preachers chose sides, when pressed—Beecher's heart lay with the temperance cause, for instance, while Finney leaned toward antislavery—often to the fury of their followers. Garrison, who had "found the Lord" under Beecher's preaching in the 1820s, published his later disaffection with Beecher in *The Liberator*: "The Dr. undertakes to 'glance at some of the perils which threaten us,' but the existence of slavery is not in the catalogue. The 'prevalence of Atheism' attracts his notice. But is not the slave system practically based upon Atheism? Does it not dethrone God, dehumanize man, blot out free agency, and overturn the moral government of the universe?"[44]

For his part, Beecher developed some resentment toward the abolitionists after an 1834 episode at Lane Seminary in Cincinnati, early in his tenure as president. Theodore Dwight Weld, then a student at the seminary and the founder of its Antislavery Society, had persuaded Beecher to open the chapel for a series of debates on slavery, during which he persuaded much of the student body to embrace Garrisonian "immediatism" and equal rights for blacks and to reject the seminary's official stance in favor of colonization. The changing winds on campus alarmed the trustees, who banned the Antislavery Society; Weld and 40 classmates, known as the "Lane Rebels," quit the school *en masse* and enrolled at Finney's Oberlin College. Beecher, whose attempts to quiet the storm proved ineffectual, blamed the strife on Weld.[45]

Tensions inevitably arise between social movements as they compete for supporters, resources, and political power. These tensions escalate, moreover, when this competition tugs at a common subgroup of citizens, like evangelical Christians, and even more so when it revolves around a common discourse, or theology, from which each side attempts to draw its own imperatives. Much of the discord between temperance and abolitionism concerns their competing conceptions of freedom. We have already seen how temperance advocates like Heman Humphrey tried to appropriate the language of slavery to character- ize alcoholism and its grip on American society—"a far sorer bondage, from which the slaves of the South are happily free."[46] Abolitionists took the more straightforward agenda of fighting for civil liberty as a spiritual good; Garrison's "Prospectus" for *The Liberator* endorsed "the emanci- pation of our whole race from the dominion of man, from the thrall- dom of self, from the government of brute force, from the bondage of sin—and bringing them under the dominion of God, the control of an inward spirit, the government of the law of love, and into the obedience and liberty of Christ."[47] Whereas the temperance movement sought to liberate the public by regulating the most private of behaviors, aboli- tionists sought to do so by enlarging political rights and bringing more people into the official franchise of the free. Activists end up resenting each other for stealing attention from what they each see as the grim- mer threat to liberty. "The prevalent use of ardent spirits in the United States is a worse evil at this moment than the slave trade ever was in the height of its horrible prosperity," chided a desperate Humphrey.

Denominational Schisms

In the span of a decade, between 1837 and 1846, each of America's three largest denominations, the Presbyterians, Baptists, and Method- ists, split into Northern and Southern factions. It vastly oversimplifies these schisms to label the sides "pro-South" versus "pro-North," or even "pro-slavery" versus "anti-slavery." For one thing, the new de- nominations were not strictly regional; they all maintained parishes throughout the United States. The theological dispute that ripped them apart, moreover, was a shade more complex than whether the church candidly approved or disapproved of American slavery. None of these national denominations, in fact, endorsed the chattel system; all three had long called for its termination, with Northern and South- ern preachers joining the cause. The difference of opinion, rather, concerned whether slaveholding itself categorically violates the law of God, a question that had implications for how the church should treat its slaveholding members (even those who had never purchased slaves). More importantly, the question drives to the heart of evangelical

Christianity: if the Bible does not categorically outlaw slaveholding, upon what authority does the church declare it to be a sin?

While a 1837 schism between "New School" and "Old School" Presbyterians did not produce a clean-cut division along the Mason-Dixon Line—21 revivalist presbyteries in the South joined the New School, for instance—two more fractures soon followed that finished the job. The initial split followed broad disagreements over revival tactics and reform priorities. In 1850, however, the New School's General Assembly called for disciplinary action against slaveholders within the denomination, prompting the Presbytery of Lexington to issue a declaration of defiance. By 1857 the tension over slaveholding broke the New School in two.[48] A common aversion to radical abolitionism kept the Old School together until war broke out in 1861. As late as December 1860 the Old School Presbyterian Henry Van Dyke was publicly blaming New Schoolers for the national crisis in his Brooklyn church, just a few city blocks away from Henry Ward Beecher's antislavery stronghold: "I trust and pray, and call upon you to unite with me in the supplication, that God would give abolitionists repentance and a better mind."[49]

The preeminent revivalist denominations, Methodists and Baptists witnessed relentless feuds over the slavery issue. For decades their central organizations affected a kind of neutrality on slavery—issuing periodic condemnations of the institution without imposing official sanctions on slaveholders—but abolitionist factions within each denomination, like the Wesleyan Methodists and the American Baptist Antislavery Convention, gained strength throughout the 1830s and early 40s, eventually pushing the denominational leadership into a hardline position. For the Baptists, it was an 1844 decision by the General Convention to disallow slaveholding missionaries that prompted Southern congregations to form their own separate alliance—the Southern Baptist Convention—in May 1845.

The Methodists' fissure opened more gradually, with some 15,000 Northerners bolting the national denomination to join the Wesleyan Methodist Church in 1844. In spite of those defections, antislavery Methodists achieved such an edge over Southerners that in 1845 they were able to gather enough votes at the General Conference in New York to defrock James O. Andrew, a Georgia bishop who had come into an unwilling possession of two slaves upon the death of his first wife. The affront to the Southern synods prompted an immediate withdrawal: at that very Conference they formed the Methodist Episcopal Church South, comprising over a half-million members. Northerners offered no resistance, working nimbly to facilitate a reallocation of common property before the Conference adjourned.[50]

The Presbyterian, Baptist, and Methodist schisms, to state the obvious, represent only the divisions among white evangelicals, most of whom remained oblivious to (or more likely complacent with) the ever-increasing gulf between white and black Christians in America. The very same decades that saw evangelicals split along territorial lines also saw the formation and early growth of the African American Church, first in the non-slave states, then absorbing Southern freemen after the war.

Across the various divides, American Christians in the 1840s and 50s agreed on one prediction—that the denominational schisms spelled trouble for the republic itself. If Christians could not maintain fellowship within a Christian nation, then it was doubtful that citizens could withstand the growing pressures of disunion. The Methodist Peter Cartwright surmised in 1856 that the split in his church "spread terror over almost every other branch of the Church of Christ, and really, disguise it as we may, shook the pillars of our American government to the center . . . [precipitating] a fearful step toward the downfall of our happy republic."[51] Had the denominations maintained unity it would certainly have given millions of citizens some compelling reasons to avoid the most gruesome conflict in American history. At the war's end, when President Lincoln proclaimed that the adversaries "read the same Bible and pray to the same God," he did not merely offer grounds for reconciliation; he exposed a theological wound at the heart of the conflict.[52]

Doctrinal Conflicts

Two conflicts over Christian doctrine—confrontations that, I have already argued, come embedded within republican theology—moved into the open as the sharpest points of division among Christians in antebellum America. The first concerned the nature and power of sin, and the other concerned the moral authority of the Bible. Both issues nagged the church in the eighteenth century, if not before, but the early nineteenth century saw the doctrinal center of gravity on each question shift enough to alter the character of American Christianity and its role in public discourse.

The changing perceptions of sin might be described, in medieval terms, as a shift from an Augustinian to a Pelagian view, or in early Protestant terms, as a shift from Calvinism to Arminianism. Augustinians and Calvinists view human sin as an inherited condition of the soul that renders it incapable of communing with God in the manner intended at Creation, the consequence of which is eternal separation from God. From this perspective flow the doctrines of "original sin"—the condition passes genetically from Adam and Eve to everyone else—and "total depravity"—people are utterly helpless in this condition apart from divine intervention. On the other side, Pelagians and Arminians view sin as having equally devastating consequences as the Augustinians do, but they characterize sin as a behavioral activity rather than as a state of being, and its grip on the human soul as external rather than internal. All people sin as a matter of course, but their power to resist temptation is merely corrupted by habit, not fatally impaired by Adam. Depravity for the Arminian is something less than total—the sinner can still freely reach out and take hold of salvation through faith in Christ. For the Augustinian, faith itself comes only through divine intervention.

Jonathan Edwards stands as the symbol of how central Augustinian theology was to evangelicals in the eighteenth century. He famously attributed the mass conversions during First Great Awakening to "the surprising work of God" and spent the last year of his life writing a dissertation entitled *The Great Christian Doctrine of Original Sin Defended* (1758).[53] The doctrines of original sin and total depravity, however, do not sit well with republican theology, which affirms the freedom of the will and the essential goodness of human nature. Without overtly rejecting Augustinianism, early expositors of republican theology like Witherspoon and Dwight distanced themselves from it by making civil morality (which even Edwards admits is achievable by the unregenerate) the essence of Christian nationhood.

Explicit rejections of Augustinianism, however, swept the evangelical church in the 1820s. Leading the charge on the academic front was Nathaniel Taylor, a student of Dwight's and a professor of didactic theology at Yale from 1822 until 1858. Conceding no scripture to the Calvinists, Taylor reinterprets one of their marquee verses—Ephesians

2:3, "For you were by nature the children of wrath"—to mean only that everybody is subject to God's wrath through their sin, and that everybody sins because they are naturally free to do so. Nature does not compel sin, he argues; it enables it. Taylor's emphatic point is that the original sin doctrine blunts revivalism by obscuring the free choice people have between God's wrath and God's salvation: "To what purpose do we preach the Gospel to men if we cannot reach the conscience with its charge of guilt and obligations to duty? And how, I ask, can this be done unless sin and duty be shown to consist simply and wholly in the acts and doings which are their own?"[54]

Charles Grandison Finney brought the critique of original sin into the mainstream of American evangelicalism. Writes one historian, "Finney viewed the [Calvinist] theology of the Westminster Confession, as far as evangelism is concerned, as a carriage driver would a swamp; it does nothing but bog it down."[55] Such anxieties, of course, overlook the historical fact that the First Great Awakening spread mainly under the preaching of committed Calvinists like Edwards, George Whitefield, and Gilbert Tennant, as Arminians like Charles Chauncey waited skeptically on the sidelines.[56] What changed in the nineteenth century were the *civic* aspirations that attended revival, and particularly the hope that the new republic could achieve national salvation through its virtue. While the doctrines of original sin and total depravity do not preclude evangelism, they do question the efficacy of social reform as a means of sanctification. It stands to reason, then, that the formal turn against Augustinianism in the American church followed the rise of republican theology as a civil religion.

The turn also gave way to innovations in revivalism, not just the growth of reform societies but also aggressive new tactics—"new measures" in period parlance—used at the revival meetings to win converts, such as the practice of calling out sinners by name and the "anxious seat," in which the repentant could receive special attention and prayer from the crowd.[57] The new measures, effective in stoking the revival, provoked a backlash from conservatives, who, this time around, encompassed the dwindling faction of preachers who still believed in original sin and total depravity.

Asahel Nettleton, a New England itinerant whose own travels saw thousands of conversions, offered the most consistent voice against both the new measures and the Pelagian shift in theology. In a defense of the doctrine of total depravity, for instance, Nettleton tries to refute the charge that the doctrine undermines free moral agency: depraved humans, he insists, "possess all the faculties which are essential to moral agency—reason, judgment, memory, will, and affections. If they were not free moral agents, they could not be the subjects of moral depravity." Conscience, Nettleton argues, "will exist in hell. It is the worm which never dies." Depravity does not imply, then, the inability to discern and perform certain moral duties, but rather a state of infidelity to the Giver of life: "By the doctrine of Total Depravity is meant that all men, by nature, are destitute of love to God, and consequently wholly sinful—or to adopt the language of [Genesis 6:5], that 'every imagination of the thoughts of their heart is only evil continually.' "[58] The doctrine does not preclude calling sinners to repentance, but such a turn of heart can only happen by the intervention of God, a divine initiative to reclaim a wayward lover: "The Bible does call upon sinners to do what it requires the Almighty power of God to influence them to do."[59]

Nettleton objected to the "new measures" because they drew upon human rather than divine power and, as such, indulged in cultic excess. Nettleton took particular alarm at the more zealous itinerants' incivility, bullying, and willingness to break up congregations. "Fire is an excellent thing in its place," he wrote in an open letter to New England divines in January 1827, "and I am not afraid to see it blaze among briers and thorns; but when I see it kindling where it will ruin fences, and gardens, and houses, and burn up my friends, I cannot be silent." Devices like the anxiety seat, in Nettleton's view, only reinforce a theological error, a belief that human efforts can penetrate a depraved heart. "Seven years ago," he recalls in a nod to his own style, "about two thousand souls were hopefully born into the kingdom, in this vicinity, in our own denomination, *with comparative stillness.*"[60]

Nettleton's letter elicited a rebuttal from Finney, who preached a sermon in Troy, New York, in which he accused his critics of spiritual deadness: "While their hearts remain wrong they will, of course, cavil; and the nearer right anything is, the more spiritual and holy, so much the more it must displease them, while their affections grovel."[61] Stung, Nettleton then went after Finney's doctrinal ambiguity:

> The sermon in question entirely overlooks the nature of true
> religion. It says not one word by which we can distinguish

between true and false zeal, true and false religion. Indeed it does not seem to hint that there can be any such thing as false zeal and false religion. If the tone of feeling can only be raised to a certain pitch, then all is well. The self-righteous, the hypocrite, and all who are inflated with pride will certainly be flattered and pleased with such an exhibition.[62]

The parry between Nettleton and Finney over the new measures soon grew into the full-fledged Presbyterian fracas, with some Congregational ministers also aligning themselves with one or the other of the factions. Lyman Beecher, a closer friend to Nettleton than to Finney, attempted to smooth things over, first by gently urging Finney to tone things down (with no success) and then by organizing a week-long convention in July 1827 that would bring the opposing parties together in search of common ground. The convention, however, which took place in New Lebanon, New York, and included Finney, Nettleton, Beecher, and 13 other clergymen, only solidified the wedge. Members of the two camps mostly traded allegations of misconduct and affirmed their respective stylistic commitments. Theology went untouched. Writes J. F. Thornbury, Nettleton's biographer, "It is not entirely clear why Finney's Pelagian tendencies had not come under scrutiny," but the absence undoubtedly reflected a shift in mainstream attitudes toward sin:

> New England theology itself was in a transition period. Modifications of the old orthodoxy were already under way at Yale, and beneath the surface there were differences between the men who stood united at New Lebanon. In fact . . . Beecher and Nettleton, who were old friends, were themselves gravitating to different centers theologically and were destined eventually to part company. Indeed, they stood together for the last time at New Lebanon.[63]

For years Beecher had quietly wrestled with the doctrines of original sin and total depravity. Back in 1822 he wrote to Nettleton, "I have noticed a leaning of my mind to heresy on this long-disputed and very difficult topic."[64] By May 1828 Beecher made his alliance with the Taylorites and the Finneyites explicit, signing a letter that urged the likes of Nettleton to stop publishing against the new measures.[65] In 1831 he buried the hatchet with Finney, inviting him to preach at his church in Boston. With Nettleton in declining health in the 1830s, the Augustinian tradition found life only on the reactionary sidelines of the revival.

The Bible Dethroned

Republican theology, in its extremis among abolitionists, pushed American evangelicals to the edge of another of their defining values—the authority of scripture—and pushed civil Christianity well over that edge. The morality of slavery, and specifically its offense against the sacred right of liberty, prompted a stark choice for believers of the Bible, which permits slaveholding and encourages slaves to submit to their masters: should republican ethics or the Bible set the nation's moral compass? Attempts to portray this as a false choice fell apart as the antislavery movement gained momentum. The force of the abolitionist argument, and its rootedness in American identity, became too hard to resist. Wrote Garrison in 1832:

> The Spirit of Liberty is no longer young and feeble . . . It is abroad with power—thundering at castle-gates and prison-doors: from revolutionizing neighborhoods, it is going on to revolutionize nations: instead of agitating a kingdom, as formerly, it is now shaking the world. Woe to those who entrench themselves behind hereditary privileges and conduct, and declare that for the crimes which they commit, their ancestors must be responsible! So long as we continue one body—a union, a nation—the compact involves us in the guilt and danger of slavery.[66]

And then in 1845:

> It is in the province of reason to search the scriptures, and determine what in them is true, and what is false—what is probable, and what is incredible—what is historically true, and what fabulous—what is comparable with the happiness of mankind, and what ought to be rejected as an example or rule of action—what is the letter that killeth, and what is the spirit that maketh alive.[67]

As Mark Noll, in *The Civil War as a Theological Crisis* (2002), puts it, "By 1860, Americans who believed in the Scriptures as unquestioned divine revelation should have been troubled by the growing number of their fellow citizens who seemed willing to live without that belief."[68]

Baptists came unstitched in 1845 as much over the authoritative status of the Bible as over the ecclesial status of the slaveholder. In the months before the Southern exodus, two of their luminaries, Richard Fuller, a Baltimore pastor, and Francis Wayland, the president of Brown University in Rhode Island, conducted a widely circulated dialogue in *The Christian Spectator* on the question of "whether it is necessarily, and amidst all circumstances, a crime to hold men in a condition where they labor for another without their consent or contract," an exchange that exposed the faltering authority of the Bible among abolitionists. Holding that "what God has sanctioned in the Old Testament, and permitted in the New, cannot be sin," Fuller challenged Wayland to "from the Bible, make out your charge that slavery is a crime."[69] Wayland's refusal came in two revealing pieces. First, he suggests ambiguity in the way that divine revelation interacts with human morality, such as in the forbearance of polygamy among the patriarchs: "It is not inconsistent with the dealings of God with men to give precepts regulating a practice in itself wrong, but concerning which he has not seen fit, at present, explicitly to reveal his will." Second, Wayland insists that God's law is imprinted with as much (if not more) authority upon the human conscience as upon the pages of scripture: "I suppose the Most High to deal with us as with beings endowed with an intelligent and moral nature; and, therefore, that he frequently makes known to us his will by teaching us the relations in which we stand, and the obligations thence resulting, without specifying to us the particular acts which he intends thereby to forbid."[70] Without rejecting the Bible in so many words, Wayland questioned its dispensational relevance to an enlightened republic.

Disavowals of scripture became gradually less equivocal among evangelicals, edging closer to Garrison than to Wayland. The Fast Day skirmish among the Brooklyn Presbyterians Henry Van Dyke and Henry Ward Beecher in December 1860 highlights the rawness to which this debate had descended. An Old Schooler, Van Dyke lays the entire blame for the national crisis at the feet of abolitionists, whose "misrepresentation and abuse" of the Bible and "utter infidelity" had generated "the strife that agitates, and the danger that threatens, our country." Abolitionism, he charges, "does not try slavery by the Bible . . . it tries the Bible by the principles of freedom. It insists that the word of God must be made to support certain human opinions, or forfeit all claims upon their faith."[71] With his ailing father sitting in the pew, Beecher struck back with the strongest confirmation of Van Dyke's fears: "When the Bible is opened that all the fiends of hell may walk through it to do mischief on the earth . . . I will let the Bible go, as God let the temple go, to the desolating armies of its adversaries." A new dispensation had arrived, complete with a new account of Jesus' resurrection: "The stone is rolled away, and he stands by the side of the sepulcher. And he calls, 'Liberty, come forth!' "[72]

IV. REPUBLICAN THEOLOGY AND THE CIVIL WAR

Given their role in the ruptures that preceded the Civil War, it should come as no surprise that the intertwined ideals of republican theology—freedom, virtue, and Christianity—would find a foothold in battle cries on both sides of the war itself. Northern and Southern patriots alike believed their side to represent the cause of liberty, and, as such, also believed that their side stood for American Christianity in the form most compatible with a free republic. Thus, as President Lincoln would later note during his Second Inaugural Address, the religious rhetoric of the North and that of the South eerily hummed along in the same key. Both invoked the causes of freedom and of Christian morality as the just ends of a righteous war.

Although it seems they would have an easier time making this case, the Northern public actually backed the war far more reluctantly than the Confederates. Ultimately, as during the Revolutionary War, rhetorical efforts to cast the conflict in religious terms helped to build support, none more so than Julia Ward Howe's popular "Battle Hymn of the Republic," which she submitted to *The Atlantic Monthly* in December 1861 as a replacement lyric for the army doggerel "John Brown's Body." The hymn designates Christ himself as the captain of the Union cause, bearing a "fiery gospel" and dispensing apocalyptic judgment on the nation's sins:

He has sounded forth the trumpet that shall never call retreat;
He is sifting out the hearts of men before his judgment seat:

Oh! Be swift, my soul, to answer Him! Be jubilant, my feet!
Our God is marching on.

Moreover, many months before Lincoln would publicly identify the
war with the cause of abolishing slavery (and perhaps inspiring him
to do so), Howe's poem connected the crucifixion of Christ with the
daily sacrifices of Union soldiers: "As He died to make men holy, let us
die to make men free."[73] Appearing in the winter of 1862, the "Battle
Hymn" was first sung in public during a commemoration of George
Washington's birthday on February 22. On the same occasion a year
later, as the war dragged on, the Presbyterian William Adams rallied his
New York congregation by urging them to "measure our nationality
as related to that kingdom of Christ, which is paramount, permanent,
and universal." The American nation, Adams insisted, in a textbook
presentation of republican theology, represents a "new order of men:
of a church ransomed and free from all political alliance—a church
reformed and untrammeled in soul and limb, of liberty regulated by
law, of institutions established by the people for self-government, self-
protection, and self-improvement."[74]

Confederates believed in the war's divine stakes from the start: "A
pure Christianity is wrapped up in this revolution," went an 1862
sermon in Greensboro, North Carolina, "and Providence is using the
South for the grand work of its preservation and extension."[75] Southern
preachers routinely drew parallels to Hebrew history, and, in particular, to the division of the northern and southern kingdoms of Israel:
"[As] David broke off from the first Israel under the reign of the house
of Saul, [Jefferson] Davis broke off from the second kingdom of Israel
under the reign of her first King, A. Lincoln."[76] Such monarchical
imagery notwithstanding, Southerners saw their social hierarchies—
including the slavery system—as grounded in biblical morality and
republican virtue, and thereby saw the egalitarian tendencies of Northern religion as morally degenerative and unsustainable for a free society. The Episcopal Bishop Stephen Elliott referred to the antebellum
decades as a "rapid moral deterioration of a nation."[77] "Let us strive
to bring back the purer days of the republic," said one preacher in an
1861 Fast Day Sermon in New Orleans, "when honest merit waited,
like Cincinnatus at his plow, to be called forth for service."[78] On this
thinking, Drew Gilpin Faust observes, the Southern secession "became

an act of purification, a separation from the pollutions of decaying northern society," in addition to a stand for the freedom of Southern institutions from Northern interference.[79]

The only Christians who did not buy into republican theology in nineteenth-century America were African slaves and freemen, and even in their religion, liberty—or at least *liberation*—took pride of place. Like white evangelicals, members of the rising black church saw themselves as a modern-day Israel. However, instead of drawing parallels to the *respublica Hebraeorum,* Africans saw their likeness among the Israelite slaves in the Book of Exodus. This, moreover, was *not* an identification they shared with whites, who to them represented the Egyptian oppressors. The driving imperative of black religion had only the most immediate horizon in view: to escape bondage and enter the Promised Land. "The Common Father of the human race," preached Absalom Jones, "has heard the prayers that have ascended from the hearts of his people; and he has, as in the case of his ancient and chosen people that Jews, come down to deliver our suffering countrymen from the hands of their oppressors."[80] When escaped slaves joined the Union army, the theme song for their regiments was "Let My People Go," a Spiritual-like number that played the war as a confrontation between Moses and Pharaoh.[81]

While freedom from slavery became an animating theme of black religion in the nineteenth century, the Lockean philosophy of limited government never did. Neither did slaves and freemen buy into the idea that America was a chosen nation by virtue of its republicanism and its Christianity. Rather, by appropriating the liberation theme of the Exodus, African Americans articulated, as Eddie Glaude puts it, "their *own* sense of peoplehood and secured for themselves a common history and destiny as they elevated their experience to biblical drama." At this point in their history, anyway, the locus of common identity among black Christians was neither ideology nor theology, but rather suffering and oppression.[82] For whites, by ironic contrast, the republican theology that had become the pervasive creed of their civil religion had also proved itself a potent source of division.

DARWIN AS ALLY,
THE SOCIAL GOSPEL
AS FOE

W hen Henry Ward Beecher told his Brooklyn congregation
in August 1877 that "freedom has been the aspiration of
our race from the beginning," he evoked the abolitionism of his youth, the preaching legacy of Lyman Beecher, his father,
and the republican theology of Benjamin Rush and Timothy Dwight.
"The liberty of the whole mass of society," Beecher testified, "is
the study which should, more deeply than any other, interest every
thoughtful man, every patriotic man, and every Christian man." On
this particular day, however, Beecher's sermon on liberty also landed a
punch in a national scuffle over labor rights, an unforeseen terrain for
the old guard. The clash was still raw, arising out of a railroad strike
that had shut down commerce from New York to St. Louis for most
of July. Beecher aimed his fire at industrial unions, blaming them for
the turmoil—and worse, for degrading American freedom through its
conscription of all railroad workers: "The liberty of the individual is
destroyed," he argued, "where men are not allowed to work when they
please, where they please, as long as they please, for whom they please,
and for what they please."[1]

The attack on unions more broadly reflects Beecher's political theology, which centered on the belief that only the free market can

advance the sacred cause of liberty and the moral progress of society, a belief grounded in the ontology of the self: "It is the American doctrine that every man is to have the full ownership of himself," he continued in that same sermon, "that he is to have every opportunity to develop himself . . . to the exercise of his powers and to the enjoyment of whatever he produces." Beecher did not stand alone in appropriating Jeffersonian ideals to defend the rise of industrial capitalism; but nor was his the only conceivable response among evangelicals to the labor movement. Prominent ministers, from Walter Rauschenbusch in Manhattan to Alexander Irvine in New Haven, gave their pulpits over to the cause of the working class as a whole, and sometimes to socialism itself. Like slavery had a generation earlier, the ordeals of the industrial economy drove a wedge through the American gospel.

What made this era unique was the post-theological context that framed its theological debates. After a century in the driver's seat, the Christian elite now fought to retain its influence over the nation's conscience. Progressive schools of thought, particularly in economics and natural science, forced a reappraisal of American religion, and its civil religion, for the modern age. The evangelical discourse on liberty and morality encountered new questions, like whether governments or markets pose the greater threat to liberty, and whether personal virtues like sobriety or instead social virtues like benevolence most characterize the godly republic. Sweeping changes in American life had destabilized long-held convictions. Who in 1776 could have envisioned the wild popularity of Henry George's *Progress and Poverty* (1879), which contended, among other blasphemies, that "ownership of land will always entail the ownership of men"?[2]

On another front, the American ideal of social progress entered an uncertain frontier with the appearance of Charles Darwin's *The Origin of Species* (1859), a study that at once affirms the idea of human advancement while casting doubt on its moral dimensions—its overarching purpose and its correspondence with personal liberty. Before they ever worried about its implications for Creationism, Protestant divines like Beecher and Rauschenbusch combed Darwinism for scientific validation of their social agendas, squeezing out any proof they could find that human beings have attained a unique moral status in the universe. Naturally, they looked to different parts of the theory, with capitalists hailing the survival of the fittest and socialists looking to unite the human race in the struggle for existence. For both sides, however, Darwin changed the conversation: American Christians, who had long embraced the imperatives of liberty and moral progress, suddenly found those concepts beholden to a new regime of meanings.

In the face of these challenges, evangelicals proved to be nimble defenders of their civil religion, offering up ready answers to the questions of the age. These answers, however, bifurcated into two distinct schools of thought—two opposing civil religions. Social class formed the line of division: bourgeois Protestants adopted the free market as the quintessence of freedom and as the engine of moral progress, while the working class rallied around a communitarian ideal known as the Social Gospel. Appealing in different ways to the American creed and to newer paradigms of progress like evolutionary biology, both theologies reconstructed the basic premise that Christianity, liberty, and a morally good citizenry depend upon each other for survival. In effect, until the mid-twentieth century evangelicals had two popular modes—one quasi-libertarian and the other quasi-socialistic—of defining these axioms. Beecher defended republican theology, emphasizing the divine intention of self-government—"every individual man is himself a whole commonwealth"[3]—while the Social Gospel aimed to recover a more communal essence of Christianity, suggesting that although "Jesus worked on individuals and through individuals, his real end was not individualistic, but social . . . His end was not the new soul, but the new society; not man, but Man."[4]

Political theology thus fragmented along a class boundary that had never before divided American Christians. To unfold the story, this chapter describes evangelicalism as it broadly stood at the turn of the century—as a cultural establishment on the wane—along with the early interaction of American Christianity with *The Origin of Species*, and the impact of industrial capitalism on social discourse. In the sweep of these confrontations, finally, emerge two opposing political theologies, each venturing its own progressive vision of republican freedom in America.

I. EVANGELICALISM IN THE GILDED AGE

For all its internal subdivisions leading up to the Civil War, Protestant evangelicalism closed out the nineteenth century at the height of cultural stature. As George Marsden maintains, "evangelicals considered their faith to be the normative American creed. Viewed from their dominant perspective, the nineteenth century had been marked by successive advances of evangelicalism, the American nation, and hence the kingdom of God."[5] After the war, revivals spread with the population into the big cities, churches grew, and denominational boundaries eased as churches across the nation adopted a common curriculum in their Sunday schools, along with a generally liberal-Arminian tilt in their theology.[6] The Evangelical Alliance for the United States of America, an interdenominational fellowship that had fallen apart before the Civil War, got revitalized in the late 1860s, attracting tens of thousands of believers to its general conferences, embracing the ecumenical spirit of American religion, and committing to the "exportation of American democratic standards" abroad.[7]

Evangelical conversion now inhabited almost entirely moral dimensions, having long since sidelined Jonathan Edwards' fixation on inward affection for God as the mark of Christian rebirth. While new disagreements opened up over the imperatives of moral advancement, almost every American evangelical agreed with the *teleological* premise of the republican tradition, namely that Christianity in the land of the free has a front-line role to play in the transformation of the human race. The prophecies of Rush, Beecher, and Finney were by now axiomatic to American religion. Josiah Strong, general secretary of the Evangelical Alliance, referred to civil liberty and reformed Christianity when he wrote in 1886: "The depositary of these two greatest blessings sustains peculiar relations to the world's future."[8]

The reform impetus of the early 1800s pivoted into new initiatives for the times. The Young Women's and Young Men's Christian Associations, for instance, aimed to provide the working class means of escape from urban vices. The groups successfully lobbied the U.S. Congress to pass anti-obscenity legislation in 1873. A YMCA superintendent, Anthony Comstock, secured an appointment from President Grant to serve as a "special agent" with the U.S. Post Office, charged with censoring smutty mail.[9] The temperance movement also hit its stride with the formation of the Women's Christian Temperance Union in 1873, a national organization that latched its campaigns against alcohol to other causes like women's suffrage and relief for the urban poor.[10]

In a telling mark of their confidence in the cultural ascent of American Christianity, evangelicals of this era devoted unprecedented resources to foreign missions, dispatching evangelists to Mexico, China, Japan, Siam, India, Persia, and the Congo. Dwight Lyman Moody presided over several summer Bible camps in the 1880s that elicited hundreds of commitments from college students to join the field. By 1910, 38 percent of all missionaries working abroad from their homeland were American Protestants.[11]

The evangelical establishment had a cast of celebrities leading it. Several pastors of large Northeastern churches, such as Henry Ward Beecher in Brooklyn and Newman Smyth and Theodore Munger in New Haven, maintained a national profile through the publication of sermons, social treatises, and devotional literature. Another New Haven divine, Alexander Irvine, made a name for himself first as an upstart pastor to trade unionists, then as a journalist and lecturer on social issues. The most renowned evangelical during this period was Moody, who, after leading the Chicago YMCA in the 1860s, discovered a gift for revivalist preaching and set out on itinerant tours to urban centers across America and Great Britain, setting records for public conversions that would go unrivaled until Billy Graham's worldwide "crusades" a century later. The most controversial voice within the Protestant establishment belonged to Walter Rauschenbusch, a long-time Baptist minister to New York's poorest who in 1907, as a professor at Rochester Theological Seminary, published the seminal articulation of the Social Gospel in his *Christianity and the Social Crisis*.

The apparent evangelical establishment, however, gave way to several shifts in American religion that would, by the 1930s, erode evangelicals' status as the bearers of American identity. The first of these was immigration. Nearly 40 million people crossed the Atlantic between the 1840s and the end of the First World War, with the influx spiking between 1900 and 1910, dramatically altering the religious landscape everywhere in America except for the rural South.[12] By 1906, Roman Catholicism was the largest single denomination in the United States, encompassing some 80 dioceses and numbering 14 million members out of a total population of 82 million.[13]

Internal ruptures also dissipated the evangelical mainstream in the early twentieth century. Racial segregation, in the North prior to the war and in the South thereafter, had already driven its wedge.[14]

The theological spectrum grew more polarized as well as a growing faction of conservatives broke off from the mainline denominations to promote the scriptural "fundamentals" of the faith.[15] Indeed, the nascent fundamentalist movement, with its emphasis on biblical literalism, dispensational theology, and its pre-millennial eschatology, offered the most blatant departure from the optimism of republican theology among Christians at the turn of the century. As Marsden explains, pre-millennialism holds that the human condition will only decay prior to the return of Christ, making fundamentalists "less hopeful concerning progress."[16] Until the late 1910s, however, this movement occupied a rearguard position in American Christianity.

Nevertheless, the two most pervasive challenges to the evangelical establishment in the late nineteenth and early twentieth centuries— the rise of industrial capitalism, with its attendant shifts in economic power, and the birth of Darwinism in the United States—did pose specific quandaries for republican theology. As such, they generated the most complex replies. Darwinism introduced new categories for understanding moral progress, while industrial capitalism brought the concept of individual liberty under fresh scrutiny.

II. DARWINISM, CHRISTIANITY, AND THE MEANING OF PROGRESS

Historians call the period from the 1880s through the 1910s the "progressive era," referring to a wave of programs, federal and otherwise, aimed at upgrading American culture. The designation vastly oversimplifies American intellectual history, which had strong progressive currents running through it from the beginning. Indeed, the idea that humanity could perfect itself, advancing toward a better future on the strength of public enlightenment, had long been the essence of American evangelicalism, the peculiar result of combining its conversion narrative with a narrative of political liberation. To be sure, the progress evangelicals envisioned was spiritual at its core, but it covered a range of social issues and came pitched in terms of modernization— urging the release of American society from the chattel system, from peasant-style liquor dependence, and from medieval vices like dueling. Until the progressive era proper, moreover, very few thought to question whether social progress and civil liberty might be at odds with one another, in large part because the republican theology of the American church held the two concepts together—upholding moral progress as the ideal fulfillment of self-government and as a goal achievable within civil society (that is, with only minimal reliance upon the state).

In addition to the structural shifts in the American economy, the 1859 publication of Charles Darwin's *The Origin of Species* intruded upon this formula at the end of the nineteenth century, forcing American Christians to rethink the meaning of progress and the methods for achieving it. In contrast to the late twentieth century, American Christians of the late nineteenth received the theory of natural selection with self-interested curiosity. The birth of Darwinism in the United States had far less to do with a "creationist" controversy and far more to do with how American thinkers, even religious thinkers, might appropriate Darwin's insights in order to advance their visions of social progress. To be sure, Christian fundamentalists would eventually smell a threat to biblicism; but at the outset the theory of natural selection hit the American public sphere as a philosophical breakthrough, giving a culture that had long believed in human progress some new categories with which to promote that agenda. The moral dilemmas that Darwinism *did* raise—whether or not history arches toward some goal, whether or not morality is a fixed entity, whether or not humans can or should engineer the progress of their species, and whether or not humans have moral freedom at all—American evangelicals were uniquely poised and eager to address. By and large they found *The Origin of Species* pliable to the enterprise of moral progress as they imagined it.

The Origin of Species

Not that Darwin himself would have endorsed this interpretation of his work. The puzzle driving *The Origin of Species* is purely scientific—How do various plants and animals take form?[17] Darwin's answer revolves around "the struggle for life"—the inclination of every creature not only to survive but also to procreate against the countervailing forces of climate, nutrient limitations, competition for those nutrients, and natural predators. Darwin presumes that "every organic being naturally increases at so high a rate, that if not destroyed, the earth would soon be covered by the progeny of a single pair."[18] It is this tension, between the instinct to multiply and the forces of annihilation, that sets the stage for evolutionary adaptations that mark the development of distinct species, a slow historical process called "natural selection." This intricate system admits to a relatively simple synopsis: the structure of every organic being has the "plastic" capacity to adapt to external conditions, adjustments that manifest in gradual genetic transformations within a species, and, finally, with the perishing of subspecies that fail to adapt for survival.[19]

Evolution Versus Progress

The earliest apprehension among American Christians had less to do with Darwin's specific challenge to Genesis 1 than with its implication that life on earth proceeds without any apparent purpose beyond mere survival—that the struggle for existence is the essence of history, even human history. Those who first took umbrage with *The Origin of Species* did so not because of its narrative dispute with the Bible but because of its Hobbesian rejection of a "final cause," or telos, of human life. "There can be no mistake as to the character of such a scheme of cosmogony," said Francis Bowen, a Harvard philosopher, in a public lecture just months after *Origin* was published: "A blind or fatalistic principle watching over a chaos of unmeaning and purposeless things, and slowly eliciting from them, during an eternity, all the order and fitness which now characterize the organized world."[20]

Darwin's earliest defenders in America thus put their strongest hand to rebutting the imputation of fatalism. Indeed, many went much further, infusing the theory of natural selection with cosmic intention—articulating a theory of "intelligent design," in late modern parlance. The effort was largely driven by progressive ideology, an inclination to extract the most compelling thesis of Darwinism—that organic life *advances*—and attach it to an Almighty agenda. "Evolution is a progressive revelation," wrote Newman Smyth in 1904, "It contains both prophesies and fulfillments."[21] Lest anyone think that natural selection lacks a final cause, Smyth argues, look no further than what the process has bestowed to the world over millions of years, including a hierarchy of "vital values"—a moral system centered on cultivating the "fitness" to live and to populate the earth.[22] At its present pinnacle it has given the world a species of animals equipped with rational intelligence, moral self-consciousness, and the ability to know and love the Creator.

In the summer of 1885 Henry Ward Beecher delivered 12 sermons to his Brooklyn congregation in defense of natural selection, building a case for its complete harmony with the faith. According to Beecher, evolution theory confirms what he (and his father, Lyman, before him) had long believed, namely that a free society of Christians represents an advanced stage of God's creation, a maturing of the *imago dei*—the image of God in man. Beecher draws on Darwin to redefine the *imago dei* itself: not as something implanted in the species, but as something "developed in human consciousness."[23] Darwin's insights, Beecher argues, offer fresh affirmation that Christian faith, both for individuals in their own lifetimes and for whole societies over many generations, is always a process: "We cannot understand God by mere enunciation; knowledge cannot fall upon us as the rain falls upon plants, nor as the light falls upon visible things of creation. The elemental qualities of the divine disposition must be evolved in us first, and the application to the divine nature is gradually unfolded to us afterwards."[24] God did not deliver the scriptures, for instance, until humanity's rational and moral faculties were sufficiently developed over those of other beasts. Even today, Beecher suggests (with a cultural chauvinism not uncommon in the progressive era), "there is a gulf fixed between the higher knowledges of human civilization and the lower range of barbaric ideas . . . Truth, fidelity, honor, purity, endurance of trials, victories over temptation, law, custom, institutions, social obligations and immunities and refined joys—all these things are familiar; they are almost alphabetic in civilization; they seem almost primary truths to us; but they are actually impossible to the inferior races of men."[25] The process of natural selection, in other words, plays out with as much consequence in the realm of social and spiritual life as it does in organic life.

Beecher draws two implications, both of which pick up on the aspirational character of republican theology. First, Beecher insists, Christian faith is still evolving, both in scope and in content: "The age of inspiration has not perished. Its sun has not set . . . A day has come when all dogmas, formulas, laws and governments of the Church must be judged by the enlightening moral consciousness of the great assembly of Christ-like men, whether in church bounds or out of them. God's Word will no longer be a shackle to impede new inspirations, but wings to lift men into that luminous atmosphere thrown up by all experiences of good men from the beginning." By framing Christianity—and, crucially, its scriptures[26]—as a work in progress, Beecher gives blessing to a rising trend within American Christianity to modernize the faith and its message.

Secondly, Beecher, like his father, points to the moral development of society as the *telos* of humanity:

> Every development of piety, every reinforcement of humanity, every development of love in strength, in breadth, in exquisite fineness, in beauty, every harmonization of the highest moral qualities, is gathering material for a clearer view of God and for a nobler humanity.[27]

To earlier generations this second point would represent nothing new: Americans had long embraced moral perfectionism as the imperative of both faith and free society. However, the arc of development had now been lengthened many times over. Whereas before the American church saw itself fulfilling a prophecy a mere 18 centuries old, Darwinists like Beecher envisioned a finale of spiritual enlightenment that had been millions of scrupulous years in the making.

Social Engineering Versus the Market

A practical question emerges, however, concerning the role society is to play in commanding change, a matter on which even committed Darwinists can differ. On the one hand, some take the fact of intellectual progress to imply a responsibility for enlightened leaders to consciously steer their culture toward improvement. Thus John Dewey engineered pedagogical reforms in colleges and grade schools, Theodore Roosevelt created a Bureau of Corporations to keep an eye on commerce, and Jane Addams established "settlement houses" to foster social development among the poor. On the other hand, some Darwinists see evolution as a phenomenon infinitely bigger than human intellect and thus dismiss social engineering as futile, even dangerous.

The extremis of evolutionary activism came into view early on: if the arc of natural selection points to the perfection of the human species (via the perishing of the weak), why not just move that process forward? The paleontologist Lester Frank Ward, for example, promoted a program of eugenics to the Biological Society of Washington in 1891:

> It is the right and the duty of an energetic and virile race of men to seize upon every great principle that can be made subservient to its true advancement, and undeterred by any false ideas of its sanctity or inviolability, fearlessly to apply it . . . From the great stirp of humanity . . . why may we not learn to select on some broad and comprehensive plan with a view to general building up and rounding out of the race of human beings? At least we should by a rigid selection stamp out the future all the wholly unworthy elements.[28]

Objectors to Darwin often made eugenics the straw man. William Jennings Bryan's argument at the Scopes trial in 1925, for instance, raised the specter of mad scientists like Ward roaming the planet with white coats and clipboards: "If taken seriously," Bryan wrote in a supplement after the trial, "and made the basis of a philosophy of life, [natural selection] would eliminate love and carry man back to a struggle of tooth and claw . . . Darwin [himself] speaks with approval of the savage custom of eliminating the weak so that only the strong will survive and complains that 'we civilized men do our utmost to check the process of elimination.'"[29] Bryan's longstanding empathy for the defenseless, in other words, drives even his antagonism toward Darwinism.

Confirmed Darwinists, however, might also make a strong case *against* social engineering. In his 1894 essay, "The Absurd Effort to Make the World Over," the libertarian William Graham Sumner advances a perfectly Darwinist argument against reformers:

> If this poor old world is as bad as they say, one more reflection may check the zeal of the headlong reformer. It is at any rate a tough old world. It has taken its trend and curvature and all its twists and tangles from a long course of formation . . . The men will be carried along with it and be made by it. The utmost they can do by their cleverness will be to note and record their course as they are carried along, which is what we do now, and is that which leads us to the vain fancy that we can make or guide the movement. That is why it is the greatest folly of which a man is capable, to sit down with a slate and pencil to plan out a new social world.[30]

Thus Darwinism, socially interpreted, cuts deep in two opposite ideological directions, supporting both progressives who want to make the world over and conservatives who instead put their confidence in the free market to separate the fit from the unfit. What they agree upon is the potential for human advancement; they differ on method. It is for this reason that the epithet "Social Darwinism" is, paradoxically, as often applied to fascist agendas of social purification as it is to *laissez-faire* antipathy for social agendas of any kind.

Freedom Versus Fatalism

Running parallel to the debate on reform, another philosophical problem that Darwinism revives concerns individual freedom. If it remains up in the air whether elites can direct the course of human development, the prospects are even grimmer for the average human beast. Darwinism offered a scientific vision of the world that reduced the game of life to one of survival, embedding every organism in a thick web of hostile conditions. The place for individual freedom in the theory of natural selection appears confined to how one adapts to the multiple threats against one's life. The organic system more or less prescribes human action.

The quandary was not merely existential, dislodging a central pillar of American cultural identity; it was also moral: if humans aren't really free, can there be accountability for one's behavior toward others? If the only code is survival, can there be such a thing as right and wrong? As explained in Chapter 5, Charles Grandison Finney had rejected original sin and predestination precisely because they negated, to his thinking, Christian faith and piety, the decisive capacity to follow God. Why preach to lost souls if they have no meaningful power to respond? In that vein, the deterministic universe described by Darwin offers an even more powerful negation in that it removes not the capacity to make decisions but rather the moral context itself.

As with the reform debate, however, Darwinism shows its suppleness, bending as easily for the believers in freedom as for its skeptics. Newman Smyth takes the question of determinism head on by looking past the struggle for existence to what that struggle has yielded: "In general," he argues, "it may be said that evolution through its age-long process has tended towards individuality . . . At the present summit of it, the individual man stands out as its supreme form, and with his face uplifted towards some radiant beyond."[31] Natural selection has, on Smyth's account, made individualism the preeminent, even teleological, value of survival, from the "laws of crystallization" in the prehistoric age to the development of "self-conscious life" among humans.

In effect, Smyth's formulation ingeniously resuscitates Scottish moral sense philosophy by locating the moral faculty as a feature of the human condition *at an advanced stage of its development*. Thus the American Christian can enjoy the pride of moral progress and the promises of liberty all at once. For the ordinary churchgoer, however, new economic realities, rather than new waves in biological science, would destabilize his long-held confidence in the freedom of the individual.

III. A NEW DISCOURSE ON FREEDOM

The rival interpretations of freedom in antebellum thought—the freedom of slaves from their owners versus that of slave-holding territories from the federal government, for instance, or the freedom of individuals from vices like alcoholism versus their freedom from public intrusion into private morality—gave way to post-bellum debates on liberty that focused almost exclusively on economic empowerment. This abrupt shift in the discourse, moreover, had little to do with the Civil War or its political outcome, except insofar as millions of former slaves joined the paid labor force (such as it was), and insofar as the union victory began to re-nationalize the American conscience. Forces beyond the war, including the rise of industrial manufacturing and farming, the consequent growth of urban centers, the influx of immigrants, the proliferation of railroads and communication wires across the continent, and above all, the concentration of capital in relatively few hands, aligned in such a way as to foster a radically new balance of power in American society.

These changes generated not just unparalleled inequalities of wealth, but also new structural vulnerabilities for American workers, and particularly farmers. Work patterns that had sustained households for centuries started, in the early 1870s, to prove susceptible to macroeconomic hazards: not just calamitous weather or war, but the failure of a single bank (in 1873, for instance) or a single railroad company (in 1893) could disrupt cash flow in ways that impoverished millions for years on end; small farmers, not to mention consumers everywhere, lived continually on the hook when it came to shipping rates set by railroad companies; and factory employees had meager bargaining leverage over their working conditions, hours, and wages. With startling speed, the American economy, which had long consisted of small, quasi-independent producers with "middling fortunes" (as Tocqueville put it in 1831), had been transformed into a plutocracy in which the worker exercised far less control over his destiny and faced a far more precarious threat of poverty.[32] By the late 1870s the political economist Henry George was spotting new, foreboding clouds over American freedom, noting that "the condition of the masses in every civilized country is, or is tending to become, that of virtual slavery under the forms of freedom . . . The laborer is robbed of the produce of his labor and compelled to toil for a mere subsistence."[33]

The Lockean bond between individual freedom and private property had solidified as an achievable ideal in North America, where, from the colonial period onward, many households maintained their own productive property and thus lived on the profit, however modest, from its fruits. As that arrangement receded in the late nineteenth century and most individuals found themselves working on *somebody else's* property, their hold on freedom itself came into doubt. Thus emerged a new discourse on American liberty, and it began with specific demands from the laboring classes. A newly formed People's Party, which had overtaken the Kansas legislature in 1890, articulated a national platform in 1892 that called for the "permanent and perpetual" union of labor forces, public ownership of railroads, a free flow of government-issued currency, a graduated income tax, and a principle of labor according to which "wealth belongs to him who creates it."[34]

While the People's Party never gained an electoral foothold beyond a few Midwestern states, its agenda largely set the terms of American class skirmishes going into the twentieth century. While trade and industrial unionism took hold in cities, rural farmers made common cause with unions in national elections, for example coalescing behind the Democrat William Jennings Bryan for president in 1896, 1900, and 1908. Bryan stood on a populist platform—a national income tax, federal regulation of industry, and (with famously cruciform overtones) resistance against a gold standard—and he fought for the social status of the common laborer, insisting that "the man who is employed for wages is as much a businessman [meriting the solicitations of government] as his employer."[35]

In response to the likes of Bryan and, more generally, to the idea that one must be economically empowered in order to be free, opponents of populism formulated what would become the most parsimonious definition of freedom in American history, namely the principle of non-interference in the market. "Civil liberty," declared William Graham Sumner, "is the status of the man who is guaranteed by law and civil institutions the exclusive employment of all his own powers for his own welfare."[36] What makes American politics fascinating on this count is that not just market winners embrace Sumner's equation of the free market with freedom itself; a critical mass of farmers and industrial workers have joined with the investor classes since the 1890s to resist Robin Hood populism, government regulation of industry, and even unionism, all in the name of American freedom. In three tries Bryan never won even the popular vote for the presidency. His overt identification with the working classes—"The Great Commoner," he was often called—never fully translated into their overt identification with him.

The reason for this is engrained in American civil religion: deference to the free market in America, even among its potential victims, comes in part on moral and theological principle. In the first place, free market ideology flows from the simplest reading of the Lockean social contract and the American credo. Never mind that neither Locke nor Jefferson ever discussed political rights against a backdrop of industrial capitalism: the imperative to limit government as the ultimate threat to individual liberty has a firm grip on the American conscience. This holds in part because the free market lends itself so well to republican theology. If civil liberty is an essential component of a godly nation, the free market becomes an essential institution to that end, as an impartial broker of morality, laying bare the virtues and vices of its players and thereby helping to cultivate virtue in society. "The institutions of civil liberty," says Sumner, by which he means the minimal state and the unregulated market, "leave each man to run his career in life in his own way, only guaranteeing to him that whatever he does in the way of industry, economy, prudence, sound judgment, etc., shall redound to his own welfare and shall not be diverted to someone else's benefit. Of course, it is a necessary corollary that each man shall also bear the penalty of his own vices and his own mistakes."[37]

Sumner's claim, furthermore, is putatively empirical, not just philosophical: in reply to the Henry Georges and W. J. Bryans of his age,
Sumner does not view the accumulation of capital as dangerous to liberty, or, for that matter, the laboring class as economically vulnerable.[38]
Indeed, like many free market apologists after him, Sumner's populism
classifies American society into *three*—not two—sectors. On top are the
inevitable (but not all-powerful) barons of industry. The real parasites
are on the bottom—"the shiftless, the imprudent, the intemperate, the
extravagant, and the vicious," whose just desserts should not be borne by
anyone but themselves. The vast majority of Americans, Sumner insists,
reside in a virtuous middle class, hardworking but justly compensated
by the free market, so long as they are left alone by the government.
Attacking welfarism in 1883, Sumner typifies this middle-class worker
as "the Forgotten Man" who gets stuck with the bill:

> Who is the Forgotten Man? He is the simple, honest laborer, ready
> to earn his living by productive work. We pass him by because he
> is independent, self-supporting, and asks no favors. He does not
> appeal to the emotions or excite the sentiments. He only wants
> to make a contract and fulfill it, with respect on both sides and
> favor on neither side. He must get his living out of the capital of
> the country. The larger the capital is, the better living he can get.
> Every particle of capital which is wasted on the vicious, the idle,
> and the shiftless is so much taken from the capital available to
> reward the independent and productive laborer.[39]

Thus, with the shift toward political economy in late nineteenth-
century discourse on liberty, the republican theology of Witherspoon,
Rush, Beecher, and Finney found secular expression in free market
ideology. For that matter, it also found expression in free market theology, but not without a fight from Christian socialists and laborites.

IV. THE SOCIAL GOSPEL VERSUS FREE MARKET FAITH

For the first time since the 1770s, American evangelicals had to drasti-
cally rethink their political theology, and to do so in a way that still resonated with the Founders' experiment while also carrying it forward.

Though Darwinism demanded—and received—a response to its philosophical dilemmas, the real crisis of conscience concerned economic justice. As it played out, political theology in the late nineteenth century bifurcated along class lines. Wealthy Protestants appointed the free market as God's moral arbiter, while working-class Christians largely (though not universally) adopted a version of socialism known as the Social Gospel.

Indeed, although American evangelicals in this period generally tilted toward a liberal theology, it might serve to conceptualize the intersection of systematic and political theology into four different quadrants in American religion: (1) liberal theologians, like Henry Ward Beecher and Newman Smyth, who also promoted the free market; (2) liberal theologians, like Alexander Irvine and Walter Rauschenbusch, who supported unionism and socialism; (3) religious conservatives, like William Jennings Bryan, who were also unionists and quasi-socialists; and (4) religious conservatives who preferred the free market. As to this final category, the quadrant for religious conservatives who actively promoted limited government and free markets sat conspicuously empty at the turn of the twentieth century. That *this* quadrant not only filled up but also came to dominate American Protestantism by the century's end is the intricate story that occupies the next chapter of this book.

With the exception of fundamentalists, the Protestants of this era still identified with the basic aims of republican theology—individual liberty, evangelical piety, and moral progress—albeit with their own divergent twists. The difference lay in how they understood each of these concepts: bourgeois Christians, for instance, located the essence of freedom in the competitive market, the heart of Christianity in virtues like sobriety and industriousness, and the goal of social progress in a prosperous economy. To many less affluent believers, the market seemed a shallow depository of freedom, virtue, and faith, not to mention a source of disempowerment and frustration. In the 1870s American Christians developed class identities and went their separate ways; working-class churchgoers found it oppressive to commune with the wealthy and to be subject to the moralism of market success. They eventually formed their own fellowships—in Sunday evening services, at the YMCA, and sometimes in their own congregations—as an escape from the "prejudices of the overly refined."[40] It was in these new communions that the Social Gospel first emerged.

Laborite Christianity

Wealthy Americans had hoped to keep the working class worshiping in the pro-market church: interclass fellowship based on a common understanding of virtue and uplift could neutralize proletarian threats to bourgeois advancement. In most urban centers it did not work out that way, and some philanthropic outreaches to laborers actually backfired, driving them deeper into their own spiritual enclaves. The YMCA's short-lived "Railroad Department" offers a case in point. In the wake of the 1877 strikes that shuttered the Northeast for three weeks, railroad executives collaborated with the Y to open up recreation halls for railroad workers—leather couches, hot coffee, and chessboards for a transient labor force. The evangelistic agenda was barely concealed: in addition to drawing railroad men away from less wholesome diversions, the railroad owners hoped to, as Winter notes, "carry the association's message of Christian manhood to the working classes." "It is very much the business of the company," declared one vice president at the time, "to make sober, moral men of our employees."[41] Specifically, they hoped to imbue their employees with a work ethic that would blunt their propensity to make demands on management. The idea was that with Bible study and mentorship programs (making positive examples of higher-ranked employees), the program could "ameliorate industrial conflict through moral reform."[42]

Rather than dissipate laborite sentiment, however, the Railroad Department at the Y gave workers a venue for strengthening their own bonds with each other. Often within months of opening, the workers would commandeer the facilities, prevailing upon reluctant Y officials to install billiard tables and smoking rooms, curtailing Bible studies, painting over the moral codes stenciled on the walls, and in several cities managing to extricate the buildings from YMCA governance altogether.[43] The experiment in laborite conversion, in the end, highlighted a dilemma for moral evangelists: to change the hearts and minds of individuals requires a grassroots engagement that must compete with (and potentially give ground to) other mentalities that have taken root. Beyond anyone's expectation, the American railroad worker had developed an identity that would mold any experience of Christianity afforded him. He had, by the end of the century, adopted a notion of social "uplift"—emphasizing fair wages and improved working conditions—which traditional Protestant notions— emphasizing sobriety and industriousness—could not overcome, even (perhaps especially) in the faux-genteel parlors of the YMCA. Indeed, the Knights of Labor in 1890 urged all railroad workers to join the Y precisely in order to quicken their sense of the "very unjust and unnecessary conditions" to which they were exposed in the workday.[44] Nothing could have been further from the intentions of those who opened these facilities.

As it happened, the Railroad Department in New Haven opened in 1878 just after a two-week revival in the city led by D. L. Moody—felicitous timing for its early membership and, consequently, for the development of the working-class church in that city. An Irish immigrant named Alexander Irvine came to lead New Haven's working class as its unofficial chaplain. Irvine's journey, in the course of his ministry, from traditional Protestantism to socialism offers a glimpse of the context in which the Social Gospel took shape.[45] Serving first at the New Haven Y, Irvine took a preaching post in 1898 at Pilgrim Congregational Church, located in the wealthy suburb of Fair Haven—close enough to the city line to draw in New Haven tenement dwellers. Straddling two different worlds under one steeple, Irvine gradually steered his Sunday evening sermons toward the working poor, exalting manual labor and displaying stereopticon images of French peasantry by the painter Jean-François Millet.[46] While uplifting the poor, Irvine said very little in his first three years to offend his wealthier parishioners; his sermons celebrated hard work and virtue and offered no slight against free enterprise. In December 1901, however, Irvine gave his morning worshipers some pause when he took sides in a public spat over the New Haven Water Company, confounding stockholders on his deacon board by calling for the company to pay taxes just like the "banana vendor" who had to shell out fees for the use of the streets.[47]

By 1902 Irvine was fully drawn into the working-class movement, routinely identifying with labor in their disputes with management. During the national coal strike that winter, while Newman Smyth and Theodore Munger upbraided the United Mine Workers from their pulpits across town, Irvine got out his stereopticon again and showed his congregation the barracks occupied by Pennsylvania coal miners alongside the Manhattan mansions that belonged to their employers. He called on workers around the country to join their local churches, not for the sake of their souls, but for the sake of the church: "I am prepared to advise that men who work with their hands go into the church of God, and create in it that which is its greatest lack: democracy of religion."[48] The Gilded Age, Irvine charged, had produced a gilded church. A salary reduction for Irvine at Pilgrim Congregational followed this accusation, and in April 1903 he resigned his post to start a new fellowship called the People's Church of New Haven.

Irvine fed his new flock, which met at a vaudeville theater, a steady diet of pro-union preaching and a "gospel of work," which dignified every trade and gave "every man and woman a career in religion, a creed of labor to be worked at every day."[49] In addition to Bible studies, Irvine led reading groups on Henry George and started a committee to discuss political issues like utility municipalization. Irvine's church, however, fell apart within two years. The congregation was poor and could ill afford to cover both building rental and pastoral salary. Moreover, the fellowship was wracked by the kind of tensions that yanked at the labor movement itself—between skilled and unskilled workers, and between laborers of different trades and industries. In the end, Irvine's attempt to draw disparate factions of the labor force into a unified communion fell short. In 1905 the People's Church disbanded; Irvine quit the ministry, joined the Socialist Party of America, and started a long new career as a muckraking journalist and novelist, publishing more than five bestselling books.

In his 1909 autobiography, *From the Bottom Up*, Irvine narrates his conversion to socialism. Following the collapse of the People's Church, Irvine's wife became pregnant; the family now resided on a modest orchard on the outskirts of New Haven, surviving "largely upon apples."[50] When delivery day arrived, "there was but five cents in the house and that was needed to telephone for the family physician." Irvine walked to a saloon in the middle of the night to find a phone, a journey that apparently consumed him with ideological panic:

> Cold sweat covered my body, my teeth chattered and my hands twitched. Socialist philosophy told me that society was in process of evolution. Democracy at heart was correcting its own evils

and, like a snake, sloughing off its outworn skin. I was part of that process. Reason pounded these things in on me but hate pushed them aside and demanded something else. I wondered that morning whether, after all, there weren't more reforms wrapped up in a stick of dynamite than in a whole life of preaching and moralizing. In that fifteen-minute walk there passed through my mind and heart all the elements of hell.[51]

After Irvine phoned the doctor, the barkeep stunned him by refusing his nickel, pouring a cup of coffee, and launching into a grateful testimony of how Irvine had changed his life with a sermon several years earlier. "I could not drink his coffee," writes Irvine, "but I shared his comradeship and as I went back home I became normal. Hate left my heart. I was beaten, in a way; but the love of mankind was a fundamental thing and the other was a mental storm that passed over and left no ill results." Whether Mrs. Irvine ever delivered her baby goes unmentioned in the memoir: the salient birth—or rebirth—that day was the Reverend's belief in the solidarity of the human race; what had for years eluded his ministry now resurfaced, if briefly, over the counter at an all-night saloon.

Socialist Theology

Irvine came to believe that American Christians needed more than just class consciousness to deal with the moral crises of the industrial age. The real imperative was for an interclass harmony that could countenance the redistribution of wealth and equal bargaining rights for workers. Many Americans saw socialism, however, as incompatible with economic and religious freedom. For their part, socialists, even in America, tended toward atheism, so commonly that Irvine himself encountered antireligious hostility when he joined the Socialist Party in 1905.[52] To identify with socialism in the early 1900s breeched political and religious creeds; if someone wanted to make it broadly acceptable to American Christians he would first need to construct a theological rationale. The Social Gospel, outlined at greatest length in Walter Rauschenbusch's *Christianity and the Social Crisis* (1907), proposes such a rationale. Rauschenbusch, the son of German immigrants, led a Baptist congregation in the 1890s in Hell's Kitchen, a blighted corner of Manhattan whose residents were perpetually "out of work, out of clothes, out of shoes, and out of hope."[53] Later, working at Rochester Theological Seminary, Rauschenbusch wrote *Christianity and the Social Crisis* "to discharge a debt . . . to these plain people who were my friends."[54] But this is no autobiography: Rauschenbusch offers the work not as a personal journey of discovery but as a biblical and historical argument for socialism. At issue is not the progress but rather the timeless justice of a civilization.

Indeed, while Rauschenbusch's book eventually outlines a plan to transform society, it opens with blunt *anti*-progressivism: "History is never antiquated, because humanity is always fundamentally the same." The premise serves as a simultaneous appeal to religious conservatives (affirming the relevance of ancient wisdom) and to Marxists: the historical constant, Rauschenbusch explains, is that humanity "is always hungry for bread, sweaty with labor, struggling to wrest from nature and hostile men enough to feed its children. The welfare of the mass is always at odds with the selfish force of the strong. The exodus of the Roman plebeians and the Pennsylvania coal strike, the agrarian agitation of the Gracchi and the rising of the Russian peasants—it is all the same tragic human life."[55]

Rauschenbusch evokes a Darwinist jungle, and then, subverting the dominant thinking of his day, pronounces it regressively cyclical, tragic, and, at the heart of the matter, an affront to God. The plight of the weak, he argues, forms the central imperative of biblical morality, from the Minor Prophets to the sermons of Jesus. Both Old and New Testament ethics concern primarily the "organic totality" of society, not just the individual, and it all points to a gospel of social redemption. In this claim Rauschenbusch takes on the moralism of American Protestants: "We are," on the one hand, "accustomed to connect piety with private virtue . . . The evils against which we contend in the churches are intemperance, unchastity, the sins of the tongue." The ancient prophets, on the other hand, "were not individualists." Injustice and oppression are the sins that consume the prophetic scrolls, and the prophets unfailingly side with the poor against the rich.[56] Seldom do they blame the poor for their poverty, while "'rich' and 'wicked' are almost synonymous terms." The lopsided wealth of ancient capitalism, furthermore, represents a departure from "primitive fairness and simplicity," a departure that God himself corrects in Bible times with statutes to restore lost land and to free indentured bondsmen. "The land belonged to Jehovah," Rauschen-busch insists, and "that is only another way of saying that it belonged to the community." The accumulation of wealth—a mark of virtue to the American Protestant—is just a sign of greed and a tool of op-pression to the ancient Hebrew divines.[57]

Rauschenbusch explains the New Testament gospel in much the same way: "The fundamental virtue in the ethics of Jesus was love," he argues, and "love is the society-making quality." Yes, Jesus aimed first at restor-ing individuals' love for the Heavenly Father, but that love, if properly reinstated, cannot but spread outward to the rest of the world. "Because Jesus believed," Rauschenbusch argues, "in the organic growth of the new society, he patiently fostered its growth, cell by cell. Every human life brought under control of the new spirit which he himself embod-ied and revealed was an advance of the kingdom of God." The Social Gospel of Jesus, in other words, is an authentic socialism in which souls, renewed in their love for God, extend that love to their fellow humans unconditionally. "Jesus worked on individuals and through individuals," Rauschenbusch explains, "but his real end was not individualistic, but social."[58]

The holism of this vision recalls the "true virtue" of Jonathan Edwards, which consisted in "benevolence to being in general." "No man shares his life with God," Rauschenbusch writes, "whose religion does not flow out, naturally and without much effort, into all rela-tions of his life and reconstructs everything that it touches. Whoever uncouples the religious and the social life has not understood Jesus."[59] Early republican theologians like Rush and Witherspoon rejected Edwardsian ethics precisely because of its burdens on individualism; it took a socialist reading of the gospels to bring Edwards' moral para-digm back into conversation.

Rauschenbusch sees the Social Gospel as that which will revitalize the transformative power of the Christian message, and for that matter, revitalize the American republic. Rauschenbusch gives the latter half of his book over to showing how socialism realizes the truest aims of human progress, individual freedom, moral virtue, and Christianity. On each front the Social Gospel redefines the terms: unlike evolu-tionary progress, socialism comes as a conversion, a sudden regener-ation of society, "by which the essential genius of Christianity is set free." Rauschenbusch also offers socialism as a recovery of freedom, but specifically as *moral* freedom from the "social forces" that degrade the players in the capitalistic machine, drawing out the worst in everyone's character and destroying the bonds of peace. Even "the great leaders of industry," he insists, "are free only within very contracted limits"—their treatment of the workers is just itself a slavish bow to a system they cannot control. As for morality, the virtues at stake are not chastity and temperance but selflessness and love for one's neighbor: "Corporate management eliminates personal sympathy and the individual sense of honor." Socialism recovers these virtues by teaching men "to value human life more than property."[60]

Republican Theology as Free Market Theology

One would not have had to walk far to hear a counterpoint to the Social Gospel in an urban pulpit. The country's foremost pastors— H. W. Beecher at Plymouth Church in Brooklyn, Theodore Thornton Munger at the United Church of New Haven, and Newman Smyth at Center Church, right next to Munger's on the New Haven Green— served up Sumnerite liberalism weekly for decades, Munger and Smyth in frequent parries with Alexander Irvine across town. The archive of their sermons offers clear evidence that the tenets of republican theology lived on, at least in the bourgeois congregations of the Northeast, where they were appropriated for the defense of the free market against the budding popularity of socialism.

The core of free market theology is the assertion that the individual, not the social organism, stands at the locus of Christian morality and American freedom. "Christianity teaches nothing," wrote Munger in *Century Illustrated* in 1887, "unless it teaches the self-sovereignty of man. Evolution crowns its process with man who acts in freedom and holds his destiny in his own hands."[61] In Beecher's words, "Every individual man is himself a whole commonwealth."[62]

Several corollaries flow from the premise, including, first, an aversion to government welfarism: "It is the duty of government to protect the people while they are taking care of themselves—that is all," wrote Beecher. Second, their individualism breeds a particular animosity toward unions: "The liberty of the individual is destroyed where men are not allowed to work when the please, where they please, as long as they please, for whom they please, and for what they please."[63] Beecher wrote these words to rebuke the railroad strikes of 1877, which, ironically, erupted largely in the absence of unions; his point, however, is ontological:

> The liberty of the individual is the one vital thing. It is the unit; and there is no computation except upon the integrity of the unit. The moment you take the individual and make him merely a part of a unit, the moment you cement him into the commonwealth as a brick is cemented into a building, so that he is not a brick but is simply an indistinguishable part of the general structure, that being the thing, and not the developments which are in him individually, then you have established an arbitrary, absolute government . . . God gave me my right to liberty when he gave me myself; and the business of government is to see to it that nobody takes it away from me unjustly.

A third corollary is an individualistic morality, focusing on indus-triousness and "manliness" and propounding the faith that the free market, in time, fairly rewards hard work and punishes laziness. "Every few years, commerce has its earthquakes," conceded Beecher during the Depression of 1873, but "when the whole story of commercial disasters is told, it is found out that they who slowly amassed the gains of useful industry, built upon a rock; and they who flung together the imaginary millions of commercial speculations, built upon the sand." And for those laborers who never see a pot of gold, hard work is its own reward: "The poor man with industry is happier than the rich man in idleness; for labor makes the one more manly, and riches unmans the other."[64]

Such comforts to the proletariat aside, Beecher's pet corollary to in-dividualism is his defense of wealth. In sermon after sermon, Beecher rebuffs the Social Gospel premise that the accumulation of wealth is anti-Christian. "To teach that the money talent is immoral or mean," he argues, "is the very way to make it so. It is far better, and far wiser, to advocate such a right use of wealth as shall justify noble young men in the pursuit of it." The rich, he assures them, "need not be ashamed to be rich":

> Even if you are a Christian, and you have but just presented your-self among the brethren to take on the vows of Christ's household, and your lips are still wet with the sacrificial wine, and the bread of

faith is still in your mouth, you need not be ashamed to say, "I am bound to serve my Lord and Master through money."[65]

Serving the Lord through money, moreover, is not just tithing and philanthropy:

> Among the appropriate uses of wealth may be mentioned that of ennobling and dignifying the household; and among the methods of doing this may be mentioned that of making it spacious and beautiful, even in its material aspects . . . I love to see a man that makes a paradiso about his house, and fills his trees with birds.[66]

Beecher's theology of wealth in part caters to his parishioners, who built his church and most of the brownstones that still array the surrounding acres in Brooklyn Heights. But it also coheres with his broader vision of moral and spiritual progress, a vision that links the advance of Christianity to the rise of modern republics. "It is impossible," he preached on Thanksgiving in 1870, "to civilize a community without riches. I boldly affirm that no nation ever yet rose from a barbarous state except through the mediation of wealth earned. I affirm that the preaching of the Gospel to the heathen will be invalid and void if it does not make them active workmen, and teach them how to make money."[67] To turn its citizens into active workmen, moreover, a Christian republic must allow them to succeed and fail in a free market, to accumulate wealth with industry, and to fall through the cracks if they don't keep up. "Are the working men of the world oppressed?" Beecher asks. "Yes, undoubtedly, by governments, by rich men, and by educated classes." But this oppression is no sin—rather, "it must be so: Only in the household is it possible for strength and knowledge and power not to oppress ignorance and weakness and helplessness."[68] The Christian republic, Beecher underscores, is *not* a family.

In April 1885 Newman Smyth broke from his usual sermons for three Sundays to engage, at the request of "several workingmen," certain "industrial questions which are fast coming to the front among the great questions of our age." Specifically, Smyth was asked to address "the claims of labor," the nascent Social Gospel movement among the New Haven working class. These claims, which he outlines in his first sermon on the subject, include the standard Marxist grievances that workers are denied a fair share of market profits and that the accumulation of capital creates a permanent class of laborers who "suffer for the sins of all higher up, and not for their own sins only."[69] Smyth's second sermon, answering the charges, cites no Bible passages at all and could very well have been written by W. G. Sumner. He simply dismisses the first grievance as overstated, estimating that "not exceeding ten percent" of the total annual product is surplus value, while "nine tenths constitute the share of the laborer."[70] As for the accumulation of capital, Smyth argues, it allows for the production of inexpensive products, which are as beneficial and uplifting to the public as low wages might be harmful. "Although there may be social injustice still lurking in the modern loaf of bread, we must search for it in the crumbs." As Sumner himself had noted, the very people who fret about capital desire, nevertheless, "to be provided with things abundantly and cheaply."[71]

As for advancing the condition of the working poor, to which Smyth devotes his third sermon, the solutions revolve around uplifting their moral character: "Any group of men whose condition needs improving must begin by improving themselves. Self-help is the first condition of all help . . . Frugality, management, self-control, temperance, purpose, pluck, persistence—these are the cardinal virtues upon which success and advancement depend in any sphere or place."[72] Labor unions are commendable so long as they "help men acquire intelligence and true information which they may use profitably in their bargaining with the world"; but "if they seek to create labor monopolies in any trade, then the great public, looking on, will have little patience with them." Smyth also proposes to ease social tensions by cultivating "public spirit," both within the Christian church and around "common social interests" like the love of one's city and country and, above all, the love of God. "That which is best and of the greatest worth in the individual man is not that which is his own, but that which he shares with others—mind, intelligence, heart, conscience, truth, and love." What man does *not* share with others, however, is his property or his economic welfare:

> As a Christian man I do not believe in any communistic heaven, either in this world or the world to come, where there shall be a constant monotony of song, and every saint shall be fed and surfeited out of a government spoon. As a disciple of the manliest of

men, who went about doing good, I believe in a manly heaven of manly service through the eternal ages.[73]

The Ambivalence of Christian Fundamentalists

The prominent divines debating economic justice in this period were, almost to a man (and woman, counting Jane Addams), theological liberals, with the conspicuous exception of William Jennings Bryan, who was as antimodernist in his religion as he was progressive in his economics. The burgeoning fundamentalist movement had emphatically little to say. Of the 90 essays in *The Fundamentals*, the series that defined the movement in the early 1910s, only one addressed socialism, and it did so with reserve. Calling it "the most surprising and significant movement of the age," Charles Erdman, a theology professor at Princeton, neither equates socialism with Christianity nor declares it incompatible. He defines socialism as "an economic theory" and then pronounces the Bible silent on questions of political economy:

> It is impossible to identify [Jesus Christ] with any social theory or political party . . . That He insisted upon justice, and brotherhood, and love, and self-sacrifice is evident: but to suggest that these virtues are the monopoly of any one political or economic party is presumptuous . . . He rebuked social sins and injustice and selfishness, but when requested to divide a possession on a certain occasion He asked, "Who made Me a judge or a divider over you?" And that question has wide implications for the present day.[74]

The thrust of Erdman's essay, appearing as it did soon after Rauschenbusch's bestseller, is against doctrinaire socialism and particularly against uniting socialism and Christianity into a common ideology. "Many Christians," he flatly notes, "do not believe that capital is the result or embodiment of robbery." Many socialists, moreover, ally themselves with "lax theories of divorce and proposals of free love which are destructive of the family and subversive of society." With these (and similar disquietudes) leveled, Erdman nonetheless affirms the basic appeal of socialism as "a serious protest against the social wrongs and cruelties of the age, against the defects of the present economic system, against special privilege and entrenched injustice, against prevalent poverty, and hunger, and despair."[75]

Moreover, Erdman declares, Christians can, with no damage to their faith, embrace statist solutions to these economic problems. Indeed, "most Christians admit the wisdom of many Socialistic proposals," he offers, and public ownership of utilities, railroads, factories, and mines may well serve the interests of a godly republic. But those debates "would not involve questions of religion, but of expediency and political wisdom, with which problems the Church has nothing to do." In any evangelical congregation, Erdman emphasizes, "a man may be an ardent Socialist and a sincere Christian, or he may be a true Christian and a determined opponent of Socialism."[76]

The rise of totalitarian communism in the 1930s and 1940s denigrated the Social Gospel brand for American Christians. By mid-century free market ideology would lay almost exclusive claim to the mantles of individual liberty, moral progress, *and* the evangelical gospel. The story of that transformation will unfold in the next chapter. In the opening decades of the twentieth century, however, no ideology had that kind of lock on the church. There was room enough, even among Christian fundamentalists, for the likes of William Jennings Bryan.

THE TRIUMPH
OF FREE MARKET
CHRISTIANITY

S peaking to fellow Republicans early in his presidency, Dwight Eisenhower evoked the "French visitor," Alexis de Tocqueville, on the American ethos:

> He patiently and persistently sought the greatness and genius of America in our fields and in our forests, in our mines and in our commerce, in our Congress and in our Constitution, and he found them not. But he sought still further and then he said: "Not until I went into the churches of America and heard her pulpits flame with righteousness did I understand the secret of her genius and her power: America is great because America is good—and if America ever ceases to be good—America will cease to be great."[1]

The Tocqueville quote became a favorite of Republican Party statesmen in the late twentieth century. Nixon used it to promote anti-obscenity measures in 1970; Reagan recited it to the National Association of Evangelicals in 1983. The renewed interest in Tocqueville among Americans luckily survived the discovery, by a college student writing a term paper in the late 1980s, that the Frenchman never actually wrote or uttered the beloved quote, or anything quite so didactic. Its original author is unknown, in fact, but the misattribution appears to originate with Eisenhower's speechwriter.[2]

Regardless of its proper source, the fact that this ode to American religion served as Republican boilerplate after 1950 points to a defining trend in American politics, namely the alliance between conservative Christians and the Republican Party. The alliance, tentatively forged in 1952 between Billy Graham and the candidate Eisenhower, achieved stability with the rise of the Christian Right movement in the late 1970s. No Republican presidential candidate has won less than 65 percent of the evangelical vote since 1980; that share is often much higher, at all levels of government and in all parts of the country.

The account of how this coalition took form involves not only strategic considerations—party operatives making a play for the religious vote—but also realignments in ideology and theology. Recent scholarship has filled in many rich details of this story, from Daniel K. Williams's *God's Own Party: The Making of the Christian Right* (2010) to Darren Dochuk's *From Bible Belt to Sunbelt: Plain-Folk Religion, Grassroots Politics, and the Rise of Evangelical Conservatism* (2011). The basic plot is simple enough: the Cold War created a unique opening in American politics for a party that stood in perfect ideological contrast to global communism—a party that would maintain a strong stance against the Soviets but also advertise the ideals of limited government, free markets, and a civil religion of traditional morality. As Democrats defended their New Deal legacy, Republicans seized the new ground. Evangelicals, who had never before coalesced behind a national political party, and who began the twentieth-century split between free market and Social Gospel factions, migrated to the Republican Party on the strength of its entire platform—Northern evangelicals in the 1940s and 1950s and Southerners in the late 1960s. Conservative Christians, in other words, resonated not only with the Republicans' moral traditionalism but also with their willingness to protect foreign mission fields from communism *and* their defense of limited government at home, against welfare programs and commercial regulation. In essence, republican theology vaulted back into circulation as a political philosophy, both within a religious community and within a major political party.

This chapter tells the religious side of the story, which unfolds in two phases with a brief but noteworthy interregnum in the middle.

The first phase, leading up to 1950, follows a theological realignment in which evangelicals became more closely associated with conservative religion, breaking away from Mainline Protestants. As evangelicals and Mainliners squared off over biblical interpretation, they also chased competing visions for American society, with evangelicals forming a reactionary bloc against the League of Nations, Darwinism in public schools, shifting moral codes, and New Deal socialism, eventually harnessing commercial radio to form a national community of conservative Christians. When the Cold War drew Republicans into their hardline anticommunism, evangelicals were poised to join them in arms, for the first time parlaying republican theology into foreign policy. Billy Graham and Dwight Eisenhower sealed the alliance in the 1950s.

Evangelicals' political ascent took a detour in the 1960s with the rise of the Civil Rights movement. The movement posed a unique challenge—how to alleviate racial discrimination—for which republican theology, and its emphasis on limited government, had limited answers. A 1963 exchange between eight Birmingham pastors and Martin Luther King highlights the predicament: the white clergy, who pursued racial justice in their own ministries, nevertheless opposed federal interventionism against Jim Crow laws and resented the embarrassment King's demonstrations visited upon their city. Their public rebuke of the imprisoned leader in April 1963 invited a rejoinder, King's *Letter from Birmingham Jail*, which, among other things, deconstructed the ministers' political theology and marginalized conservative evangelicals from the great social justice debates of the 1960s.

Evangelicals' brief exile from influence, however, saw enough social and political change—the sexual revolution, the drug culture, the welfare state, mounting taxes and regulation, the *Roe vs. Wade* decision, not to mention a string of humiliating setbacks in the Cold War—to fuel a revival of the old republican theology. In the late 1970s free market ideologues, anticommunists, and moral traditionalists teamed up to transform the Republican Party into the seat of the American right wing. The "New Right" movement, mobilized by such organizations as the Moral Majority, succeeded in attracting Southern Baptists (loyal Democrats since the 1840s) into the GOP and in establishing a reliable voting bloc of conservative Christians who were as fired up about tax cuts as they were about overturning *Roe*.

As effectively as republican theology has held this alliance together, its longevity has also brought into daylight the tensions it encompasses—between libertarianism and moralism (over gay marriage, among other issues), between free market and social justice types in the church, between the older and younger generations of evangelicals, and between the gospel of individual conversion and the swampy politics of reform. The New Right, while reestablishing republican theology as the civil religion of American evangelicals, has also prompted many evangelicals to rethink the basics of their political theology.

I. THE CONSERVATIVE REALIGNMENT

Evangelicalism, as a label, migrated to its present lodging among conservative Christians between 1919 and 1942. When the century began, the term "evangelical" fit comfortably within diverse wings of American Protestantism, encompassing both the Social Gospel and that of free market liberalism. In fact, just about the only Protestants who did *not* as readily identify as evangelicals in the early 1900s were the fundamentalists, whose grim eschatology shunned the perfectionism that animated Christian thinking at the time. Fundamentalists, George Marsden notes, believed that "the decline of civilization was inevitable."[3] By the 1940s, however, "evangelical" had become almost synonymous with Christian fundamentalism (or at least generally conservative theology), and the movement had not only grown in size and stature but had found a powerful voice in American politics. To boot, these conservative evangelicals championed free market capitalism, moral reform, and American global leadership as vigorously as they did biblical fidelity and evangelism. In other words, conservative evangelicals came full circle from the founding era, reuniting with republican theology in nearly its original dimensions and applying it to beckon a new era of American ascendancy.

How did this realignment come about? Cold War politics certainly solidified the trend in the late 1940s, but an open feud between liberal and conservative Protestants forms the long-running subtext. Starting with a disagreement over the League of Nations in 1919, fundamentalists and Mainliners did public battle for cultural primacy in America, a struggle that culminated in a standoff over radio broadcasting rights in the 1940s. Along the way, the evangelical mantle shifted to conservatives more exclusively than at any time since the First Great Awakening. Liberals, who came to associate that mantle with tasteless radio hucksterism, simply let it go. When the National Association of Evangelicals (NAE) formed in 1942 to defend the rights of fundamentalist broadcasters, nobody questioned to whom the term belonged. The key battles in this saga reveal an indicative pattern: the rise of conservative evangelicalism coincided with its embrace of Americanism and eventually its fervent identification with republican theology.

Fundamentalists and the League of Nations

What set the stage for the Mainline/fundamentalist rupture, and for the latter's resurgence, was the birth of the Federal Council of Churches in 1908. The Council rose out of the ashes of the Evangelical Alliance, which had united revivalists under a quasi-Calvinist confession since 1846 but had dissipated as American Christianity grew more liberal.[4] In deliberate contrast, the Federal Council took for its basis "the spirit of fellowship, service, and cooperation" among all Christian churches in America; its charter, drafted at Carnegie Hall in New York City in 1905 and later ratified by every American denomination except for the Southern Baptists, omitted all references to doctrine.[5] To not join the Council in 1908 was to take a stand not only against its ecumenism but also against the evangelical ethos of the times.

The politics of the Federal Council were broadly progressive from the start, promoting Social Gospel initiatives in big cities and the prohibition movement nationally. In 1919 the Council even sent its own representative to the Paris Peace Conference to endorse President Wilson's pitch for a League of Nations. *The Christian Century*, the Council's major periodical, enveloped the League into a broad evangelical vision for reforming the world. "It is the prime business of the church," went the typical editorial, "to create the conscience for civilization . . . The question at Versailles is, shall the world go on in the old immoral international life, or shall we boldly launch on a new era of moral internationalism?"[6] Wilson himself was given space to defend the League in *The Christian Century*, and he used his column to sensitize American clergy to "the great world processes."[7]

More importantly, however, the League of Nations debate also marked the entry of Christian fundamentalists into American politics.[8]

Rebutting the Council's internationalism on theological grounds, Christian conservatives managed to strike a nationalist chord with the general public and helped to secure the treaty's defeat in the U.S. Senate. Eschatology lay at the heart of their opposition: dispensational theology holds that the "end times" will see the rise of a world empire against the church of Christ, and the dispensationalists of 1919 came to see such an empire prefigured in the League of Nations. A leading dispensationalist, Arno C. Gaebelein, called the League a "great delusion" hatched by "the god of this age, Satan, to lull a secure world to sleep."[9] Dispensationalists believe, furthermore, that the redemption of civilization that Wilson sought in the League could only truly come about after the final return of Christ and that for humans to devise it themselves presumed upon the authority of God.[10] From these doctrinal objections fundamentalists built a more populist case against U.S. membership in the League that raised the specter of "unholy alliances" with European Catholics, Arab Muslims, and Asian Buddhists, a sentiment that resonated with the isolationist mood in postwar America. Not only did the treaty go down in flames, American voters proceeded to sweep Wilsonian progressives out of national office in the elections of 1920.

The Scopes Trial

Fundamentalists next took their antimodernist fight into state capitals, seeking to outlaw the teaching of evolution in public schools. The first big legislative victory came in March 1925 with the passage of the Butler Act in Tennessee, the law under which John T. Scopes was prosecuted in Dayton later that summer in a trial sensationalized by fundamentalists and secularists alike.[11] The legal results of the trial—Scopes' conviction, later vacated—have been long overshadowed by the redacted court transcript, in which Scopes' attorney, Clarence Darrow, called the prosecuting attorney, William Jennings Bryan, to the witness stand to squeeze him on the inconsistencies of Genesis—an exchange immortalized in Jerome Lawrence's *Inherit the Wind* (1955).

Liberal Mainliners, who had preached "theistic evolution" for 65 years, took pains to reject the Darwin-versus-Jesus stakes of the trial, reserving their harshest words for the fundamentalists who provoked it with their activism—and then failed to meet the intellectual challenge. Referring to the "amateur dramatics at Dayton," *The Christian Century* treated Bryan's embarrassment on the witness stand as symptomatic of broader ignorance among conservatives, ignorance that, they worried, opens all of Christianity up to modernist ridicule: "There is a scholarly and convincing argument to be made for the conservative position . . . but Mr. Bryan is manifestly unable to make this argument, for he has neither the mind nor the temper for the task."[12] Mainliners' unsparing treatment of Bryan—the populist hero of the Social Gospel, who had stood with them in the League of Nations dispute just six years earlier— exposes the magnitude of their alarm over the rise of fundamentalism. Even at the start of the trial *The Christian Century* mocked Bryan as a showboat, "having just the sort of time he enjoys." By contrast, when Bryan collapsed and died in Dayton just after the trial ended, *Moody Monthly*, a journal published by the conservative Moody Bible Institute, lionized him: "We have mourned the death of many public men, but there is something different in our mourning for William Jennings Bryan . . . We never voted for him for President. His politics were not ours, but on almost every great moral question it seemed to us that he was always right . . . He has put courage into the hearts of some of our spiritual leaders. He has shamed cowards."[13]

Religious Responses to the Great Depression

A third fundamentalist foray into the public sphere concerned the New Deal. The July 1933 issue of *Moody Monthly*, which circulated just after the first whirlwind of New Deal legislation, opens a window onto the Mainline versus conservative approaches to economic philosophy in the post-Beecher era. In it the editors reviewed a new Federal Council memo, *Our Economic Life in the Light of Christian Ideals*, which called for "a more democratic distribution of wealth and income" and which outright condemned the profit motive, declaring Christianity "hostile to any system founded on the private interest of the individual." The theological core of the Council's argument was the egalitarian fellowship of early Christians as recorded in the Acts of the Apostles, Chapter 4, in which believers are seen selling their worldly possessions and distributing "to each as any had need."[14]

Making the case against socialism (and against the redistributive efforts of the New Deal), *Moody Monthly* flatly rejected the Acts 4 paradigm for the unregenerate world. The Acts 4 model, *Moody* argued, applies only to the local church, and "regenerated men do not need specialists in economics and industrial relations to teach them how to treat one another." Evangelical salvation, in other words, distinguishes modern socialism from Acts 4 egalitarianism in an elemental way: "Whereas socialism would be obligatory," in the early church the sharing "was voluntary."[15]

By emphasizing the voluntary nature of Christian benevolence against the rising collectivist ethos, conservative evangelicals took a decisive step toward filling a long-empty quadrant in American Protestantism— fundamentalist free marketism—and toward recovering republican theology in its eighteenth-century form, as a religious rationale for limited government. As with Rush, Witherspoon, and Beecher, however, evangelicals in the 1930s made an open exception to their anti-collectivism when it came to personal morality. The health of the republic depends upon the moral virtue of its individual citizens, they maintained, and after a decade of decrying speakeasies, divorce, and gambling, *Moody Monthly* laid blame for the Great Depression on America's moral decline. "America's greatest sin," a pastor wrote in the same 1933 issue, "and the *real* cause of the present depression, is forgetting God."[16] There *is* a collectivist solution to the country's problems, in other words, but it involves reforming the nation's spiritual life, not redistributing its wealth.

Radio and the Birth of a New Evangelical Community

What fundamentalists of the early 1930s lacked in their republican theology was the optimism of the early evangelicals—the "advancing splendors of prophetic day"—that cadenced the poetry of the founding era.[17] Evangelicals in the Roosevelt years sang the glum lyrics of decline—"the nations and the world must reap what they sow"—and actually took a measure of vindication in the Depression. "Those of us old enough" to remember the heydays of Progressivism, wrote one pastor in 1933, "cannot fail to recall the intolerant optimism which was then an almost universal vogue. Anyone who doubted that the world was entering upon a millennium of happiness and good living was a 'pessimist,' and such an epithet was about the worst that could be flung."[18] Conservatives' taste for augury grew partly out of their dispensational theology, which prophesies total destruction before redemption at the end of time. Their pessimism acquired a special edge in the 1920s and 30s in reactive stance against the modernists.

Fundamentalism, however, does have a "good news" component, namely personal salvation in Christ. The circumstances of the Great Depression, combined with the mass communication potential of radio broadcasting, offered fundamentalists a chance to reintroduce the nation to the old gospel of Whitefield, Edwards, Nettleton, and Moody. Radio evangelists like Paul Rader out of Chicago, Aimee Semple McPherson and Charles Fuller out of Los Angeles, and hundreds of smaller-wattage broadcasters reached living rooms across America with daily calls for repentance from the late 1920s through the 50s. Federal policy, which reserved free public-service air time for ecumenical religious programs, effectively diverted fundamentalists into commercial broadcasting. Thus, unlike the Mainline radio preachers, conservative evangelists *had* to attract listeners and private donors, an onus that gave rise to live music, riveting testimonials of conversion, and, above all, the reassuring "self-certainty" of the fundamentalist mindset. Evangelists even managed to introduce a measure of hope and good cheer into their broadcasts: Rader's daily *Breakfast Brigade* greeted listeners with a jingle that promised that his sermon would be "sugar in your coffee and honey on your bread." By 1948, more than 1,600 fundamentalist programs flooded the American airwaves, none of them subsidized by the government.[19]

In consequence of its popularity, radio evangelism transformed religious life in the 1930s and 40s. It helped to build, first of all, a national community of fundamentalist Christians.[20] It also concentrated the enterprise of evangelism among theological conservatives, as Mainliners shunned the emotionalism of on-air appeals for conversion and money. If there was a single decade in which the word "evangelical" fell from the ecumenical skies to the fundamentalist island, it was the 1930s, and its flight path was a bandwidth of radio waves. Above all, radio created an institutional platform for the power struggle between liberals and conservatives over the soul of American Christianity. From the late 1920s into the 40s, officials in the Federal Council of Churches (some of whom sat on the boards of NBC and CBS) aggressively sought to limit the broadcasting reach of conservative evangelists. They helped to craft the sustaining-time policies that chased conservatives into commercial broadcasting in the first place; by the 1940s they were urging stations to cease selling air time to religious programs altogether—and urging the federal government to criminalize the practice.[21]

Liberals' concerns were both ethical and theological. As even some
evangelicals admitted, commercialized preaching lent itself to racket-
eering (as it would with "televangelism" in the 1980s). The *Christian
Century* in 1944 charged that "many insincere and unauthorized 'evangelists' are making a handsome living" off their listeners' checks, an
accusation evangelical broadcasters took to heart when they drafted a
code of conduct later that year.[22] The longer-range fear, however, was
theological: liberal Protestants perceived their waning influence over
American culture after decades of ascendancy. "The public gets a dis-
torted and one-sided picture of current religious thinking," the *Century* complained in the same editorial, "because most [Christian radio]
programs follow the ultraconservative fundamentalist pattern"—this in
spite of the fact that Mainliners could get sustaining time on the air at
no charge and had no legal barriers to competing with conservatives on
the commercial dial. The Federal Council's only hope of containing
radio evangelism was to put an end to commercial religious programming, a goal the pursuit of which would only energize and mobilize
the new evangelical movement.

National Identity, Ideological Leanings

The radio battles gave birth to the NAE in 1942, a conservative
answer to the Federal Council that gave radio evangelists representation from Rockefeller Plaza to Capitol Hill and also formalized the
battle lines within American Christianity, allowing conservatives to
speak with one voice in the public sphere. In the opening years of the
NAE, that voice belonged to Harold J. Ockenga, the organization's
first president, the longtime pastor of Park Street Church in Boston,
and an early patron of Billy Graham. Ockenga's inaugural address in
St. Louis, delivered before several hundred conservative pastors, vented
a scathing critique of the Federal Council and the "terrible octopus of
liberalism, which spreads itself throughout our Protestant Church."[23]
Ockenga declared American Christianity in a state of crisis and blamed
this crisis on liberalism and secularism, which had unleashed "a tidal
wave of drunkenness, immorality, corruption, dishonesty, and utter
atheism."[24]

What is most striking about Ockenga's call to arms, however, is its
explicit recovery of republican theology. Ockenga drew politics and
religion together with an analogy that saw government and religion

forming the two banks of a river in which flows the economic life of the nation. For most of American history, Ockenga argued, the solid banks of republicanism and Christian virtue tamed the rushing river of free enterprise and private industry; but the twentieth century saw both the "disintegration of Christianity" and a stunning new flow of capital to fund old-fashioned vices. "As a result," Ockenga concluded, "one bank of the river began to deteriorate while the river rose." To contain the flood, moreover, government attempted, "by the increase of bureaus," to regulate the ensuing chaos, thus upending the republican tradition. "Because our religion failed we have had a revolution in our political form . . . Unless we can have a true revival of evangelical Christianity, able to change the character of men and build up a new moral fiber, we believe Christianity, capitalism, and democracy, likewise, to be imperiled."[25]

That Ockenga sounds like an early American revivalist here is significant: like evangelicalism, republican theology had been gradually stretched to cover the whole map of American Christianity. Abolitionists and their foes alike had exploited its logic in the nineteenth century, as did market theologians and even Social Gospelers in the twentieth century. With the launch of the NAE, however, evangelicalism and republican theology together snapped back to the corner of the map where conservative Christianity and limited government ideology coexist. That the new organization set out to save "Christianity, capitalism, and democracy" all in the same revival reflects a core belief that these institutions are joined in their fates—that freedom, limited government, and virtuous Christian living are codependent. It also reveals a recommitment to the American project among fundamentalist Christians, who not long before had positioned themselves as outliers to American culture. Now, seizing an opportunity to redefine this culture, conservative evangelicals emerged as its greatest champions.

Anticommunism as an Evangelical Cause

Nothing, not even the Depression or the war against Hitler, forced Americans to rethink their place in the world more urgently than did the march of Soviet communism in the late 1940s. Stalin's sphere of influence, enlarged by the spoils of the Potsdam Conference and by the Chinese Revolution, presented a strategic and cultural threat to the United States—strategic in the new balance of power taking shape on the world stage, cultural in its implications for American identity. The Soviet system represented to many Americans the exact antithesis of their republic—post-religious in its moral foundations and totalitarian in its politics. That such a system could gain a footing in every corner of the globe carried prophetic connotations, even among quasi-religious Americans: either the American model—a religious people living under a free government—was losing its appeal in the modern age, or that ideal was the last great hope against a global terror and had to be defended at its core. The stakes of this dilemma could not have offered up a better opportunity for evangelicals to reassert their relevance to the American experiment, and to do so on the terms that had worked so well at the founding, namely those embedded in republican theology.

Upon this narrative began the evangelical revival that conservative pastors had called for in St. Louis in 1942. The headlining preacher in this revival had not actually attended that convention, as he was still a junior at Wheaton College at the time. By 1950, however, Billy Graham had preached repentance and salvation to nearly 1 million people across the United States, including at an 18-day rally in Boston organized by Harold Ockenga that reached 105,000 listeners, and at a convention in Los Angeles in the fall of 1949 that stretched on for 72 meetings over eight weeks, with 350,000 attendees and over 3,000 reported conversions.[26] Graham's Los Angeles revival put him on the covers of *Life*, *Time*, *Newsweek*, and the *London Illustrated* and launched a six-decade preaching career that took him to every inhabitable continent.

Graham's gospel was famously direct, simple, and soul-searching—"Is Heaven your home tonight?" he would ask his listeners.[27] But his sermons came pitched in tune with the times and with American culture, and he managed to draw his audience into a cosmic narrative, both as individuals *and* as members of a nation set apart by God. What surged into a call to personal repentance always began with an indictment of the city he was preaching in and of the nation at large; to make a personal decision for Christ, moreover, had geopolitical implications. The rise of communism, in the early Billy Graham sermons, presented more than a diplomatic quandary; it was a warning from God to all Americans. Graham's Los Angeles campaign began two days after it was reported that the Soviet Union had developed its own atomic bomb. In his first sermon of the campaign, on September 25,

1949, Graham referred to the "stark, naked fear" gripping the country as reason enough to urge a national repentance for sins, beginning in the depraved city of Los Angeles:

> An arms race, unprecedented in the history of the world, is driving us madly toward destruction! And I sincerely believe that it is the providence of God that He has chosen this hour for a campaign— giving this city one more chance to repent of sin and turn to a be- lieving knowledge of the Lord Jesus Christ.[28]

Degeneracy in the "City of Angels," Graham continued, encompassed a humanistic film industry, rising street and domestic violence, sen- sual billboards, cocktail bars, divorce, lax church attendance, and teen- age delinquency—all patterns that reflected the trajectory of the entire country: "Our high school and college young people are going to the dogs morally, encouraged by the press and radio across this Nation."[29] The state of affairs, moreover, marked a departure from the godly roots of American culture and as such carried serious implications for the dawning Cold War:

> The world is divided into two sides. On the one side we see Communism; on the other side we see so-called Western culture. Western culture and its fruit had its foundation in the Bible, the Word of God, and in the revivals of the Seventeenth and Eighteenth Centuries. Communism, on the other hand, has decided against God, against Christ, against the Bible, and against all religion. Communism is not only an economic interpretation of life—Communism is a religion that is inspired, directed, and moti- vated by the Devil himself, who has declared war against Almighty God. Do you know that the Fifth Columnists, called Communists, are more rampant in Los Angeles than any other city in America? We need a revival![30]

Graham then connected the theological dots: when God's people come to resemble their enemies, it is the design of God to deliver his people into the hands of those very enemies. That the Soviets have acquired the capacity to annihilate Los Angeles in minutes made divine sense to Billy Graham: Americans living in that city no longer lived as citizens worthy of a free republic. "Unless God's people turn to Him and the city repents, we are going to see the judgment of God come upon us."

The more hopeful half of his sermon—an invitation to receive salvation in Christ—completes the account of why Billy Graham's preaching style struck a chord with mid-century Americans. Graham offered not only a First Great Awakening kind of redemption—personal salvation from sin and death—but also a Second Great Awakening kind of promise—of American triumph. "Let Christ come into your heart and cleanse you from sin," he urged; but he also reminded his listeners of the "tremendous social implications" of a mass revival: "Do you know what came out of past revivals? The abolishment of slavery came out of revival. The abolishment of child labor came out of revival."[31] In the closing months of the 1940s, what hung in the balance was the fate of Western civilization itself. More than military might or diplomatic resolve, Graham argued, an evangelical revival in a city like Los Angeles was the key to victory for democracy in the Cold War. Graham's optimism, however, stood in contrast to the Jeremiahs of the previous generation. Interviewed on Moody radio at the height of his early revivals, Graham was asked, "Is there hope for America's spiritual survival?" Yes, he answered, "I believe at this very moment, there is moving across the nation toward religion and back to the faith of our fathers. And I sincerely believe that the only hope of our present day is to re-inject into American society the moral stamina which can be brought about by spiritual rearmament."[32] In essence, Graham led two revivals at once: a revival of traditional evangelical conversions among American Christians and a recovery of republican theology and American patriotism among conservative Christians.

A Platform and a Party

Having found their voice, American evangelicals found their way back into national politics riding the tailwinds of the resurging Republican Party, which also centered its platform on a muscular anticommunism. Nothing chased evangelicals and Republicans into each other's arms faster than President Truman's dismissal of Douglas MacArthur from his command on April 11, 1951. Truman's decision, over the General's defiant campaign to carry the Korean War into China, touched every nerve that evangelicals and Republicans had in common: it left the 1949 Chinese Revolution, which had doubled the communist map, uncontested by the West. Abandoning China to the Communists, furthermore, sealed off the borders to what Christian missionaries had found to be a ripe harvest for evangelism.[33] Generating palpable heat from evangelicals, the debacle was Truman's undoing—he soon aborted his plans to run for reelection—as well as a major blow to the national Democratic Party, which had enjoyed nearly unrivaled control of Washington since 1933. The knights of the New Deal now found themselves blundering into a reputation for weakness against communism, a label that made Democrats decreasingly acceptable to the growing bloc of evangelical voters. The time was ripe for realignment.

Evangelicals and Republicans made their romance official in the election of 1952. Daniel K. Williams credits Billy Graham (among others) with recruiting Dwight D. Eisenhower, the retired general, to run for president as a Republican. That the Democrats nominated Adlai Stevenson, a Unitarian who was divorced, made the choice even easier for evangelical voters. After splitting their vote evenly between Truman, Thomas Dewey, and Strom Thurmond in 1948, conservative Christians broke for Eisenhower by over 60 percent (on the strength of Northern support more than Southern), handing the general an easy victory on themes of restoring traditional values and reasserting American muscle in the Cold War. Republicans achieved majorities in the House and Senate as well.

Graham's agenda was to recover Christian moralism in the public square, and in this he found a willing partner in Eisenhower, who pushed Congress in 1954 to approve a new airmail stamp bearing the words "In God We Trust" and to revise the Pledge of Allegiance to affirm the nation's status "under God," proposals that won broad support as cultural armaments against the spread of communism. Evangelical reaction to these largely symbolic victories mixed approval with caution. *Moody Monthly* rejoiced that "as thousands of pieces of mail enter atheistic countries every day, the stamp will prove a wonderful testimony to our confidence in God as a nation." And they predicted that the amended Pledge would point young citizens to a "moral law, absolute because it comes from [God]." However, the editors also warned that simply "conceding that we are 'under God' does not make us a Godly nation or give right standing in His sight . . . No nation—or individual—can be right with God except on God's own terms, and they are trust in Jesus Christ and dependence on His work."[34]

Statements like these reveal the lingering ambivalence of fundamentalists toward politics. Civic relevance for American evangelicals has always depended upon their willingness to embrace the intersection of faith, virtue, and the free republic—the basic formulation of republican theology. Evangelical resurgence in the mid-twentieth century proved no exception to this rule, as evidenced in the sermons of Ockenga and Graham. Unlike their counterparts in the nineteenth century, however, evangelicals in the twentieth stood their ground on conservative fundamentals—the primacy of the scriptures and the importance of personal conversion to faith in Christ. Thus, even as Republicans in the 1950s sought to build on their alliance with this new constituency, the constituents themselves resisted all compromise on the articles of faith—a stubbornness that undoubtedly added decades to the full formation of this alliance. Not until the late 1970s would anything as durable as the "New Right" emerge among religious conservatives.

II. CIVIL RIGHTS AND THE LIMITATIONS OF REPUBLICAN THEOLOGY

No sooner had conservative evangelicals reclaimed a voice in national politics when the Civil Rights movement took center stage. Evangelicals' abrupt return to the political wilderness in the late 1950s stemmed from their failure to engage the Civil Rights movement and its leaders. The movement itself posed an interesting challenge to evangelicals and their republican theology, as it did to the political system at large. The cause of advancing race equality did not map cleanly onto the ideological battles that had dominated American politics since the 1910s. Progressivism, for instance, lends itself as easily to cultural chauvinism (and racial segregation along with it) as it does to themes of social equality. Free market conservatives, moreover, are no likelier to support integration, particularly to the extent that such mandates are handed down from Washington to the states, as in the *Brown* case of 1954. Neither political party had a particular concern for civil rights in the 1950s: Democrats still retained the large Southern factions that had opposed racial equality since the age of Jefferson. Republicans, who had sprung to life in 1854 on an antislavery platform, gave up on equal rights for blacks as soon as Reconstruction ended in 1876. GOP interest in calming racial tensions in the 1950s stemmed mainly from Cold War concerns about anti-American propaganda abroad.

American Christians, furthermore, had only grown more segregated since the abolition of slavery. Objections to social comingling between the races found ostensible support in the New Testament warning against *heterozugeo,* or being "unequally yoked." Indeed, for the express purpose of preventing racial intermarriage, in fact, the conservative Bob Jones University in South Carolina started rejecting applications from African Americans in 1963 (BJU admitted married blacks starting in 1971 and unmarried blacks in 1975, and formally dropped its ban on interracial dating in 2000).[35] Many Southern white Christians expressed their fear of forced integration in political rather than social terms, referring to the threats to local church autonomy, free association, and private property.[36]

The more liberal *Christian Century,* which employed Martin Luther King as an editorialist in the 1950s, had taken something of a stand for racial equality in the 1940s, encouraging black domestic workers, for instance, to demand higher pay.[37] When national evangelical figures like Billy Graham embraced the cause of civil rights, however, they did so guardedly, pinning their hopes to a slow and voluntary integration that would emanate from the church rather than from the federal government. Their voluntarism kept faith with republican theology, which sees the church as the primary agent of moral reform, and which sees individual freedom—rather than social equality—as the highest political good. Almost no evangelicals, North or South, approved of the disruptive tactics of the Civil Rights movement—the disobedience, the lunch counter sit-ins, and the protest marches—that activists found necessary to awaken the American conscience. Evangelicals' outspoken discomfort with the movement's strategies, combined with their hopes for a gradual and painless resolution to racial issues, pushed conservative evangelicals to the fringe of this defining issue of the 1950s and 60s, exposing once again the conflicts within republican theology when it comes to moral reform.

The Birmingham Eight

The dilemmas of republican theology played out no more vividly than with the "Birmingham Eight," an ad hoc group of white clergymen who in 1963 attempted to allay racial frictions in the city, reproaching whites for their bigotry as well as Civil Rights leaders for their provocations, earning hostility from their own parishioners, vandalism and death threats from the Ku Klux Klan, and, with lasting significance, an apostolic rejoinder from Martin Luther King in his *Letter from Birmingham Jail*. The group, which convened on only three occasions (twice at the Tutwiler Hotel in Birmingham and once at the White House with President Kennedy), by no means spoke for the evangelical community writ large. It was an Episcopal bishop, George Murray, who called the first meeting, and his compatriots included Bishop Joseph Durick of the Catholic Church and Rabbi Milton Grafman. Only two of the eight, the Southern Baptist Earl Stallings and the Presbyterian Ed Ramage, had any affiliation with the National Association of Evangelicals. Taken as a whole, however, their sermons, ministries, and joint statements all bear the defining marks of republican theology, albeit with a Southern white twist. Like most of their regional peers, the Birmingham Eight valued individual virtue—and particularly gentility—over social justice; they placed greater faith in the church than in government to sanctify cultural mores; and they nonetheless cherished the basic integrity of the American system. Lawlessness, more than anything else, offended their sensibilities. "There is no freedom where there is no law" was a common mantra in their pulpits.[38]

The limitations of this theology in the face of racial injustice would be the subject of King's *Letter*; but the first stand these ministers took was, in fact, against segregationists, and it bore immediate consequences. The inauguration of Alabama Governor George Wallace on January 14, 1963, brought his promise to preserve "segregation now, segregation tomorrow, and segregation forever," in defiance of the federal courts if necessary. Meeting for lunch at the Tutwiler two days later, the ministers issued a sweeping reproof, declaring, first of all, that "hatred and violence have no sanction in our religious or political traditions," and second, "that there may be disagreement concerning laws and social change without advocating defiance, anarchy, and subversion." The ministers also took a broad stand for Lockean equality, noting that "no person's freedom is safe unless every person's freedom is equally protected" and that "every human being is created in the image of God and is entitled to respect as a fellow human being with all basic rights, privileges, and responsibilities which belong to humanity."[39]

By no means did these words endorse the racial integration efforts that had descended from Washington, D.C. over the previous decade.

On the contrary, the ministers expressed empathy toward the "many sincere people" troubled by court-mandated integration, and at least two of the eight held the view that racial harmony and justice could be achieved in a segregated city. Nevertheless, the statement, published in every Birmingham paper later that week, was enough to generate "an outpouring of vicious letters and harassing midnight phone calls" directed at each of the men. Picking up on the hair triggers of Cold War political theology, segregationists branded even the vaguest reference to the common image of God or the brotherhood of man as Marxism in disguise. "These so-called Christians," went the typical reaction, "are, as a matter of fact, Socialists." Thus the Tutwiler band of clergy, with not one socialist among them, nonetheless wandered into a no man's land of Southern religion.

Neither in their statement of January 16, nor in any subsequent communiqué, did the ministers reach out to civil rights leaders for support; the effort would have proved futile had they tried. The general dearth of moderate voices in Birmingham was precisely what drew Martin Luther King and his associates to the city in 1963. Alabama's largest city exhibited Jim Crow at its worst, with segregation permeating every sphere of commerce, a depressed economy keeping racial tensions on edge, and a longtime city manager named Bull Connor who handled racial protest with police dogs and fire hoses. Even as residents attempted to soften the city's image, replacing the Connor regime with a new city council system in 1963, King looked to Birmingham for its extremism. Moderation was King's worst enemy: to shake the nation's conscience the Civil Rights movement needed true ramparts to storm, and Birmingham offered those ramparts. "If we can crack Birmingham," said King, "we can crack the South."[40]

King arrived in the city to lead demonstrations in early April, days after the election that booted Bull Connor from city government. Fortuitously, Connor challenged the election results in court and maintained control over the police and fire departments for several more weeks. One journalist quipped that Birmingham had "two mayors and a King." Playing right into King's hand, Connor secured an injunction prohibiting the civil rights march planned for Good Friday, April 12, and personally ordered King's arrest after three blocks of illegal marching. The marchers refused bail. On the night that Christians around the world marked the crucifixion and burial of Jesus, Martin Luther

King was precisely where he intended to be—entombed in the "Dark City" of Southern racism.[41]

In one final turn of fortune, local religious leaders handed King an opportunity to assume not only the image of Christ but also the voice of Paul. The Birmingham Eight convened at the Tutwiler for a second time on April 12, the day of King's arrest. Irked at the distraction from the city's good-faith (if gradualist) reforms, the ministers vented their frustration with the civil rights leaders, referring to them as "outsiders" and deploring their provocations. "Just as we formerly pointed out that 'hatred and violence have no sanction in our religious and political traditions,'" they snapped, "we also point out that such actions as incite to hatred and violence, however technically peaceful those actions may be, have not contributed to the resolution of our local problems." Rather, the ministers commended "certain local negro leadership which has called for honest and open negotiation of racial issues in our area."[42] Whatever the clergy meant by such "negotiations," King took the ministers' diffidence toward him as a teachable moment on a grand scale. Remaining in his cell for more than a week, King scratched out a reply to the ministers' statement on the margins of the newspaper on which he read it. His reply is perhaps the widest-ranging defense of civil disobedience ever published and serves up a critique of republican theology on par with the best Social Gospel manifestos.

King begins the *Letter from Birmingham Jail* with a defense of his status as an outsider. "I am in Birmingham because injustice is here," he explains. "Just as the Apostle Paul left his village of Tarsus and carried the gospel of Jesus Christ to the far corners of the Greco-Roman world, so am I compelled to carry the gospel of freedom beyond my own home town." He brings his personal apologia to an ontological point: "Injustice anywhere is a threat to justice everywhere. We are caught in an inescapable network of mutuality, tied in a single garment of destiny." This latter statement opens up a case for social justice as the essence of divine justice, and grounds for why the pursuit of civil rights warrants the breaking of local laws. Racial segregation, King argues, along with any statutes that uphold it, categorically violates God's law because it "distorts the soul and damages the personality. It gives the segregator a false sense of superiority and the segregated a false sense of inferiority." Virtue—not just material fortune—hangs in the balance. As such, King argues, it must be resisted by any peaceful means available, even if unlawful.[43]

King commends the Birmingham ministers for supporting local "negotiations" but maintains that the national Civil Rights movement is necessary to empower Birmingham's blacks for a meaningful role in such discussions. "Too long has our beloved Southland been bogged down in a tragic effort to live in monologue rather than dialogue." A focus on achieving local fellowship misses the larger, deeper-seated dynamics of group domination and oppression. Some "individuals," King concedes, "may see the moral light and voluntarily give up their unjust posture," but "it is an historical fact that privileged groups seldom give up their privileges," a fact that will forever negate the type of progress proposed by whites who seek racial harmony without a grand reform of local commerce and municipal life.[44]

Republican Theology and Civil Rights

King's personal affront to the Birmingham Eight overlaps with the basic theological disagreement between them. The white clergymen truly believed that the only way to break the lock of racism on the hearts of bigots is to foster interracial friendships and that the best way to achieve racial integration is to cultivate within the black community virtues that whites associate with social uplift, like gentility and sobriety. The local church, they believed, was ideally suited to both tasks. Indeed, the ministers believed that federal integration efforts, by undermining the voluntarism of these outreaches, disrupted rather than advanced the necessary transformation of souls on both sides of the color line.

Members of the Birmingham Eight privately conveyed their resentment over King's dismissiveness and his apparent ignorance of their many years of labor toward racial healing and social uplift for blacks in Birmingham. This labor reflected their republican theology. Charles Carpenter, the oldest and most conservative of the group, who once predicted that "if we can just make enough Christians integration will take care of itself," also had the most proactive track record on race relations. In the early 1950s Carpenter chaired a biracial committee that worked on improving facilities for African Americans in Birmingham and hiring more black police officers.

To be sure, Carpenter's committee operated in deference to Jim Crow; it nonetheless faced hostility from segregationists, so much so after the *Brown* decision in 1954 that it disbanded rather than open its boxes full of hate mail. Carpenter blamed the *Brown* ruling for forcing the issue too hard and too fast.[45]

The most dramatic test of the ministers' republican theology came on Easter Sunday 1963, two days after the march, while King sat in jail. In a second front of demonstrations, Birmingham's civil rights leaders dispatched a small group of African Americans to cross the thresholds of two prominent white churches, First Baptist and First Presbyterian, standing three blocks apart on 21st Street. As it happens, both churches were led by members of the Birmingham Eight, and whatever their disapproval of King's Good Friday march, Earl Stallings and Ed Ramage took no exception to welcoming blacks into their own congregations. A photograph of Stallings cheerfully greeting the visitors on the steps of First Baptist made the *New York Times* the next morning. The real theological test, however, was to follow: the congregations of First Baptist and First Presbyterian were not nearly as prepared to welcome blacks into fellowship as their pastors. One member at First Presbyterian described the Easter service as a "rolling wave of static electricity standing everyone's hair on end." Stallings and Ramage immediately took the brunt of harassing phone calls and letters; Ramage found his tires slashed later that week and by October had been chased out of town, taking a new position in Houston, Texas.[46]

Stallings saw the moment as an opportunity to shepherd his church into a new era of interracial fellowship. After all, as republican theology goes, the church should stand at the vanguard of moral reform for the larger society. In May, Stallings preached a sermon in which he compared passivity on racial injustice to Pontius Pilate's treatment of Jesus, and then called on First Baptist to unequivocally affirm an "open-door" policy. Although the members narrowly passed his resolution on May 22, the vote opened a rift within the congregation that never healed. The subsequent months, while seeing no further black attendance, did see persistent infighting among the members and punishing notoriety for Stallings, who on one occasion suffered an uppercut to his jaw in the church sanctuary from a visiting white supremacist. By 1965 Stallings had fled to a new post in Marietta, Georgia; in 1970 integrationist sympathizers peeled off from First

Baptist and held Sunday services in Milton Grafman's synagogue. In 1984 the remaining members of First Baptist Church of Birmingham sold the property and moved the operation to the all-white suburb of Homewood, ensuring by geography what they could no longer uphold as policy.[47]

Hence a belief in the church as the engine of moral reform does not come with a guarantee that such reform will proceed with efficiency and ease, even *within* the church. On the cause of civil rights, indeed on their narrower goal to achieve interracial fellowship within the church, evangelicals simply missed the boat. Conservative evangelical churches in America are only slightly more integrated in the early twenty-first century than they were in the mid-twentieth.

The challenges of republican theology are made all the more clear when it stands in contrast to King's political theology. King's theology, in fact, has an explicitly social dimension that conservatives, because of their republican commitments, cannot countenance. While republican theology links the moral virtue of the citizen with the freedom of the state, it leaves the shaping of society—relations of class, race, and gender—to divine providence. If anything, pro-market theology allows that relations of social power might *reflect* the distribution of virtue. King refutes this thinking not only by acknowledging the presence of dominant and oppressed groups within a free society, but also by noting the effect these power relations have on moral virtue. The *Letter*'s most devastating claim for republican theology is that the liberty to discriminate on the basis of race "distorts the soul and damages the personality," both for the discriminator and the discriminated. In King's political theology, social structure is not a byproduct of but rather an influence on the Christian integrity of individuals. He salutes those Birmingham preachers, including Earl Stallings by name, who welcomed blacks into their churches; and he generally affirms the church's potential to transform society from the bottom up, pointing to the early Christians living in the Roman Empire. But King dismisses the American church at large as a "weak, ineffectual voice with an uncertain sound," whose reluctance to challenge social hierarchies undermines its gospel witness and perverts the American soul. To recover its leadership the church must pursue a more radical agenda of social transformation.[48]

III. THE RISE OF THE NEW RIGHT

Billy Graham and other national evangelical leaders kept their silence in the spring of 1964 while Congress debated, filibustered, bartered, and eventually passed the Civil Rights Act, which forbids businesses and municipalities from discriminating on the basis of race and gender. *Moody Monthly,* a journal not normally shy in its political and social commentary, published not one editorial on the historic bill, for or against.[49] While proponents of republican theology might ordinarily protest the bill's extension of federal power into private commerce, they had been caught short in the tumult of the previous year, their ideology impotent in the face of entrenched racial discrimination. After the bill passed, Graham issued a statement of support: "I think that many of the peaceful demonstrations have aroused the conscience of the nation . . . [and have] brought about new, strong, tough laws that were needed many years ago."[50] Evangelicals' acquiescence to the new reality reflected their broader predicament: they believed in small government and in independent, influential churches, but they did not want to be seen as opponents of racial justice. At this particular juncture, Graham seemed to acknowledge, an alternate band of religious leaders—and a responsive federal government—had to take the lead in reforming the nation's morals. Retreating to the back bench of American politics, evangelicals made no dent one way or the other in Lyndon Johnson's landslide presidential victory in November 1964.

This is not to say, however, that the ideas and values that had been driving evangelicals back into politics receded from evangelical culture. On the contrary, wherever the evangelical church was thriving in America, so was the belief in limited government and free market capitalism. Darren Dochuk's *From Bible Belt to Sunbelt* tells the story of evangelicalism's resurgence in Southern California in the 1950s and 60s on the backs of recent transplants from the Deep South. "Texas theology's encounter with a Southern California style," writes Dochuk, "forged a vigorous cultural force, one that melded traditionalism into an uncentered, unbounded religious culture of entrepreneurialism, experimentation, and engagement—in short, into a Sunbelt creed."[51] The creed—part "gospel of wealth," part republican theology—resounded from pulpits across Orange County and also formed the basis of a local but well-funded movement to launch private Christian schools (at every grade level, including college), simultaneously taking a stand against the growth of government *and* asserting the moral standards of the evangelical community. In its organizational capacity, Dochuk notes, this California movement marked an early stage of the New Right and helped to propel Ronald Reagan to the governorship in 1966.

What germinated at the local and state level in the 1960s went national in the 1970s, as events and social changes created conditions for a broad revival of evangelical politics, as closely linked to republican theology as ever before. By the late 1970s evangelical churchgoers had been galvanized into a kind of political activism not seen since the 1830s; what is more, they had forged an enormous coalition in national politics with free market capitalists, anticommunists, and conservative Roman Catholics, all under the growing cabana of the Republican Party.

What particularly drew *evangelicals* into the "New Right" movement—over major hurdles like their anti-Catholicism and their longtime registration as Democrats (at least in the South)—was an ideology that brought coherence to their reactionary sentiments. The New Right rhetoric, set forth by various preachers and perfected by presidential candidate Ronald Reagan in 1980, was, in substance, doctrinaire republican theology. It saw limited government and Christian morality as the defining elements of America's founding and ascendance and saw the desertion of those values in the twentieth century as the cause of America's decline. "We have gone backward," wrote one religious activist in 1976, "and left the course of freedom."[52] More positively, it held that this decline could be reversed through moral, social, and political reform. Thus republican theology became Republican ideology: the New Right movement sought to scale back the welfare state and the taxes used to fund it, reduce governmental authority over schools and businesses, and appoint judges who would take a stand for traditional morals. This agenda was crafted not just to appeal to a wide range of "middle-American" voters but also to hold together as a philosophy of governance, backed by a long theological tradition. Above all, the New Right rhetoric was crafted to recover the optimism of the original founding, pointing voters to a relatively simple formula for restoring American greatness and recapturing the sheen of what Reagan (quoting the Puritan settlers) called "the shining city on a hill."[53]

Reengagement

An often-overlooked but vital detail in this story is that conservative Roman Catholics, and not Protestant evangelicals, were the first to organize against the moral shifts of the 1960s and to connect the "culture war" to a fight against big government. Their most prominent efforts ranged from the Right to Life League (America's first anti-abortion organization, organized by Catholic bishops in 1968) to Phyllis Schlafly's crusade against the Equal Rights Amendment and Paul Weyrich's Heritage Foundation, founded in 1973, which pioneered grassroots fundraising for socially conservative politicians. Indeed, during these early years evangelical leaders kept their distance from right-wing activism precisely because of the potential association with Catholics. Jerry Falwell wrote that he believed "being yoked with unbelievers for any cause was off limits."[54] In pronounced contrast to Roman Catholics, both Protestants and free market conservatives exhibited ambivalence to the abortion issue in the years before *Roe*: Ronald Reagan loosened abortion restrictions as governor of California in 1967; the Southern Baptist Convention urged other states to do the same; in various editorials in the late 1960s *Christianity Today* offered qualified support for "therapeutic" abortion rights.[55]

The *Roe vs. Wade* decision of 1973, which liberalized abortion rights dramatically, overturning laws in over 30 states, shocked the evangelical community into a far more reactionary stance. Leaving aside its previous equivocations, *Christianity Today* charged the Supreme Court with "rejecting the almost universal consensus of Christian moral teachers through the centuries on abortion" and warned that "Christians should accustom themselves to the thought that the American state no longer supports, in any meaningful sense, the laws of God, and prepare themselves spiritually for the prospect that it may one day formally repudiate them and turn against those who seek to live by them."[56] Evangelical leaders began to make a case for engagement in public affairs. The theologian Francis Schaeffer, who made a late career converting hippies into Calvinists at his Switzerland retreat, L'Abri, wrote a best-selling treatise, *How Then Shall We Live? The Rise and Decline of Western Thought and Culture* (1976), which framed *Roe* as just the latest crack in the moral foundation of Western civilization. Schaeffer calls believers to an urgent response: "As Christians we are not only to know the right worldview . . . but consciously to act upon that world-view so as to influence society in all its parts and facets across the whole spectrum of life."[57]

The evangelical community, virtually silent at the national level since the 1950s, recovered its voice on the theme of national repent-ance. In 1976, Jerry Falwell, who had founded Liberty Baptist College five years earlier as an act of higher-education separatism, took the college choir on a national "I Love America" tour, evangelizing state capitols with tributes to America's heritage mixed with warnings about her future.[58] In that same year Bill Bright, who had long evangelized college students through his Campus Crusade for Christ, distributed a new pamphlet, "Your Five Duties as a Christian Citizen," which en-couraged young people to pray, register to vote, and "help elect godly people."[59]

Bicentennial Theology

What ultimately shepherded evangelicals into national politics, and especially into the GOP, was a revival of republican theology. In 1976, the year of America's bicentennial, several popular books appeared that linked American-style liberty to Christian morality and urged a reasser-tion of the latter on behalf of the former. Schaeffer's *How Then Shall We Live?*, for instance, credits the Protestant Reformation of the sixteenth century with not only recovering scripture in the Christian church but also with bringing about the era of individual freedom in Western politics. Reformed cultures could enjoy individual liberties, Schaeffer argues, precisely "because there was [voluntary] consensus based upon the absolutes given in the Bible, and therefore values within which to have freedom, without these freedoms leading to chaos."[60] Schaeffer's point is that liberty cannot survive the loss (or absence) of this moral consensus. The vanishing of the Christian worldview in the twentieth century, he warns, is "progressively preparing modern people to accept manipulative, authoritarian government."[61] Schaeffer's evidence runs from the boom of Marxist-Leninism across Europe and Latin America to the rising culture of dependency in the United States—in particular, the crutches of recreational drugs and public welfare programs. As cul-tures grow weaker morally, goes Schaeffer's algebra, government must of necessity grow stronger. In this light the *Roe* decision is not merely an affront to traditional morals; it exemplifies the "arbitrary" rule of government in a society that lacks a moral foundation.[62]

The bookstores carrying Schaeffer's volume quickly sprouted others reinforcing the same political theology, often in more pamphlet-style prose, and with a patriotic emphasis on the American founding. *One Nation under God* (1976) by Rus Walton, editor-in-chief for the evangelical publishing company Third Way, offers the typical prescription: "Maximum individual freedom is most generally found within those nations where the laws of men are most in harmony with the laws of God . . . Freedom demands—depends upon—self-discipline from both the governed and the governing."[63] The American founding fathers, Walton argues, "staked the future of all our political institutions upon the capacity of mankind for self-government; upon the capacity of each and all of us to govern ourselves, to control ourselves, and to sustain ourselves according to the Ten Commandments of God."[64]

Schaeffer and Walton ventured essentially the same argument for the mutual dependence of Christian virtue and political liberty that is ventured by all the disciples of republican theology that came before—from John Witherspoon and Benjamin Rush to Charles Grandison Finney, the Beechers, Harold Ockenga, and Billy Graham. That none of these republican theologians ever cite each other (indeed, writers like Walton are far more likely to quote James Madison and Thomas Jefferson as theological authorities) reveals one of the most curious features of the tradition, and one of the main reasons the tradition has eluded documentation. Republican theology is an intellectual tradition only in the continuity its ideas have exhibited over time, not in its inhabitation of a self-referential canon. It speaks to the decentralized character of American evangelicalism that its elites do not often quote each other or otherwise ossify their forebears' place in history. Though Finney maintained national fame for several decades in the early nineteenth century, for instance, his name is barely known among ordinary evangelicals today. Certain *ideas*, nevertheless, have been drilled into the psychology of American Christianity from the earliest days of the republic. That the doctrines of republican theology get periodically revived *without* a corresponding revival of old Lyman Beecher sermons only underscores how deeply embedded this tradition comes in the worldview of American evangelicals.

New Right Apparatuses and Candidates

A surprising turn in the late 1970s gave the Republican Party a renewed appeal to evangelicals. When former Georgia Governor Jimmy
Carter won the Democratic nomination for president in 1976, he appeared to offer evangelical Christians the chance of a lifetime—to elect
the first openly "born-again" Christian to the Oval Office, a Southern
Baptist Sunday school teacher who spoke about his faith with an ease
unheard of in a presidential campaign.[65] The ironic surprise is how
dissonantly Carter's political theology ultimately resonated with that
of the emerging New Right movement. For conservative Christians
looking to the White House for leadership against abortion, gay rights,
sex education, drugs, welfare, and high taxes, Carter proved a comprehensive disappointment. Carter supported the Equal Rights Amendment, conferred with gay rights activists, made no efforts (legislatively
or with judicial appointments) to curtail abortion, withdrew the tax-
exempt status of private Christian schools, and expanded the federal
bureaucracy to include a new Department of Education, which fun-
neled federal tax dollars to support the "secular humanist" agenda.
"Since the educational system has been taken over by humanism," rued
a prominent San Diego pastor in 1979, "and since humanism is an offi-
cially declared religion, we find the government establishing a religion
and giving the high priest a position in the president's cabinet."[66]

Months into Carter's presidency, evangelicals mobilized to take
moral reform into their own hands. Disenchantment with the president
only served to catalyze the movement. Emulating Roman Catholic
activism of the previous decade, evangelicals launched the "Save the
Children" campaign against homosexual rights in Miami, an unsuc-
cessful statewide proposition to roll back gay rights in California, and
a highly successful bid to elect several anti-abortion candidates—all
Republicans—to Congress in the 1978 midterms. Failure proved as
galvanizing as victory: in early 1979, Robert Grant, a pastor who led
the California campaign against gay rights, pulled its disparate supporters into a unified network called Christian Voice. Attracting substantial donations even in its early months of existence, Christian Voice
pursued a strategy modeled after the Heritage Foundation, producing
"Moral Report Cards" for members of Congress and channeling cash
to elect high achievers. Christian Voice's report cards tracked not only

obvious moral issues like gay rights and abortion, but also tax policy and foreign policy (a soft stance against the USSR, for instance, was as damaging as support for the Equal Rights Amendment).[67]

Just months later, in June 1979, Falwell, a Southern Baptist so conservative he still preferred to be called a "fundamentalist" rather than an "evangelical," launched Moral Majority, a second New Right organization that aimed at electing moral conservatives to national office. Falwell had already earned stripes in the culture wars, but only from the home base of his mega-church in Virginia. Thomas Road Baptist started a private Christian grade school in the early 1970s, as well as Liberty Baptist College, conservative antidotes to the secular education. In 1978 Falwell dipped his toe into local politics, organizing opposition with other Southern Baptists to a referendum to legalize racetrack gambling in Virginia.[68]

According to Williams, it was Paul Weyrich of the Heritage Foundation and Francis Schaeffer who privately persuaded Falwell to create an alliance that would include non–Southern Baptists, even Catholics, Jews, and Mormons, in its membership, and that would also dive into the swamp of national party politics.[69] Falwell's consent, long in coming, reflected a triumph of republican theology, an admission that the essence of American Christianity lay not in a crucicentric gospel but rather in a broad moral consensus and a commitment to limited government. Defined in this way, American Christianity covered a large swath of the public—a "moral majority" who could, if unified, wield significant influence in American politics.

Moral Majority's domino-like accomplishments in 1980 and 1984 cannot be overstated. Working through a tight network of conservative clergymen, Falwell registered millions of first-time voters in the basements of their churches. In response, enterprising Republican candidates up and down the ballot began to add social conservatism to their free market commitments. Southern Baptists, who had been faithful Democrats since the 1840s, switched their party registration virtually *en masse*. The Republican National Convention in 1980 adopted a platform that for the first time opposed the Equal Rights Amendment, called for the overturning of *Roe vs. Wade*, and explicitly rejected any policy "which would give the federal government more power over families." Falwell, who attended the convention, boasted that the GOP platform "could easily be the constitution of a fundamentalist Baptist

Church."[70] At unprecedented levels candidates for office courted the New Right vote at churches and community prayer breakfasts.

The movement caught no bigger fish than former California governor Ronald Reagan, who, as a veteran defender of the free market, easily mastered the cadences of republican theology. "I believe this nation hungers for a spiritual revival," Reagan declared when he announced his presidential candidacy in November 1979. "She hungers to once again see honor placed above political expediency; to see government once again the protector of our liberties, not the distributor of gifts and privilege. Government should uphold and not undermine those institutions which are custodians of the very values upon which civilization is founded—religion, education and, above all, family."[71] Reagan captured 67 percent of the evangelical vote in 1980 and 80 percent in 1984, swamping Carter and later Walter Mondale in landslide victories. Republicans achieved a majority in the Senate for the first time since the early 1950s, and their caucus displayed a more reliable conservatism than ever before.

While these electoral gains yielded little by way of moral reforms (only one of President Reagan's three additions to the Supreme Court proved a reliable vote against abortion rights, for instance), Reagan was able to weave his other conservative achievements—tax cuts, deregulation, and a new arms race with the Soviets—into the broader narrative of the New Right movement, persuading evangelicals that their traditional values were once again on the ascent in America. "I want you to know," Reagan told the National Association of Evangelicals in 1983, echoing the phony Tocqueville quote, "that this administration is motivated by a political philosophy that sees the greatness of America in you, her people, and in your families, churches, neighborhoods, communities—the institutions that foster and nourish values like concern for others and respect for the rule of law under God." The NAE address famously urged evangelicals to get behind a military buildup against the "evil empire" of communism and to comprehend the arms race as a "struggle between right and wrong, and good and evil."[72]

The New Right has achieved permanence both as a social movement and as a Republican Party machine. No Democratic presidential candidate has come close to winning the evangelical vote since 1976. The movement has changed hands and tweaked strategies only modestly in subsequent decades. Reagan's theology remained its creed.

In the 1990s Pat Robertson's Christian Coalition, managed by Ralph Reed, served as the primary vehicle of electoral activism among religious conservatives. Since 2009 Reed has led the Faith and Freedom Forum, whose network of pastors and church laity built upon the running lists of members from the previous three decades. Reed's strategy, both for the Christian Coalition and the Faith and Freedom Forum, is holistic, focusing resources on state legislative races and local initiatives in addition to congressional campaigns and the Republican presidential primary.

The religious ecumenism of Reed's operation is purified only by an explicit commitment to republican theology. Faith and Freedom's website trumpets "common sense values" like "respect for the sanctity and dignity of life, family, and marriage as the foundations of a free society," "limited government, lower taxes and fiscal responsibility to unleash the creative energy of entrepreneurs," and "free markets and free minds to create opportunity for all." The Faith and Freedom Forum played a key role, working phones and registering new voters, in returning Republicans to the governorships of Virginia and New Jersey in 2009 and to the House of Representatives in 2010.[73]

Far beyond its electoral activism, the New Right movement has spawned numerous organizations aimed at raising public awareness of moral issues and advocating conservative values in the public square, such as the Family Research Council, founded in 1981, and the Traditional Values Coalition, founded in 1984, both of which mobilized support for successful ballot initiatives against gay marriage in 2004 and 2008.[74]

IV. LINES OF FRACTURE IN EVANGELICAL POLITICS

In spite of (or perhaps because of) its electoral successes, the New Right coalition breeds at least three types of conflict in American society, all of which manifest tensions embedded with in republican theology. Within the alliance, libertarians and moral conservatives clash over ideology and issues, fulfilling a conceptual tension built into the movement. The New Right also disaffects members of the evangelical community who hold to alternative political values, particularly on the "evangelical left." A third kind of friction, between religion and politics at large, comes to the surface whenever religious activists pause to consider the costs and dividends of their political engagement. Even the most committed believers in republican theology get stymied by the political process.

Libertarianism Versus Christian Moralism

The diffusiveness of the New Right coalition has made for journalistic fodder ever since the fall of communism, when the global enemy to republican theology suddenly vanished, and when Ronald Reagan, its consummate champion, retired from politics. "Republicans," goes the prediction, "have built a sprawling, wobbly tent in which libertarians, Christian moralists and suburban business owners all pretend to have similar goals . . . That tent is too flimsily constructed to stay up forever."[75] Analysis of this kind underestimates how readily these groups snap into electoral alignment as a reactionary force, as they did in 1994 (coalescing against President Clinton's plan for universal health insurance), in 2002 and 2004 (against national security threats from Islamic groups), and in 2010 (against President Obama's health care plan). Even the Tea Party movement of the early 2010s, which styles itself as a defender of Constitutional liberties, finds broad support among evangelicals and backs candidates, like Congresswoman Michele Bachmann of Minnesota, who espouse both small government and morally conservative values.[76]

Still, if reports of the New Right's self-immolation tend to prove premature, the cognitive dissonance of the movement is difficult to escape. Political theologies aside, libertarianism and Christianity are distinct traditions with diverging ends. It does not take much to expose the tensions between them. When he ran for vice president in 2012, for instance, the Republican Paul Ryan publicly struggled to reconcile his Christian faith with his devotion to Ayn Rand, the mother of modern libertarianism. In her anti-statist novels of the 1950s, Rand promoted "objectivism," a kind of free market atheism, and referred to organized Christianity as "the best kindergarten of communism possible." Ryan, who would give out copies of *Atlas Shrugged* (1957) as Christmas presents and speak at Ayn Rand conventions, gradually tempered his enthusiasm and tried to recast his economic conservatism in more religious terms: "If somebody is going to try to paste a person's view on epistemology to me," he told the *National Review*, "then give me Thomas Aquinas, don't give me Ayn Rand," a rhetorical shift that, according to one Rand scholar, offered "a window into the ideological fissures at the heart of modern conservatism."[77]

The free market and religious wings of the New Right have not just ideological but policy differences as well, sometimes handing Democrats an opportunity to exploit the wedge. Several issues in contemporary politics mark this fault line, including military interventionism, aid to Israel, government subsidies for faith-based charities, recreational drug policy, and, with perhaps the greatest realigning potential in the 2010s, same-sex marriage. Opposition to gay civil rights fueled the early formation of the Christian right in the 1970s; by 2008 organizations like Focus on the Family, the Liberty Counsel, the American Family Association, and the Traditional Values Coalition had successfully lobbied over 40 states, including California, to enact legal (and sometimes constitutional) bans on same-sex marriage.[78] Most often it was a well-articulated republican theology—not just traditional values, but a rationale linking those values to individual liberty—that bolstered this initiative. "If same-sex marriage were legalized," went the New Right warnings, "all employers, public and private, large or small, would be required to offer spousal benefits to homosexual couples . . . Individual believers who disapprove of homosexual relationships may face a choice at work between forfeiting their freedom of speech and being fired."[79]

The movement against same-sex marriage, however, gave way in 2008 to a countermovement in favor of legalization, led in part by the civil libertarians who normally align with Christian conservatives. The Cato Institute, a libertarian think tank with longstanding ties to Republicans, came out in favor of privatizing marriage altogether, but announced that if the government must privilege marriage at all, it should do so equally for hetero- and homosexual couples.[80] Theodore B. Olson, the Solicitor General under President George W. Bush (and the widower of Barbara Olson, a prominent right-wing author), shocked fellow Republicans in 2009 when he joined the legal team to oppose California's ban on gay marriage in Federal court, but his voice was soon joined by others in the Republican Party, including Ken Mehlman, the former party chairman, and Dick Cheney, the former vice president.[81]

The New Right Versus the Evangelical Left

A second line of fracture runs within the evangelical church. Not all American evangelicals support a right-wing, pro-capitalist view of government. The very same decades, in fact, that saw the rise of the New Right also witnessed a resurgence—miniature, but viable—of Social Gospel Christianity among otherwise conservative evangelicals. The most durable group on the evangelical left is the "Post-Americans," now known as Sojourners, led by Jim Wallis since 1971. Wallis came to left-wing politics by way of student protests in the late 1960s, an involvement that initially led him away from Christian faith. A spiritual reawakening in 1970 moved Wallis, undiminished in his opposition to war, racism, and capitalistic excess, to pursue these issues as a divinity student at Trinity Evangelical Seminary just north of Chicago. On Trinity's campus, Wallis launched debates on the theology of social justice and formed the People's Christian Coalition with 24 classmates. Declaring their fellowship "with the exploited and oppressed, rather than the oppressor," the members of Wallis's coalition set up a communal residence in a poor Chicago neighborhood and produced the first issue of the *Post-American* in September 1971. The issue's cover featured a picture of Jesus wearing a crown of thorns and shackled to an American flag draped around his shoulders.[82]

The *Post-American* regularly denounced the evangelical establishment and lamented the state of American Christianity, deploring "the disastrous equation of the American way of life with the Christian way of life." Its politics were reliably leftist—anti-war, anti-corporation, pro-union, and pro-civil rights. In an era of political ambivalence among evangelicals the Post-Americans chided believers for their complacence in a corrupted system. At the same time, however, Wallis and his compatriots explicitly rejected the secular humanism of the New Left, and even the soft liberalism of Mainline Christianity. They emphasized personal conversion and small-group prayer in addition to social restructuring. They drew as much inspiration from Francis Schaeffer as Christian right leaders would later in the decade. Their critique of industrial capitalism covered not only its social inequalities but also its moral degeneracy: "We protest," wrote Wallis in 1971, "the materialistic profit culture and technocratic society which threaten basic human values."[83]

Post-American's readership grew to 20,000 by 1976, mostly among college-age evangelicals. As Swartz writes, "The Post-Americans had clearly tapped into a substantial market of angst-ridden evangelicals searching for authentic faith."[84] Jim Wallis dropped out of seminary in 1972 to tour college campuses—both Christian and secular. In 1975 his Coalition restyled itself as the more biblical-sounding "Sojourners" and moved its operations to Washington, D.C., where it could work in closer proximity to national policymakers. A smattering of evangelical elites, from the Oregon Senator Mark Hatfield to the Anglican cleric John Stott, embraced the Sojourners and their leftist priorities. Stott, who served as a contributing editor to *Post-American*, used the magazine to argue that believers in the incarnation of Christ should recognize its *moral* implications, which "summon us freely to renounce our wealth for the sake of others who are poor."[85] Indeed, a snapshot of evangelical politics in 1975 might well have suggested an imminent revival of Social Gospel activism among young conservative Protestants.

That American evangelicals instead rallied to precisely the opposite cause—anti-welfare, pro-market revivalism—speaks to the inherent appeal of republican theology within that community. As such, the ascent of the New Right also elevated the discord between Sojourners and the evangelical establishment. Wallis lavished skepticism on the New Right from the beginning, even publishing an "exposé" of the movement in early 1976, entitled "The Plan to Save America: A Disclosure of an Alarming Political Initiative by the Evangelical Far Right."[86] The piece generated bad blood between Wallis and other evangelical leaders for next several decades. As late as 2004 Jerry Falwell accused Wallis of being "about as evangelical as an oak tree."[87]

Wallis's more recent appeals to younger evangelical leaders, like Rick Warren of Saddleback Community Church in California, Bill Hybels of Willow Creek Church in Illinois, and Tim Keller at Redeemer Presbyterian in New York, have periodically succeeded in putting social issues like poverty relief on their ministry agendas. His persistent criticism of liberal Democratic candidates for their religious tone-deafness, moreover, eventually paid off when Barack Obama went out of his way to court evangelical voters in 2007 and 2008.[88] President Obama's agenda, however—the Federal stimulus, the automaker bailout, and the push for universal health care—mobilized a conservative reaction that adopted a 1980-style republican theology for its intellectual core, reviving the specter of godless socialism as a rallying cry against big government. By 2010 the right wing of American politics had rebounded with the traditional constituencies—operating under new names like the Tea Party and the Faith and Freedom Coalition—driving its electoral successes. Republican theology regained its strength, in other words, and Jim Wallis quickly reverted to playing defense for the American left.

The New Right Versus Generations X and Y

Perhaps the most fateful consequence of these first two points of strain is a generational divide over politics within the evangelical church. On issues like homosexual marriage, recreational drug policy, environmental regulation, affirmative action, labor rights, and social welfare spending, Americans born after 1976—across all religions— exhibit more "liberal" attitudes than their parents. This means, of course, a more libertarian proclivity on sexuality and drugs and a more collectivist outlook on economics—the precise antithesis of republican theology.[89] What is more, preliminary evidence suggests that evangelical *politics*, more than its theology, is driving young people away from the church, and perhaps away from the faith itself.

Robert Putnam and David Campbell, in a 2010 survey of American religion, draw this conclusion by correlating two unmistakable trends: (1) the sharp rise of nonreligious Americans since 1990 and (2) the growing antipathy among Americans toward New Right activism. On the first trend, Putnam and Campbell point out that proportion of Americans who answer "none" to the question "What is your religious affiliation?" held remarkably steady at 6 percent between 1950 and 1990, surviving the "seismic society shocks" of the sexual revolution, the Vietnam War, and the age of hippie culture. Indeed, the evangelical revival of the late 1970s, what they call the "first aftershock" of the 1960s, helped to keep that proportion low. However, starting in 1990, when the Baby Boomers' own children started to reach adulthood, "the fraction of Americans who said they were 'none' suddenly began to rise," tripling to 18 percent in 2008. The number reached 24 percent in 2012. The trend amounts to a "second aftershock" of the mid-century crisis, one that is perhaps more significant than the first.[90]

Observing that the "nones" tend to be young, that the young tend to be more socially progressive, and that the same survey reveals much greater skepticism toward the influence of religion on politics than in 1980, Putnam and Campbell suggest that the aversion to the church among many young people, though they are still "open to religious feelings and ideals," may be rooted in their "unease with the association between religion and conservative politics."[91]

The hypothesis needs testing. For one thing, even Putnam and Campbell concede that attrition in conservative evangelical churches is far less severe than in Roman Catholic and Mainline congregations. Still, they warn, "if the broader appeal of conservative sexual morality emblazoned on the evangelical banner continues to wane, the evangelical movement may face a dilemma . . . over how much to accommodate religious views to modernity. Continuing to sound the public trumpet of conservative personal morality may be the right thing to do from a theological point of view, but it may mean saving fewer souls now than it did a generation ago."

Corwin Smidt, who, like Putnam and Campbell, has also measured a shift in attitudes toward moral and political issues among young evangelicals (along with evangelicalism's relative success in the retention of young worshipers), ventures a slightly different forecast for evangelical politics in America. The relative size of the evangelical community with the American population, Smidt predicts, will remain fairly constant in the coming decades, and, "regardless of what happens politically, it is likely that evangelicals will continue to exhibit a relatively high level of involvement in civic life." Civic engagement, Smidt insists, is deeply engrained in the American evangelical conscience. What *will* change, he suggests, is the level of "political cohesion" among evangelicals—the extent to which evangelical voters hew to the ideals of the New Right—and not just because of the "expanded political agenda" of younger evangelicals, but also because of ethnic diversity within the church.[92]

Christianity Versus Politics

A final type of friction to emanate from the New Right movement concerns evangelical frustration with the limits of politics. Even as libertarians and Social Gospel evangelicals harbor misgivings over the Christian Right's narrow moral agenda, Christian Right leaders lament how little of that agenda they have been able to accomplish. Expectations of recovering traditional values in American society by scaling back government and empowering the private sphere have fallen short on multiple fronts: not only have political reforms proved difficult to achieve, but the liberalization of American moral culture has proved nearly impossible to thwart. Empirical evidence has largely failed to vindicate republican theology as an effectual mode of governance. In spite of the New Right's electoral successes, nearly every metric of importance to conservative evangelicals—divorce rates, teen pregnancy, abortions, drug use, and pornography sales—has drifted further from their stated ideals since 1980. On some issues, such as opposition to gay civil rights, legislative victories have actually provoked a backlash in public opinion.

In 1999, in the wake of the Monica Lewinsky sex scandal (and President Clinton's clear-cut survival of it), two original board members of the defunct Moral Majority, Cal Thomas and Ed Dobson, wrote a postmortem for the New Right, *Blinded by Might*, in which they admit broad failure to reform American society. They begin by recounting, somewhat bitterly, the exhilaration of 1980, an election that not only elevated Reagan to the White House but also gave Republicans a majority in the Senate *and* remade that caucus in a more conservative mold. According to Thomas and Dobson, a post-election rally at Liberty Baptist College attracted reporters from the *Washington Post* and *The New York Times* as well as cameras from NBC, ABC, and CBS. The college pep band played "Hail to the Chief" when Jerry Falwell took the stage:

> We had the power to right every wrong and cure every ill and end every frustration that God-fearing people had been forced to submit to by our "oppressors," whom we labeled secular humanists, abortionists, homosexuals, pornographers, and "liberals." We opposed them all with the righteous indignation we thought came directly from God. We opposed them because we knew they were the reason America was in decline. And we had been raised up by God himself to reverse that decline.[93]

The vindication conservative evangelicals felt in 1980, the new access they received to the White House and other halls of power, and the mutual affection they enjoyed with Reagan gradually gave way to the realization that the task of reforming a nation's moral culture is a taller order than it might seem. "That was twenty years ago," Thomas and

Dobson write of their victory, "and today very little that we set out to do has gotten done. In fact, the moral landscape of America has become worse." They don't blame Reagan, Falwell, or any particular strategic error; rather, Thomas and Dobson cite the fallacy of believing that politics holds solutions to deep moral problems: "We failed not because we were wrong about our critique of culture, or because we lacked conviction, or because there were not enough of us, or because too many were lethargic and uncommitted. We failed because we were unable to redirect a nation from the top down. Real change must come from the bottom up or, better yet, from the inside out."[94] The dream of fusing First Great Awakening conversionism with Second Great Awakening moral reform, in other words, was doomed from the start.

EPILOGUE

Somewhere on the map of evangelical thought in America—perhaps controlling less acreage than they would like—reside the philosophers, those academics who identify as traditional Christians and who speak to issues relating to God and public life. The list is tight-knit and includes Protestant and Catholic authors from all over the English-speaking world. Scholars like Stanley Hauerwas, Oliver O'Donovan, Joan Lockwood O'Donovan, Alasdair MacIntyre, N. T. Wright, John Witte Jr., John Milbank, Alvin Plantinga, Nicholas Wolterstorff, Charles Taylor, and the late Dallas Willard and Jean Bethke Elshtain come to mind, along with an expanding directory of their students. Writing in a world that largely assumes the values of liberalism to be axiomatic (i.e., that takes John Rawls, if not John Locke, as the center of gravity in political philosophy), these Christian thinkers seek to recover the Hebrew and Christian scriptures, as well as Augustinian and Thomistic theology, into the conversation and to bring these literatures to bear on the liberal context. At issue in their writings are not only the epistemological assumptions of modernity but also deep questions of political theology concerning the legitimacy of the state, the justification of violence, the possibility of natural rights, and the feasibility of defining the "good life" in a world that sees the individual as sovereign. This tiny corner of the academy is still large enough to witness serious disagreements—on just war, for instance, and on the theological viability of natural rights.

None of the major Christian philosophers of the last half century, however, has ever emerged as an apologist for republican theology as it has been described in this book. To be sure, the internal ambiguities of republican theology resist a perspicuous defense. But the ethical gap between the academy and the church reaches further: nearly every Christian philosopher working in the academy finds some way to condemn the selective libertarianism into which American evangelicals have settled. Whatever its lineage in eighteenth-century moral philosophy, republican theology no longer has any foothold among Christian theorists, perhaps explaining why it so rarely gets treated as a full-blown tradition in academic publications.

THE DEBATE ON NATURAL RIGHTS

The debate on individual rights serves to illustrate this widespread unease with the premises of republican theology. Among Christian scholars, both proponents and skeptics of natural human rights find fault with the philosophy of limited government and particularly with the idea that this philosophy represents the true biblical position on justice. This is a striking fact given the intensity of their disagreements on the larger moral questions. The debate itself began in the late twentieth century when thinkers like MacIntyre, Hauerwas, and the O'Donovans started invoking Christianity against the ethical framework of liberalism, taking express aim at its abiding conviction that individual humans possess natural rights. Though each of these authors takes a different tack, the common thrust of their critique is that the assumption of natural, "God-given" rights not only lacks a scriptural foundation but, worse, distorts how God intends to relate to humanity and how he wishes humans to relate to each other. The concept of rights, argues MacIntyre, "lacks any means of expression in Hebrew, Greek, Latin, or Arabic, classical or medieval, before about 1400, let alone in Old English, or in Japanese even as late as the mid-nineteenth century . . . The truth is plain: there are no such rights, and belief in them is one with belief in witches and unicorns."[1] This belief, furthermore, bends the Christian narrative of justice away from the recognition of sin and the hunger for redemption, reducing the gospel to a footnote and the church to an exercise in isolated piety.

Arguing that Christianity makes itself "irrelevant" when it adopts the value system of individual rights, Hauerwas urges Christians to more fully comprehend their membership in "God's kingdom," finding their core identity in the church.[2] This mode of identity demands a rejection of individualism and the social contract mentality: "We are not individuals who come into contact with others and then decide our various levels of social involvement . . . our individuality is possible only because we are first of all social beings."[3] The church, on this view, is a community with a divine calling in a fallen world—a calling to reveal to that world an image of redemption in Christ:

> What makes the church the church is its faithful manifestation of the peaceable kingdom in the world . . . It does this by having the patience amid the injustice and violence of this world to care for the widow, the poor, and the orphan. Such care, from the world's perspective, may seem to contribute little to the cause of justice, yet it is our conviction that unless we take time for such care neither we nor the world can know what justice looks like . . . For the world has no way of knowing it is a world without the church pointing to the reality of God's kingdom.[4]

The O'Donovans aim for a similar recovery of the church as the locus of justice in the world and for the recovery of love as the central imperative of justice.[5] In stressing love, they insist (much as Jonathan Edwards did in the 1750s) that this human obligation is twofold—to selflessly love God *and* neighbor: "Take away love for God," warns Oliver O'Donovan, "and the ontological parity which makes true neighbor-love possible is upset." This means, moreover, that the love of neighbor must be active, not passive, and must recognize that the neighbor, like oneself, "is a being whose end is in God." Justice, in other words, is not about respecting the boundaries of individual sovereignty, or even about attending to the material needs of individuals. To love as God intends is to pursue the redemption of humanity in Christ, which is why "there is only one society which is incorporated into the Kingdom of God . . . and that is the church."[6] As such, the assertion of natural rights is not only theologically suspect but also subversive to the love obligation and to morality in general. Joan Lockwood O'Donovan posits that "the modern liberal concept of right belongs to the socially atomistic and disintegrative philosophy of 'possessive individualism.'"[7] While Oliver O'Donovan grants that "the language of subjective rights" might have a "perfectly appropriate and necessary place within a discourse founded on law," he stresses that modern, post-Christian culture mistakenly takes rights to be "original, not derived," a move that dissolves the "unity and coherence" of divine justice in favor of an indefinite plurality of subjective rights.[8]

Against this trend in Christian philosophy, Wolterstorff has taken a resolutely pro-rights stance, insisting that natural human rights, far from representing a novelty of modern individualism, are, in fact, moored in the Bible. Wolterstorff's argument is not that the Bible lays out a full-blown natural rights theory but rather that its "background framework of conviction," from the Hebrew scriptures into the New Testament, holds that justice among earthbound humans matters to God and that it chiefly concerns the equitable distribution of "intrinsic life-goods," goods to which ordinary humans have a rights-like claim.[9] This conviction comes into view whenever the scriptures attend to the cries of the poor, as they do in Hebrew law, the Psalms, Old Testament prophecy, and the sermons of Jesus. The repeated injunctions to help the downtrodden, as well as the vow that God himself will lift them up, come freighted with the premise that God intends for people to flourish on the earth and that both one's internal virtues *and* external needs to this end have moral worth in the divine scheme of justice: "The goods constitutive of a person's well-being," Wolterstorff argues, "are what God desires for that person's life."[10] It follows that the love commandment has for its basic content the pursuit of justice, which entails, all throughout the scriptures, the allocation of those essential "life-goods"—both spiritual *and material*—to all people. "The prophets and psalmists do not argue the case that alleviating the plight of the lowly is required by justice. They assume it."[11]

From this conception of justice Wolterstorff draws an argument for natural, inherent rights: if God intends for humans to live a "good life" and creates within the human condition certain desires to that end, then the objects of those desires are "not merely intrinsically prefer-able, but intrinsically good." If, moreover, God regularly called on ancient societies to rectify inequitable divisions of those goods, then one may infer that humans have a rights-like claim to those goods. "If one thinks of well-being in terms of the well-going life," writes Wolterstorff, then "one has no difficulty in recognizing virtues along with rights in one's moral framework."[12] The rights are natural, inherent, universal, and God-given because the desire for them is natural, inherent, universal, and God-given. Wolterstorff also rebuffs the idea, promoted by Hauerwas, that the church is the only true locus of justice in the fallen world, insisting that government, even secular government, remains a viable instrument of God for the achievement of justice among humans. "Government," in Wolterstorff's view, "serves an indispensable coordinating function" that aims at the "common good," in large part by protecting and vindicating the rights of the vulnerable.[13]

Wolterstorff does not attempt to saddle the Bible with an enumeration of these rights, but one can already surmise that his idea of what humans are entitled to extends far beyond individual autonomy. The scriptural concern for distributive justice in material goods (and its relative lack of focus on republican civil rights) suggests as much. Thus, while Wolterstorff rejects, on one side, the anti-rights theology of McIntyre, Hauerwas, and the O'Donovans, he also rejects, on the other side, a liberal framework that grounds human rights on individual self-sovereignty and elevates personal freedom above all other goods. Even more decisively, Wolterstorff rejects republican theology, which contends for limited government on the basis of human virtue. Republican theology supports at least two fallacies on Wolterstorff's reasoning: first, it predicates human rights on the moral capacity of humans instead of, as Wolterstorff does, on the God-given *needs* of humans living in the world; second, it concludes that limited government is inherently more just, a proposition that makes little sense if justice entails the redistribution of goods and the collective protection of the defenseless.

Indeed, in the years after finishing his book on rights, Wolterstorff has made a mission of assailing the reductionism of evangelical politics in America, traveling the world in search of more expansive (and more biblical, in his view) visions of justice among social activists abroad. For instance, after interviewing members of the *Asociacion para una Sociedad mas Justa* (ASJ), a Christian legal assistance group in Honduras, Wolterstorff contrasts *its* political theology with that of "Tea Party" evangelicals in America. The ASJ sees government as responsible for protecting the land and labor rights of the poor and therefore works with the government and through the justice system in Honduras to help victims of oppression to assert their rights. The ASJ, Wolterstorff points out, does not "content itself with dispensing aid and charity to victims; it holds government officials responsible. But it also does not content itself with issuing denunciations; it assists officials in carrying out their task."[14]

EVANGELICAL POLITICS IN AMERICA: NEW DIRECTIONS?

If evangelical philosophers today stand arrayed against Lockean theology, signals are more mixed elsewhere on the map of American evangelical thought. Among social activists, journalists, and even some clergy there are at least some signs that republican theology does not hold as firm a lock on the evangelical conscience as the electoral performance of the New Right might suggest. Certainly cultural misgivings with free-market capitalism are getting voiced with greater urgency. Wealth and materialism, which were once openly encouraged by free-market defenders like Henry Ward Beecher in the late nineteenth century, come in for frequent condemnation in the twenty-first, particularly when it is seen insulating affluent American churches from global poverty. "If our lives do not reflect radical compassion for the poor, there is reason to wonder if Christ is really in us at all," writes David Platt, an Alabama pastor in *Radical: Taking Your Faith Back from the American Dream* (2010).[15] "If American Christians just tithed," notes Ronald J. Sider in *The Scandal of the Evangelical Conscience: Why Are Christians Living Just Like the Rest of the World?* (2005), "they would have another $143 billion available to empower the poor and spread the gospel," more than enough "to provide access to essential services like basic health care and education for all the poor of the earth."[16]

Evidence points to the emergence of an organized "evangelical left"—or at least a "new evangelical" movement—that functions beyond the activities of Jim Wallis and the Sojourners. The New Evangelical Partnership for the Common Good, for instance, founded in 2010 by Richard Cizik, a former vice president for governmental affairs at the National Association of Evangelicals, supports lobbying efforts as well as research and publishes commentary on a range of policy issues, often taking positions in opposition to those of the New Right. "We stand against needless human suffering due to lack of health care," the group announces in its mission statement, also describing itself as "deeply involved in efforts to address major environmental challenges facing our world, including climate change, species loss, and green energy." On the issue of marriage, the group aims to "strengthen the fading institution" but not with a firm stance against gay marriage: "We do not believe that denigrating the dignity and denying the human rights of gays and lesbians is a legitimate part of a 'pro-family' Christian agenda."[17] The Partnership lists on its website 13 partner organizations, including Evangelicals for Social Action, the National Faith and Justice Network, and Jubilee USA. Marcia Pally, in *The New Evangelicals: Expanding the Vision of the Common Good* (2011), depicts these groups as an expanding critical mass of voices that aim to shift evangelical politics in America away from the "prototheocratic yearnings" of the Christian Right.[18]

Even among figures long associated with Christian conservative politics, there is growing unease with the ideological burdens of the New Right, and in particular the fusion of small-government economics with big-government moralism. Michael Gerson, the former speechwriter for George W. Bush and a columnist for *The Washington Post*, takes frequent aim at the Tea Party movement for its stiff posture against the federal government, bewailing the popularity of Ayn Rand's objectivist philosophy—"a freedom indistinguishable from selfishness"—among conservatives and even betraying some weariness with the "culture wars" that have captivated evangelicals since the late 1970s.[19] When Pope Francis suggested, in September 2013, that the Roman Catholic Church has historically overemphasized its opposition to abortion and contraception, Gerson applauded: "Ethical religion without love is arid and misleading. Relationships—with God and your neighbor—come first."[20]

Beyond his own apparent misgivings, Gerson senses that American evangelicals at large have entered a "period of transition" to a new era in political theology. Looking to 2009 polling data on evangelical attitudes, Gerson senses ideological fluidity within the church: "It is an exciting moment, when new movements and institutions are taking shape. It is also a precarious moment—a moment when apparently small flaws could eventually lead to large cracks."[21] Thus it falls to people like Gerson—committed Christians who are also canny students of American politics—to chart the way forward.

What Gerson puts forward is a political theology that emphasizes collective responsibility—promoting traditional values within a patently communitarian framework, one that also supports environmental protection, a social safety net, and aid to victims of AIDS and to inhabitants of the developing world.[22] It is a vision construed broadly enough to invite the qualified approval of a Hauerwas *and* a Wolterstorff; and it is certainly a vision that tracks more agreeably with the activism of Richard Cizik than with the activism of Ralph Reed. Gerson's approach might be a libertarian's nightmare, but he maintains that it speaks to a generation of evangelicals who "want their brand of politics to be less partisan and bitter than in the past . . . as well as more high-minded and more firmly rooted in principles"—in Christian (rather than strictly American) principles, he seems to imply.[23]

This book casts a skeptical light on Gerson's intuition and on the potential for the deeper debates among the likes of Wolterstorff, Hauerwas, and the O'Donovans to shape evangelical political theology in America. Certainly the book reveals *why* American evangelicals now and again consider revising their civil religion, and as such invites new proposals. Republican theology is a bundle of contradictions waiting to unravel at any moment. It is rooted in assumptions concerning sin and redemption that defy evangelical doctrines, and in moral imperatives that explicitly marginalize the Bible. It aligns believers with ideologues and interest groups who care little about their moral priorities. It sets believers up for inevitable frustrations—a century of resistance to the temperance movement, for example, and the collapse of Prohibition after it passed, not to mention the bitter dénouement of the New Right during the Clinton years and the advance of gay marriage in the twenty-first century.

For all its incongruities, however, the history of republican theology is one of a resilient and dominant tradition. None of its viable alternatives has ever attracted widespread commitment within the evangelical community for very long. Whenever it seems that its moment has passed, along come the political and cultural conditions for a revival. Indeed, its appeal has expanded beyond the evangelical electorate in recent decades to include many conservative Roman Catholics. The simplest explanation for this consistency—that evangelicals have figured out that ideological conformity is the key to power for like-minded players in a political system—leaves unexplained why republican theology, and not some other alternative, would have become that locus of conformity among conservative Christians.

This book does not leave that question a mystery. What accounts for the durability of republican theology is the very feature that would point to its weakness, namely its contrary impulses. A school of thought based on opposing principles, it turns out, can actually draw strength from those oppositions, much in the same way that a political faction might expand its power in coalition with its adversaries. Republican theology combines three broadly attractive principles—the protection of individual rights, the aspiration toward personal virtue, and the prospect of a divinely blessed nation. The fallacies of joining these principles into one theology are overshadowed by the sheer attraction of each principle to many religious Americans. It is not just that republican theology brings evangelicals into coalition with others; rather, the theology appeals to different (even divergent) elements within their own psyche as American Christians. The desire to be free—and to enjoy one's wealth and mobility—all under the cover of republican government and Christian virtue makes an intellectual tradition that holds all that together irresistible.

NOTES

Introduction

1. David Badash of the New Civil Rights Movement broke the story on the organization's website (http//:thenewcivilrightsmovement.com/breaking-billy-graham-endorses-romney-then-scrubs-site-calling-mormonism-a-cult/politics/2012/10/12/51106, accessed on March 5, 2013).

2. "Should the Billy Graham Evangelistic Association have Removed Mormons from 'Cult' List?" *Christianity Today*, October 19, 2012 (http://www.christianitytoday.com/ct/2012/october-web-only/should-billy-graham-have-removed-mormons-from-cult-list.html, accessed on March 5, 2013); Steven P. Miller, *Billy Graham and the Rise of the Republican South* (Philadelphia: University of Pennsylvania Press, 2009), 2.

3. Daniel K. Williams, *God's Own Party: The Making of the Christian Right* (New York: Oxford University Press, 2010), 27, 91.

4. Jean-Jacques Rousseau, *The Social Contract and Other Later Political Writings*, trans. Victor Gourevitch (Cambridge: Cambridge University Press, 1997), 150–151.

5. Johann N. Neem, "A Republican Reformation: Thomas Jefferson's Civil Religion and the Separation of Church from State" in Francis D. Cogliano, ed. *A Companion to Thomas Jefferson* (West Sussex: Blackwell Publishing, Ltd. 2012), 105–106.

6. Robert N. Bellah, "Civil Religion in America," in *Daedalus* Vol. 96, No. 1 (Winter 1967).

7. See Alexis de Tocqueville, *Democracy in America* (1835), Part II, Chapter 9; Max Weber, "Church and Sects in America" (1904); see also Robert N. Bellah, "Civil Religion in America," in *Daedalus* Vol. 96, No. 1 (Winter 1967).

8. Andrew R. Murphy, *Prodigal Nation: Moral Decline and Divine Punishment from New England to 9/11* (New York: Oxford University Press, 2009), 10.

9. Michelle Boorstein and Scott Clement, "Romney Won Over White Evangelicals, Catholics, but They Weren't Enough to Win Race," *The Washington Post*, November 7, 2012.

10. An anonymous comment post on politicalforum.com in reaction to the May 2012 passage of a gay marriage ban in North Carolina (www.politicalforum.com/current-events/246945-n-carolina-passes-amendment-ban-same-sex-marriage-9.html, accessed on March 10, 2013).

11. Allan Brawley, "When Will the Christian Right Return to the Teachings of Their Gospel?" Huffington Post, March 11, 2012 (www.huffingtonpost.com/allan-brawley/will-christian-right-return-to-social-gospel_b_1333327.html, accessed March 10, 2013).

12. David J. Dunn, "Voting My Religion: The Hypocrisy of the 'Christian Right,'" Huffington Post, June 29, 2012 (www.huffingtonpost.com/david-j-dunn-phd/voting-my-religion-the-hy_b_1637034.html, accessed on March 10, 2013).

13. Jim Wallis, *God's Politics: Why the Right Gets It Wrong and the Left Doesn't Get It* (San Francisco: Harper Collins, 2005), 3.

14. "About the Faith and Freedom Coalition," http://ffcoalition.com/about/, accessed on January 25, 2012.

15. Ibid.

16. Lyman Beecher, *The Memory of Our Fathers* (1827), printed in *Sermons Delivered on Various Occasions* (Boston: T.R. Marvin, 1828), 296–297.

17. Of the recent studies, Dochuk's comes closest to recognizing the deeper ideological attachments—as opposed to merely tactical alignments—that American evangelicals have with economic conservatism. The "pre-history" of the New Right, on Dochuk's reading, revolved around California evangelicals, including many recent transplants from the South seeking entrepreneurial opportunity, whose subsequent "leap from Depression-era poverty to middle-class respectability left them convinced of capitalism's Christian virtues" [Darren Dochuk, *From Bible Belt to Sunbelt: Plain-Folk Religion, Grassroots Politics, and the Rise of Evangelical Conservatism* (New York: W.W. Norton, 2011), 168].

18. Abraham Keteltas, "God Arising and Pleading His People's Cause, or The American War in Favor of Liberty" (1777), printed in Ellis Sandoz, ed. *Political Sermons of the American Founding Era, 1730–1805* (Indianapolis: Liberty Fund, 1991), 598.

19. Os Guinness, *A Free People's Suicide: Sustainable Freedom and the American Future* (Downers Grove, IL: InterVarsity Press, 2012), 99.

20. Christian Smith, *Christian America? What Evangelicals Really Want* (Berkeley: University of California Press, 2000), 7.

21. Andrew R. Murphy, *Prodigal Nation: Moral Decline and Divine Punishment from New England to 9/11* (New York: Oxford University Press, 2009), 52.

22. D. Michael Lindsay, *Faith in the Halls of Power: How Evangelicals Joined the American Elite* (New York: Oxford University Press, 2007), 2.

23. Michael Lienesch, *Redeeming America: Piety and Politics in the New Christian Right* (Chapel Hill: The University of North Carolina Press, 1993), 21.

24. Cf. Edward Gilbreath, *Reconciliation Blues: A Black Evangelical's Inside View of White Christianity* (Downers Grove, IL: InterVarsity Press, 2006), 139; and Rick Santorum, *It Takes a Family: Conservatism and the Common Good* (Wilmington, DE: ISI Books, 2005).

25. Alexis de Tocqueville, *Democracy in America*, trans. George Lawrence (New York: Harper, 1988), 449.

26. James E. Block, *A Nation of Agents: The American Path to a Modern Self and Society* (Cambridge, MA: The Belknap Press of Harvard University Press, 2002), 21.

27. James A. Morone, *Hellfire Nation: The Politics of Sin in American History* (New Haven: Yale University Press, 2003), 5.

28. George McKenna, *The Puritan Origins of American Patriotism* (New Haven: Yale University Press, 2007), 5.

29. David Sehat, *The Myth of American Religious Freedom* (New York: Oxford University Press, 2011), 2.

30. The term itself was certainly not born on the pages of this book. As I will discuss at somewhat greater length in Chapter 4, the American historian Donald D'Elia describes the theological innovations of Benjamin Rush, and particularly his fusion of Christian and political thought, as "republican theology." However, D'Elia confines the scope of this version of republican theology to the peculiar formulations of Rush, rather than suggesting the outlines of a broader tradition that predates or outlives the Philadelphia doctor.

31. Stanley Hauerwas, *The Peaceable Kingdom: A Primer in Christian Ethics* (Notre Dame: University of Notre Dame Press, 1983), 103.

32. Nicholas Wolterstorff, *Justice: Rights and Wrongs* (Princeton University Press, 2008), 236.

Chapter 1

1. Evangelicals, who have given more than 70 percent support to every Republican candidate for president since 1980, are regularly called the "pillar" of the conservative Republican coalition. Cf. John C. Green, *The Faith Factor: How Religion Influences American Elections* (Westport, CT: Praeger Publishers, 2007), 43.

2. Daniel K. Williams, *God's Own Party: The Making of the Christian Right* (New York: Oxford University Press, 2010), 171–179.

3. Darren Dochuk, *From Bible Belt to Sunbelt: Plain-Folk Religion, Grassroots Politics, and the Rise of Evangelical Conservatism* (New York: W. W. Norton, 2011), 168–170, 196. Dochuk also notes an irony: California's "pristine capitalism" relied heavily on U.S. military spending in the 1950s and 60s.

4. David Bebbington, *Evangelicalism in Modern Britain: A History from the 1730s to the 1980s* (Grand Rapids: Baker Book House, 1989), 1.

5. http://www.lausanne.org/en/documents/lausanne-covenant.html, accessed August 9, 2013.

6. Bebbington, 3.

7. George Marsden, *Understanding Fundamentalism and Evangelicalism* (Grand Rapids: Eerdmans, 1991), 36–38.

8. Corwin E. Smidt, *American Evangelicals Today* (Lanham, MD: Rowman & Littlefield, 2013), 57.

9. http://religions.pewforum.org/pdf/report-religious-landscape-study-appendix2. pdf, accessed August 9, 2013.

10. See Bruce Hindmarsh, *The Evangelical Conversion Narrative: Spiritual Autobiography in Early Modern England* (Oxford University Press, 2005) for a discussion of how conversionism shaped American intellectual culture during the First Great Awakening.

11. Paul Freston, *Evangelicals and Politics in Asia, Africa, and Latin America* (New York: Cambridge University Press, 2001), 11.

12. Peter Beyer, "From Far and Wide: Canadian Religious and Cultural Diversity in Global/Local Context," in Lori G. Beaman and Peter Bayer, *Religion and Diversity in Canada* (Boston: Brill, 2008), 23–25.

13. Smidt, 70 (statistics based on the Pew Forum Religious Landscape Survey, 2007).

14. Nancy T. Ammerman, "American Evangelicals in American Culture: Continuity and Change" in Steven Brint and Jean Reith Schroedel, eds. *Evangelicals and Democracy in America* (New York: Russell Sage Foundation, 2009), 45–49.

15. Robert D. Putnam and David E. Campbell, *American Grace: How Religion Divides and Unites Us* (New York: Simon & Schuster, 2010), 279.

16. Smidt, 67–68, 122.

17. Corey Robin, *The Reactionary Mind: Conservatism from Edmund Burke to Sarah Palin* (New York: Oxford University Press, 2011), 4–5.

18. Cf. Milton Friedman, *Capitalism and Freedom* (Chicago: University of Chicago Press, 1962); Ayn Rand, *Atlas Shrugged* (New York: Random House, 1957).

19. John Locke, *Two Treatises of Government* (Cambridge: Cambridge University Press, 1960), 323, 330.

20. Referring to the well-known second paragraph, which begins with the statement, "We hold these truths to be self-evident, that all men are created equal, that they are endowed by their Creator with certain unalienable Rights, that among these are Life, Liberty, and the pursuit of Happiness. That to secure these rights, Governments are instituted among Men, deriving their just powers from the consent of the governed" (*The Unanimous Declaration of the Thirteen United States of America*, in Congress, July 4, 1776).

21. Intellectual historians have engaged in at least two different kinds of debate concerning Locke's influence on the American founding. The first concerns the relative *importance* of Locke's thought, with historians like Caroline Robbins (*The Eighteenth-Century Commonwealthman,* Harvard University Press, 1961) flicking Locke into a much broader constellation of Whig thinkers in the seventeenth century, and political theorists like Thomas Pangle (*The Spirit of Modern Republicanism,* University of Chicago Press, 1988) and Steven Dworetz (*The Unvarnished Doctrine,* Duke University Press, 1990) insisting on Locke's centrality to the American experiment. A second debate revolves around the precise *nature* of Locke's contribution: C. B. Macpherson, in *The Political Theory of Possessive Individualism* (Clarendon Press, 1962), argues that Locke provides the theoretical groundwork for unfettered capitalism, while James Tully argues almost precisely the opposite—that Locke was actually a proto-collectivist—in *A Discourse on Property* (Cambridge University Press, 1980). This book cannot possibly cover the ground necessary to weigh in on these debates, although it proceeds with sensitivity toward them. As to translating Locke's political economy, I accept Jerome Huyler's formulation that Locke is neither a possessive individualist nor a collectivist but instead a republican who urges individuals to "live in society and under law, secure in person and property, dealing with others by mutual agreement to mutual advantage" (*Locke in America: The Moral Philosophy of the Founding Era,* University Press of Kansas, 1995, 148). As to Locke's influence on the American founding, I will argue that his moral philosophy came to American audiences with a Scottish inflection—that is, within a tradition that fleshed out the concept of republican virtue to a far greater extent (and with a more explicit reliance on Protestant Christianity) than Locke had.

22. Lee Richard Adams and Charles Strouse, "Those Were the Days" (New Tandem Music Co., 1971).

23. Smidt, 133.

24. Michael O. Emerson and Christian Smith, *Divided By Faith: Evangelical Religion and the Problem of Race in America* (New York: Oxford University Press, 2000), 96, 173–176.

25. Sam Reimer, *Evangelicals and the Continental Divide: The Conservative Protestant Subculture in Canada and the United States* (Montreal: McGill-Queen's University Press, 2003), 126–127.

26. In Portuguese: "Não fica bem a gente passar bem e o outro carestia/ ainda mais quando se sabe o que fazer e não se faz," from the opening lines of the hymn "Barnabé," by Guilherme K. Neto, 1985 [*Hinário para o Culto Cristão* (Rio de Janeiro: Junta de Educação Religiosa e Publicações, 1991), 496].

27. Rudolf von Sinner, *The Church and Democracy in Brazil: Towards a Public Theology Focused on Citizenship* (Eugene, OR: Wipf & Stock, 2012), 225–231, 255–259.

28. Andrew R. Murphy, *Prodigal Nation: Moral Decline and Divine Punishment from New England to 9/11* (New York: Oxford University Press, 2009), 10.

29. Increase Mather, "An Earnest Exhortation to the Inhabitants of New-England" (Boston, 1676), quoted in Murphy, 19–20.

30. Alexis de Tocqueville, *Democracy in America,* tr. George Lawrence (New York: Doubleday, 1969), 243.

31. David Sehat, *The Myth of American Religious Freedom* (New York: Oxford University Press, 2011), 8. See also James A. Morone, *Hellfire Nation: The Politics of Sin in American History* (Yale, 2003), which traces both the private morality movements and the Social Gospel tradition back to the Puritans. Jon A. Shields, in *The Democratic Virtues of the Christian Right* (Princeton, 2009), offers a more Tocquevillian take on evangelical activism, crediting the phenomenon with fostering a more participatory democracy, by mobilizing certain citizens into the public sphere and by inculcating "deliberative norms . . . especially the practice of

civility and respect, the cultivation of real dialogue by listening and asking questions, the rejection of appeals to theology, and the practice of careful moral reasoning" (2).

32. Paul Starr, *The Creation of the Media: Political Origins of Modern Communication* (New York: Basic Books, 2004), 242–244.

33. Francis A. Schaeffer, *Complete Works* (Westchester, IL: Crossway Books, 1985), 5:254.

34. Since 1998, for instance, conservative activists have successfully lobbied the electorate in 21 states to vote for constitutional amendments banning same-sex marriage.

35. Ron Paul, Comments at the Republican Presidential Debate, Myrtle Beach, SC, May 5, 2011, http://www.youtube.com/watch?v=G4AUUYFeB9c (1:20), accessed March 21, 2012.

36. Michael Gerson, "Ron Paul's Land of Second-Rate Values," *The Washington Post*, May 9, 2011, http://www.washingtonpost.com/opinions/ron-pauls-land-of-second-rate-values/2011/05/09/AFD8B2bG_story.html, accessed March 21, 2012.

37. Jim Wallis, *God's Politics: Why the Right Gets It Wrong and the Left Doesn't Get It* (San Francisco: Harper Collins, 2005), 211.

38. Smidt, 165.

39. Smidt, 195–197.

Chapter 2

1. What these thinkers agree on is the necessity of certain beliefs to serve as a moral anchor for a free society. They differ widely on the proper substance of civil religion, although none of them sees traditional Christianity as viable. Machiavelli, for instance, views the observance of cult worship in ancient Rome to be "among the first causes of happiness in that city"—not because its sound cosmology, but because "it caused good orders." If later Christian empires had succeeded in inspiring the same general deference to divine will, Machiavelli reasons, "the Christian states and republics would be more united, much happier than they are" [Niccolo Machiavelli, *Discourses on Livy*, trans. Harvey C. Mansfield and Nathan Tarcov (Chicago: University of Chicago Press, 1996), 35–37]. Rousseau also admires the galvanizing force of pagan cults and deplores the emasculating distractions of Christian otherworldliness, but he goes a step farther than Machiavelli, distilling the features of an ideal civil religion down to simple dogmas: republics succeed when their citizens believe in a "provident Deity, the life to come, the happiness of the just, the punishment of the wicked, and the sanctity of the social contract and the laws" [Jean-Jacques Rousseau, *The Social Contract and Other Later Writings*, trans. Victor Gourevitch (Cambridge: Cambridge University Press, 1997), 150–151]. Jefferson, an unorthodox Christian who famously argued for the "wall of separation between church and state," made belief in the freedom of conscience itself a civil religion, erecting a public university in Virginia that lacked a theology department precisely to cultivate that belief [see Johann N. Neem, "A Republican Reformation: Thomas Jefferson's Civil Religion and the Separation of Church from State" in Francis D. Cogliano, ed. *A Companion to Thomas Jefferson* (West Sussex: Blackwell Publishing, Ltd. 2012)]. Similarly, the twentieth-century progressive John Dewey puts forth "the democratic ideal" as a "vital moral and spiritual ideal in human affairs" and suggests that achieving "common faith" around this ideal is only possible if religious fundamentalists surrender their commitment to "a separation of sheep and goats, the saved and the lost; the elect and the mass" [John Dewey, *A Common Faith* (New Haven: Yale University Press, 1934), 84].

2. Schmitt coined the term for a more ironic usage than how most other scholars use the term today. For Schmitt, *politische theologie* refers to what modern political concepts owe linguistically to old theological paradigms, rather than to a political philosophy that

still adheres to theological commitments. "All significant concepts of the modern theory of the state," he writes, "are secularized theological concepts." Thus, for instance, the modern concept of "sovereignty" traces its roots to a particular vision of God. By noting its debts to theology, however, Schmitt seeks mainly to underscore modern philosophy's ability to outlast those debts and break free from their constraints. "The development of the *nineteenth-century* theory of the state displays two characteristic moments," Schmitt notes: "the elimination of all theistic and transcendental conceptions and the formation of a new concept of legitimacy." The religious provenance of the new concepts, in other words, has significance only from a socio-historical angle. Political philosophy, Schmitt posits, is now strictly *post-theological*; the ancestors are all dead and buried [Carl Schmitt, *Political Theology: Four Chapters on the Concept of Sovereignty*, translated by George Schwab (Cambridge, MA: MIT Press, 1985), 36, 46, 51]. That political theology remains in use today bespeaks its migration to a more intuitive meaning, one that recognizes the continued vitality of the world religions and their engagement in politics. Scholars generally use political theology to refer to "a specifically theological program concerned to place questions of the political order in more universal perspectives . . . [reflecting] the interests of particular religions" [John F. Wilson, "Common Religion in American Society," in Leroy S. Rouner, ed. *Civil Religion and Political Theology* (Notre Dame, IN: University of Notre Dame Press, 1986), 111]. Even contemporary fans of Schmitt recognize this new conventional meaning: "We are likely to associate political theology," writes Paul Kahn, "with those who insist that America return to its origins as a 'Christian nation'" [Paul W. Kahn, *Political Theology: Four New Chapters on the Concept of Sovereignty* (New York: Columbia University Press, 2011), 4].

3. Robert N. Bellah, *The Broken Covenant: American Civil Religion in Time of Trial* (New York: Seabury Press, 1975), 27.

4. Bellah, "Civil Religion in America," *Daedalus* Vol. 92, No. 1 (Winter 1967), 5, 18.

5. Richard Rorty, *Contingency, Irony, and Solidarity* (Cambridge: Cambridge University Press, 1989), 86.

6. James W. Ceaser et al., *Nature and History in American Political Development: A Debate* (Cambridge, MA: Harvard University Press, 2006), 6.

7. John Rawls, *Political Liberalism* (New York: Columbia University Press, 1993), 139, 149.

8. Stephen K. White, in yet a third possible formulation, offers the concept of a "weak ontology," a malleable philosophy of human nature that can provide a foundation for ethical-political life while remaining in a "horizontal circuit of reflection, affect, and argumentation." Distinct from both the American founders' appeal to the law of nature and from Rawls's consensus-building, and adamantly denying all reference to religious dogma, White's weak ontology has a "tentative, experimental aspect": "One must patiently bring it to life," White argues, "by working it into one's life." Thus, without yielding to Rorty's agnosticism, White nonetheless insists that public philosophy is a fluid work-in-progress [see White, *Sustaining Affirmation: The Strengths of Weak Ontology in Political Theory* (Princeton: Princeton University Press, 2000), 11–12].

9. Andrew M. Greeley, "Civil Religion and Ethnic Americans," *Worldview* (February 1973), 24.

10. Quoted in Benestad, 153.

11. Wael B. Hallaq, *An Introduction to Islamic Law* (New York: Cambridge University Press, 2009), 28–30.

12. Hefner, 27–35.

13. Max Weber, "The Social Pathology of the World Religions" (1915), in H. H. Gerth and C. Wright Mills, *From Max Weber: Essays in Sociology* (New York: Oxford University Press, 1946), 280.

14. Cf. Brad Gregory, *The Unintended Reformation: How a Religious Revolution Secularized Society* (Cambridge, MA: The Belknap Press of Harvard University Press, 2012).

15. Alexis de Tocqueville, *Democracy in America*, trans. George Lawrence (New York: Harper, 1988), 449.

16. Anthony Pinn suggests that while various liberation theologies "have taken hold in the same geography and make use of similar resources on occasion . . . there is little evidence of 'cross-fertilization,' or dialogue" [Pinn, "Black Theology," in Stacey M. Floyd-Thomas and Anthony Pinn, eds. *Liberation Theologies in the United States: An Introduction* (New York: New York University Press, 2010), 33].

17. "Black Theology," A Statement by the National Committee of Black Churchmen, June 13, 1969 (adopted at the annual convocation in Oakland, California), printed in James H. Cone and Gayraud S. Wilmore, eds. *Black Theology: A Documentary History* (Maryknoll, NY: Orbis Books, 1993), 38.

18. Walter Rauschenbusch, *Christianity and the Social Crisis* (Louisville: Westminster Press, 1991), 60–61, 65.

19. Rauschenbusch, 356.

20. Jim Wallis, *God's Politics: Why the Right Gets It Wrong and the Left Doesn't Get It* (San Francisco: Harper Collins, 2005), 31.

21. Mark Noll, *America's God: From Jonathan Edwards to Abraham Lincoln* (New York: Oxford University Press, 2002), 14.

22. Abraham Kuyper, "Calvinism: Source and Stronghold of Our Constitutional Liberties" (1873), in James D. Bratt, ed. *Abraham Kuyper: A Centennial Reader* (Grand Rapids: Eerdmans, 1998).

23. Ronald Reagan, "Speech to the National Association of Evangelicals, Orlando, FL, March 8, 1983," http://www.nationalcenter.org/ReaganEvilEmpire1983.html, accessed on March 20, 2012.

24. George Washington, "The Speech of George Washington, Esq., Late President of the United States, on His Resignation of That Important Office" (R. Edwards, 1796), 12.

25. Rus Walton, *One Nation Under God* (Old Tappan, NJ: Fleming H. Revell, 1976), 51.

26. Timothy Dwight, *Greenfield Hill: A Poem* (New York: Childs and Swaine, 1794), 167.

27. Whittaker Chambers, *Witness* (New York: Random House, 1952), 17.

28. Revelation 21:5; Lyman Beecher, "The Memory of Our Fathers," in *Sermons Delivered on Various Occasions* (Boston: T.R. Marvin, 1828), 293.

29. Beecher, 295.

30. Ibid., 295–296.

31. Ibid., 296–297.

32. Ibid., 297, 301.

33. Ibid., 305–318.

34. Ibid., 309.

35. For example, R. Albert Mohler, president of Southern Baptist Theological Seminary, contends that Christian witness must come to grips with—and build up a visible resistance to—the shifting ground of moral epistemology in late modernity: "One of the most important things we have to understand," Mohler said on his weekly podcast, *Thinking in Public*, in January 2011, "is the trajectory of moral change within a society. And when you look at the trajectory, it's not coming towards us; it's going away from us. The younger you go in our society the more likely you're going to find a diminished understanding of a commitment to natural marriage and a biblical notion of restraints upon human sexuality"; R. Albert Mohler, on *Thinking In Public*, January 20, 2011, http://www.albertmohler.com/2011/01/24/moral-argument-in-modern-times-a-conversation-with-robert-p-george-2/, accessed on March

20, 2012. Michael Horton, of the more Calvinistic Westminster Theological Seminary, takes the side of gospel-driven preaching, critiquing "the Pelagian tendency of popular Christianity in our day, what [sociologist] Christian Smith calls 'moralistic, therapeutic deism,'" and urging Christians to "start with the gospel" in their ministry to the wider world; Michael Horton, *Christless Christianity: The Alternative Gospel of the American Church* (Grand Rapids: Baker Books, 2008), 48, 197.

36. Locke, John, *Two Treatises of Government* (New York: Cambridge University Press, 2005), 271.

37. Ibid., 278–282.

38. Ibid., 350–351.

39. Nathan Tarcov, in his analysis of Locke's *Some Thoughts Concerning Education* (1692), notes that Locke advocated "a gentlemen's education . . . supportive of the politics he taught. It forms men of business and affairs. They are physically fit and courageous, able to be soldiers if necessary. But, much more important, they are willing and able to concern themselves with their estates, perhaps even with trade, and to be active and informed in public affairs." Nevertheless, Tarcov stresses, Locke envisions education as a strictly private and domestic concern: "Locke not only appealed to parents rather than to government; he appealed to parents to educate their children at home rather than at schools . . . Education is exclusively entrusted by [Locke] to the authority that lacks the power of life and death" [Nathan Tarcov *Locke's Education for Liberty* (Lanham: Lexington Books, 1999), 4–5].

40. Augustine, *Confessions*, trans. John K. Ryan (New York: Doubleday, 1960), 49.

41. John Calvin, *Institutes of the Christian Religion* (1536), trans. Ford Lewis Battles, ed. John T. McNeill (Philadelphia: Westminster Press, 1960), 258.

42. Samuel Finley, "Christ Triumphing and Satan Raging, a Sermon on Matthew 12:28" (Philadelphia: Samuel Mason, 1741), 14.

43. See George Whitefield, *Seventy-Five Sermons on Various Important Subjects* (London: W. Baynes, 1812), 185, 337.

44. "Christian faith," says John Wesley, "is a sure confidence which a man hath in God, that through the merits of Christ his sins are forgiven, and he is reconciled to the favor of God." John Wesley, "Salvation By Faith," in *The Works of the Reverend John Wesley* (New York: J. Collard, 1833), 14.

45. "Whatever men's reasoning may suggest, if the children of God fairly examine their own experiences—if they do God justice, they must acknowledge that they did not choose God, but that God chose them. And if He chose them at all, it must be from eternity, and that too without anything foreseen in them. Unless they acknowledge this, man's salvation must be in part owing to the free-will of man; and if so, Christ Jesus might have died, and never seen the travail of His soul in the salvation of one of His creatures. But I would be tender on this point, and leave persons to be taught it of God. I am of the martyr Bradford's mind. Let a man go to the grammar school of faith and repentance, before he goes to the university of election and predestination." George Whitefield, *Journals* (London: Banner of Truth, 1960), 491.

46. Benjamin Rush, in L.H. Butterfield, ed. *Letters of Benjamin Rush* (Princeton: Princeton University Press, 1951), 490; Rush quotes Luke 9: 56.

47. Nathaniel W. Taylor, *Lectures on the Moral Government of God* (New York: Clark, Austin & Smith, 1859).

48. Nathaniel W. Taylor, "'Concio ad Clerum,' A Sermon Delivered in the Chapel of Yale College, September 10, 1828" (New Haven: Maltsby & Hallock, 1842), 6–8.

49. Ibid., 37.

50. That believers disagree with each other on the role of morality in the Christian gospel reflects, as is often the case in such disagreements, mixed signals within the biblical

text itself. One need not look further than the undisputed letters of Paul to find mixed signals on the question of morality. Paul's earliest letter, I Thessalonians, is notable for its almost total lack of *paranesis*, or moral exhortation. He includes a brief warning against "fornication" (4:3-6—New Revised Standard Version, 2222), but mostly urges his readers to take hope in the imminent *parousia*, or "day of the Lord"—a day they can all look forward to with happy anticipation, "for you are all children of light and children of the day" (5:2-5—NRSV, 2223). One gets the impression in this early letter that God's timetable for human salvation does not leave the saints very much to spare for ethical reflection. By contrast, in Paul's final, or at any rate later, undisputed letter to the Romans, *parousia* gives way to *paranesis*. The return of Christ goes barely mentioned (obliquely in 13:11–12 and in 16:20) and in its place come extensive and specific moral exhortations—dozens of ethical imperatives, dealing with everything from charitable giving (12:13) to race relations (15:7), all under the general exhortation not to be "conformed to this world, but [rather] transformed by the renewing of your minds, so that you may discern what is the will of God—what is good and acceptable and perfect" (12:2—NRSV, 2132) [*The Harper Collins Study Bible*, New Revised Standard Version (New York: Harper Collins, 1993)].

51. Lyman Beecher, "A Reformation of Morals Practicable and Indispensable, 1812," printed in *Sermons Delivered on Various Occasions* (Boston: T.R. Marvin, 1828), 81.

52. Jonathan Edwards, *The "Miscellanies"* (ed. Thomas A. Schafer; vol. 13 of *The Works of Jonathan Edwards*; New Haven: Yale University Press, 1994), 310.

53. A brief disclaimer on biblical interpretation is in order here, particularly when it comes to the construction of ethical norms: this study does not venture any authoritative assertions on the application of scripture text to modern morality. Indeed, I agree with the New Testament scholar Bert Harrill, who notes that *all* moral inferences from the Bible reflect "the agency and contingency of the interpreter," often at great distance from the original literary context [see Albert J. Harrill, *Slaves in the New Testament: Literary, Social, and Moral Dimensions* (Minneapolis: Fortress Press, 2006), 1]. The scripture references in this section are intended only to flag the complexity that attends the application of scripture to morality, particularly when it comes to ranking certain moral imperatives above others.

54. Joan Lockwood O'Donovan, "Natural Law and Perfect Community: Contributions of Christian Platonism to Political Theory," *Modern Theology*, V. 14, No. 1 (January 1998), 20. See also Alasdair MacIntyre, *After Virtue: A Study in Moral Theory* (Notre Dame: University of Notre Dame Press, 2007); Stanley Hauerwas, *After Christendom? How the Church Is to Behave If Freedom, Justice, and a Christian Nation Are Bad Ideas* (Nashville: Abingdon Press, 1991); and Oliver O'Donovan, *Resurrection and Moral Order: An Outline for Evangelical Ethics* (Grand Rapids: Eerdmans, 1986).

55. Nicholas Wolterstorff, *Justice: Rights and Wrongs* (Princeton University Press, 2008), 353.

56. Wolterstorff, 135.

57. Cf. Exodus 20–23; Leviticus 1–7, 11–27; Deuteronomy 10–28; Matthew 5–7; and I Corinthians 5–14.

58. Cf. Matthew 5.

59. Cf. Proverbs 31:5.

60. Cf. Romans 3:9–20.

61. John Locke, *Two Treatises on Government* (New York: Cambridge University Press, 2005), 271, 323.

62. John Witte, Jr., *The Reformation of Rights: Law, Religion, and Human Rights in Early Modern Calvinism* (New York: Cambridge University Press, 2010), 61.

63. Jesus says, for instance, "You have heard that it was said, 'You shall not commit adultery.' But I say to you that everyone who looks at a woman with lust has already committed

adultery with her in his heart. If your right eye causes you to sin, tear it out and throw it away; it is better that for you to lose one of your members than for your whole body to be thrown into hell" (Matthew 5:27–29, NRSV, 1867).

64. Locke, 386–388.

65. Cf. Exodus 21:15–17; Exodus 22:19; Exodus 31:15; Leviticus 20:13, 27; Numbers 1:51; Deuteronomy 13:5; Joshua 6:17, 8:26, 10:28–40, 11:11–12.

66. Leviticus 1–7.

67. Leviticus 23.

68. Leviticus 25:23–34.

69. Leviticus 25:8–22.

70. "As much land as a man tills, plants, improves, cultivates, and can use the product of, so much is his property. He by his labor does, as it were, enclose it from the Common." Locke, 290–291.

71. Cf. Genesis 24:35, Deuteronomy 28:1–14, Proverbs 10:22, Proverbs 13:22, Ecclesiastes 2:24.

72. Cf. Mark 10:17–31, Luke 1:51–53, Luke 6:20–21.

73. Matthew 19:24 (NRSV, 1893).

74. Leviticus 25:23 (NRSV, 192).

75. John Winthrop, "A Model of Christian Charity," in Perry Miller, ed. *The American Puritans: Their Prose and Poetry* (New York: Columbia University Press, 1956), 79–80.

76. Ecclesiastes 5:15 (NRSV, 993).

77. Matthew 6:19–20 (NRSV, 1869).

78. Cf. I Corinthians 7:20–22, Ephesians 6:5–6, Colossians 3:22–24, I Timothy 6:1–2, Titus 2:9–10.

79. See Exodus 6–12; Leviticus 23;45; Joshua 9; 2 Kings 17 and 25.

80. Romans 6:6–8 (NRSV, 2123).

81. Judges 19–20.

82. Eric Nelson, *The Hebrew Republic: Jewish Sources and the Transformation of European Political Thought* (Cambridge, MA: Harvard University Press, 2010), 37.

83. See, for example, Samuel Langdon, "The Republic of the Israelites an Example to the American States," in Ellis Sandoz, ed. *Political Sermons of the Founding Era, 1730–1805* (Indianapolis: Liberty Fund, 1998), 941–967. More recently, the Texas libertarian Ron Paul shocked the Faith and Freedom Coalition in June 2011 when he devoted his Conference address to a biblical exposition on Hebrew republicanism and limited government: "It was a patriarchal society; it was a family-driven society, but there were always going to be arguments and conflicts. So these conflicts were taken, not to the government, but to somebody who was chosen to be a judge and a respected person that respected the law and respected their traditions. But a time came—there was always temptation, even as Israelites were leaving Egypt . . . but there was this effort made under Samuel: People came and said, 'You know, we want somebody to come and take care of us; we want a king.' And Samuel strongly objected to it. He explained to them, 'You do not want a king; that will substitute for God . . . The king will take your young people, your young men to fight war, the young women to be used in the government. They're going to tax you and they're gonna overburden you. And you're going to have to work so much time—25 percent, 35 percent, 45 percent, of the time, for the king . . .'" Ron Paul, "Speech to the Faith and Freedom Coalition Conference and Strategy Briefing," June 4, 2011, http://ronpaulflix.com/2011/06/ron-paul-video-at-the-faith-freedom-coalition-conference-june-4th-2011/#show-transcript, accessed on March 23, 2012.

84. Romans 13:1–4 (NRSV, 2133).

85. John 18:36 (NRSV, 2049).

Chapter 3

1. Cf. Sacvan Bercovitch, *The Puritan Origins of the American Self* (New York: Cambridge University Press, 1974).

2. George McKenna, *The Puritan Origins of American Patriotism* (New Haven: Yale University, 2007), 2, 7. See also Sacvan Bercovitch, *The Puritan Origins of the American Self*, and James A. Morone, *Hellfire Nation: The Politics of Sin in American History* (New Haven: Yale University Press, 2003).

3. John Witte, Jr., *The Reformation of Rights: Law, Religion, and Human Rights in Early Modern Calvinism* (New York: Cambridge University Press, 2010), 23.

4. "And the Lord God commanded the man, 'You may freely eat of every tree of the garden, but of the tree of the knowledge of good and evil you shall not eat, for in the day that eat of it you shall die.'" Genesis 2:16, *The Harper Collins Study Bible, New Revised Standard Version* (New York: Harper Collins, 1993), 8.

5. Exodus 20:1–21ff., NRSV 115–116.

6. "Now the Lord said to Abram, 'Go from your country and your kindred and your father's house to the land that I will show you. I will make of you a great nation, and I will bless you, and make your name great, so that you will be a blessing. I will bless those who bless you, and the one who curses you I will curse, and in you all the families of the earth shall be blessed.'" Genesis 12:1–3, NRSV 20.

7. "Thus says the Lord of hosts, 'I took you from the pasture, from following the sheep, to be prince over my people Israel; and I have been with you wherever you went, and have cut off all your enemies from before you; and I will make for you a great name, like the name of the great ones of the earth. And I will appoint a place for my people Israel and will plant them, so that they may live in their own place and be disturbed no more; and evildoers shall afflict them no more, as formerly, from the time that I appointed judges over my people Israel; and I will give you rest from all your enemies. Moreover, the Lord declares to you that the Lord will make you a house. When your days are fulfilled and you lie down with your ancestors, I will raise up your offspring after you, who shall come from your body, and I will establish his kingdom. He shall build a house for my name, and I will establish the throne of his kingdom forever.'" 2 Samuel 7:8–13, NRSV 477.

8. Michael Horton, *God of Promise: Introducing Covenant Theology* (Grand Rapids: Baker Books, 2006), 52–53.

9. Galatians 3:23–26, NRSV 2187.

10. On the comparison between Ishmael and Isaac, for instance, Calvin writes: "As in the house of Abraham there were two mothers, so are there also in the Church of God. Doctrine is the mother of whom we are born, and is twofold, Legal and Evangelical. The legal mother, whom Hagar resembles, gendereth to bondage. Sarah, again, represents the second, which gendereth to freedom; though Paul begins higher, and makes our first mother Sinai and our second Jerusalem. The two covenants, then, are the mothers of whom children unlike one another are born; for the legal covenant makes slaves and the evangelical covenant makes freemen." In drawing the analogy to the Church of Rome he says, "This designation, 'the mother of us all,' reflects the highest credit and the highest honor on the Church. But the Papists are fools and twice children, who expect to give us uneasiness by producing these words; for their mother is an adulteress who brings forth to death the children of the devil; and how foolish is the demand that the children of God should surrender themselves to her to be cruelly slain!" John Calvin, *Commentaries on the Epistles of Paul to the Galatians and Ephesians*, trans. William Pringle (Grand Rapids: Baker Books, 2005), 137–141.

11. Cf. Augustine, *Against Two Letters of the Pelagians.*

12. John Calvin, *Institutes of the Christian Religion*, trans. Ford Lewis Battles (Philadelphia: Westminster Press, 1960), 244–245.

13. Calvin, *Institutes*, 684.

14. The gospel, Calvin maintains, "is a doctrine not of the tongue but of life. It is not apprehended by the understanding and memory alone, as other disciplines are, but it is received only when it possesses the whole soul, and finds a seat and resting place in the inmost affection of the heart" (*Institutes*, 688).

15. "When Scripture bids us act toward men so as to esteem them above ourselves, and in good faith to apply ourselves wholly to doing them good, it gives us commandments of which our mind is quite incapable unless our mind by previously emptied of its natural feeling" (*Institutes*, 693).

16. Calvin, *Institutes*, 176–177.

17. Ibid., 1012.

18. Ibid., 1487.

19. Witte, 4.

20. Michael Walzer, *The Revolution of the Saints: A Study in the Origins of Radical Politics* (Cambridge: Harvard University Press, 1965) 65.

21. Romans 13:1, NRSV 2133.

22. Witte, 122–124.

23. Johannes Althusius, *Politics Methodically Set Forth, and Illustrated with Sacred and Profane Examples*, trans. Frederick S. Carney (Edinburgh: Eyre & Spottiswoode, 1964), 34.

24. Althusius, *Politics*, 2; see also Thomas O. Hueglin, "Covenant and Federalism in the Politics of Althusius" in Daniel J. Elazar and John Kincaid, eds. *The Covenant Connection: From Federal Theology to Modern Federalism* (Lanham, MD: Lexington Books, 2000), 31–54.

25. Witte, 193.

26. Eric Nelson, *The Hebrew Republic: Jewish Sources and the Transformation of European Political Thought* (Cambridge, MA: Harvard University Press, 2010), 37.

27. Althusius, *Politics*, 19.

28. "Having undertaken," they wrote, "for the glory of God and advancements of the Christian faith . . . a voyage to plant the first colony in the northern parts of Virginia, do by these presents, solemnly and mutually, in the presence of God and one another, covenant and combine ourselves together in a civil body politic, for our better ordering, and preservation and furtherance of the ends foresaid." *The Mayflower Compact*, in Melvin I. Urofsky and Paul Finkelman, *Documents of American Constitutional and Legal History* (New York: Oxford University Press, 2008), 9.

29. John Winthrop, "A Model of Christian Charity" (1630), in Perry Miller, *The American Puritans: Their Prose and Poetry* (New York: Columbia University Press, 1956), 83.

30. "The care of the public," Winthrop argues, "must oversway all private respects, by which, not only conscience, but mere civil policy, doth bind us. For it is a true rule that particular estates cannot subsist in the ruin of the public." Winthrop's communitarian vision extends both to religious and economic life: "We must be knit together, in this work, as one man. We must entertain each other in brotherly affection. We must be willing to abridge ourselves of our superfluities for the supply of others' necessities. We must uphold a familiar commerce together in all meekness, gentleness, patience and liberality. We must delight in each other; make others' conditions our own; rejoice together, mourn together, labor and suffer together, always having before our eyes our commission and community in the work, as members of the same body." Winthrop, 82–83.

31. Edwin S. Gaustad, *Roger Williams* (New York: Oxford University Press, 2005), 10–14.

32. Mark Noll, *America's God: From Jonathan Edwards to Abraham Lincoln* (New York: Oxford University Press, 2002), 40.

33. In 1638 a "Covenanter" movement in Scotland had succeeded in establishing Presbyterianism as the state religion. Presbyterianism constructs a national church from semi-autonomous congregations; it composes a central government from parish representatives, and its members covenant with each other on the basis of a doctrinal confession rather than a liturgy (or mode of worship). The Covenanter victory, as it happens, is what had forced Charles I to convene Parliament in the first place (attempting to enforce his own liturgy on the whole kingdom, he needed to money to fight the Scots); the new English Parliament therefore saw an alliance with the Scottish Church as both politically and religiously vital and invited its leaders to join the Westminster Assembly.

34. The Westminster Confession of Faith, XXXI.3, as quoted in G. I. Williamson, *The Westminster Confession of Faith* (Philadelphia: Presbyterian and Reformed Publishing Company, 1964), 247.

35. Ibid., 244.

36. John Owen, "A Vision of Unchangeable Mercy in Sending the Means of Grace to Undeserving Sinners, A Sermon Preached before the House of Commons on April 29, 1646," in *Works of John Owen*, ed. Thomas Russell (London: Richard Baynes, 1826), XV:5–49, 31–32.

37. John Owen, "Righteous Zeal Encouraged by Divine Protection, with A Discourse About Toleration, and the Duty of the Civil Magistrate About Religion, thereunto annexed" (*Works of John Owen*, XV:157–253), 181.

38. Thomas Hobbes, *Leviathan* (Indianapolis: Hackett, 1994), 259–260.

39. Ibid., 366.

40. Hobbes uses "covenant," as Calvinists do, to describe a broad range of agreements, including lopsided arrangements in which "one of the contractors may deliver the thing contracted for his part and leave the other to perform his part at some determined time after" (*Leviathan*, 82). By "contract" Hobbes implies an equal and immediate exchange of goods or rights.

41. Hobbes, 85.

42. John Locke, *First Tract on Government* (1660), printed in Locke, *Political Essays*, ed. Mark Goldie (Cambridge University Press, 1997), 7–8.

43. Ibid., *First Tract*, 9.

44. Locke's association with the Earl of Shaftesbury offers the most plausible explanation of his liberal turn in the 1660s.

45. John Locke, *A Letter Concerning Toleration*, 1689 (Indianapolis: Hackett, 1983), 50–51.

46. William Leechman, Preface to Francis Hutcheson, *A System of Moral Philosophy*, reprinted from the 1755 edition (Bristol: Thoemmes Press, 2000), xxxvi.

47. Francis Hutcheson, *A System of Moral Philosophy*, reprinted from the 1755 edition (Bristol: Thoemmes Press, 2000), 20.

48. Ibid., 24.

49. Ibid., 43–47.

50. Ibid., 46–50.

51. Ibid., 36.

52. Ibid., 58.

53. Joseph Butler, *Fifteen Sermons Preached at the Rolls Chapel, 1726* (Glasgow: R. Uie, 1769), 54, 63, 99, 131.

54. Adam Smith, *A Theory of Moral Sentiments* (Indianapolis: Liberty Classics, 1976), 9.

55. Ibid., 31, 178.

56. Ibid., 184–185.

57. Hutcheson, 37.

58. Ibid., 60.

59. Jonathan Edwards, *Dissertation on the Nature of True Virtue*. Printed in *The Works of Jonathan Edwards*, ed. Paul Ramsay, (New Haven: Yale University Press, 1989), 540.

60. George Marsden, *Jonathan Edwards: A Life* (New Haven: Yale University Press, 2003), 259.

61. Nathaniel Niles, *Two Discourses on Liberty* (Newbury Port: I. Thomas and H. W. Tinges, 1774), 55–56.

Chapter 4

1. As Mark Noll notes, "The republicanism of the early US provided a vocabulary for resisting British tyranny, offered a framework for the Constitution, and established norms for public behavior in the new nation" [*America's God: From Jonathan Edwards to Abraham Lincoln* (New York: Oxford University Press, 2005), 55].

2. Abraham Keteltas, "God Arising and Pleading His People's Cause," preached in Newbury-Port, Massachusetts, October 5, 1777, printed in Ellis Sandoz, ed. *Political Sermons of the American Founding Era, 1730–1805*, (Indianapolis: Liberty Fund, 1991), Vol. 1, 597–598.

3. See also Mark Noll, *America's God: From Jonathan Edwards to Abraham Lincoln* (Oxford: Oxford University Press, 2002).

4. In response to the moral sense philosophy of the Scottish Enlightenment, Edwards wrote *A Dissertation on the Nature of True Virtue* (1757), in which he argues that human virtue consists in "benevolence to being in general," a holistic love for God and for all of God's creation. Articulating a hyper-Calvinist position, Edwards sets "true virtue" as a moral standard to which no human can measure up, thus revealing the need for divine grace. Ordinary virtues that keep societies peaceable derive from self-love and human reason, Edwards argues. A full analysis of Edwards' argument appears in Chapter 3 of this book. Even Edwards' closest associates, such as Samuel Hopkins and Joseph Bellamy, found this epistemology extreme and unworkable and set about revising it even as early as the 1760s; their efforts appear later in this chapter.

5. Quoted in L. H. Butterfield, *John Witherspoon Comes to America: A Documentary Account Based Largely on New Materials* (Princeton, 1953), 50.

6. Benjamin Rush to John Witherspoon, March 25, 1767, Quoted in Butterfield, *John Witherspoon Comes to America* 34. Witherspoon came under intense pressure from all quarters to take the job. John Rodgers, a New York pastor and College trustee, followed up the letter of offer with another explaining, "The President of the College of New Jersey will not only have it in his power to serve the interests of Christ in the most enlarged and effectual manner by training up youth for the gospel ministry in this wide extended country, but he will sit revered as the head of the Presbyterian interest already great and daily growing in these Middle Colonies" (Butterfield, 22). Archibald Wallace, an Edinburgh merchant and fellow evangelical, urged Witherspoon "to obey the call" (Butterfield, 24), and Thomas Randall, a pastor at Perthshire in the Highlands, wrote Witherspoon to say that "When I heard . . . of your being called to the presidency of N. Jersey College, I judged it a matter of thankfulness to God, as I have long thought it the intention of Providence (after our abuse of our great mercies and our dreadful degeneracy from real religion) to fix the great seat of truth and righteousness in America" (Butterfield, 29). Richard Stockton, a College trustee who visited the Witherspoons in the spring of 1767, wrote in April: "I am pained when I think of the consequences of your determining against us" (Butterfield, 38).

7. Aaron Burr, Sr. died in 1757 at age 41, Jonathan Edwards in 1758 at age 54, Samuel Davies in 1761 at age 37, and Samuel Finley in 1766 at age 51. The College's letter of offer to Witherspoon detailed the "*singular* circumstances" of each death and highlighted the "clear and wholesome air" of Princeton, "which we can assure you is as healthy here as in any part of N America." William Peartree Smith to John Witherspoon, November 19, 1766, quoted in Butterfield, 8.

8. John Witherspoon to Benjamin Rush, August 14, 1767, quoted in Butterfield, 50.

9. In his *Autobiography*, Rush does mention that he "lamented often in the presence of [Witherspoon's] wife his not accepting of the charge of the Jersey College, and obviated such of the objections as she had formerly made to crossing the ocean," but such entreaties cannot have sounded new to Elizabeth Witherspoon. See *Autobiography of Benjamin Rush* (Princeton University Press, 1948), 50–51.

10. See John R. McIntosh, *Church and Theology in Enlightenment Scotland: The Popular Party, 1740–1800* (East Lothian, Scotland: Tuckwell Press, 1998), 19–20.

11. John Witherspoon, *Ecclesiastical Characteristics, or, the Arcana of Church Policy*. Printed in *The Selected Writings of John Witherspoon*, ed. Thomas Miller (Carbondale: Southern Illinois Press, 1990), 65–84.

12. V. Lansing Collings, *President Witherspoon: A Biography* (Princeton: Princeton University Press, 1925), 71.

13. John Witherspoon, *Lectures on Moral Philosophy*, ed. Jack Scott (Newark: Associated University Presses, 1982), 66.

14. Ibid., 78–80.

15. Witherspoon, *Lectures on Moral Philosophy*, 109.

16. Scottish Presbyterians like Francis Hutcheson devised moral sense philosophy in the 1730s in order to forge a position that incorporated Locke's case for natural liberty with a farther-reaching moral epistemology. Moral sense, on this compromise, entails the self-discovery of higher virtues through the natural capacity humans have to take delight in their own character. It is not that humans possess innate knowledge of an exogenous moral law, which would reject Lockean ethics: rather, humans discover (and are drawn to) behaviors and frames of mind—virtues in the most aesthetic sense—that make their souls more beautiful. A fuller analysis of Hutcheson in his Calvinistic context appears in Chapter 3 of this book.

17. Ibid., 80.

18. In his sermons Witherspoon emphasizes the role of Christian clergy in the shaping of private and public virtue: "Teachers and rulers of every religious denomination," he said in a Thanksgiving Sermon of 1782, "are bound mutually to each other and to the whole society, to watch over the manners of their several members." Quoted in Jeffry H. Morrison, *John Witherspoon and the Founding of the American Republic* (University of Notre Dame Press, 2005), 23.

19. Witherspoon scholar Jeffry H. Morrison is unsurprised that Witherspoon worked so quickly to undermine the Edwardsian tradition in Princeton: "Except for agreement on the basic theological tenets of Calvinism, Witherspoon was opposed to Edwards on almost every front. Edwards was a New Light Revivalist, Witherspoon an Old Side Presbyterian who may have had grave doubts about the religious enthusiasm that swept the Princeton campus in the early 1770s; Edwards was a philosophical idealist while Witherspoon an uncompromising realist. Edwards found it necessary to attack the moral sense epistemology of Francis Hutcheson, while Witherspoon always remained a firm believer in the moral sense." See Jeffry H. Morrison, *John Witherspoon and the Founding of the American Republic* (University of Notre Dame Press, 2005), 63. While this perspective may shed some light on why many Old

Side Presbyterians, like Ezra Stiles at Yale, embraced Witherspoon's arrival in 1768, it overlooks Witherspoon's even greater appeal to the New Light trustees, his biting critiques of Hutcheson in works like Ecclesiastical Characteristics, and the general tenor of his ministry in Scotland.

20. Even the early trustees of the College of New Jersey had envisioned a role for the academy in training statesmen: "Though our great intention was to erect a seminary for educating ministers of the Gospel, yet we hope it will be a means of raising up men that will be useful in other learned professions—ornaments of the State as well as the Church." This vision was far from realized prior to Witherspoon's arrival. See Thomas Jefferson Wertenbaker, *Princeton: 1746–1896* (Princeton: Princeton University Press, 1946), 19–20.

21. John Fea, "'The Chosen People of God': Presbyterians and Jeffersonian Republicanism in the New Jersey Countryside," *American Nineteenth Century History* (Autumn 2001), 4–5. Fea points to a notebook of one Ebenezer Miller, a young student of Rev. Jonathan Freeman, who received a degree from Princeton in 1809, as an illustration of this dual commitment: "Miller's notebook makes clear that 'conscience' and the 'moral law of God' were two different sources of virtue, but they were not unrelated." Fea continues, "The relationship between the moral law of the Calvinist God, and the inherent moral sense afforded to all humans, including those in a 'fallen state,' provided an ideological underpinning for the way in which rural Presbyterians approached the moral life of the early American republic." Politically, the Cohansey Presbyterians were not only ardent revolutionaries; they were Jeffersonian republicans for several generations thereafter. Fea notes that the Cohansey town of Fairfield broke for Jefferson's electors nine to one in the election of 1800 (Fea, 3, 9–10).

22. John Witherspoon, *The Dominion of Providence Over the Passions of Men, A Sermon Preached at Princeton on the 17th of May, 1776*, printed in Ellis Sandoz, ed. *Political Sermons of the American Founding Era, 1730–1805* (Indianapolis: Liberty Fund, 1998), I:545.

23. Witherspoon, *Dominion of Providence*, 549.

24. Donald D'Elia, "The Republican Theology of Benjamin Rush," Pennsylvania History (Vol. 33, No. 2), 1966, 196.

25. Benjamin Rush, *The Autobiography of Benjamin Rush* (Princeton University Press, 1948), 163.

26. Finley worked as an itinerant evangelical preacher before founding the West Nottingham Academy as a pre-seminary training ground in 1744. Among other memories of his time at West Nottingham, Rush recalls Finley's sermons on "the most striking and intelligible evidences of the truth of the Christian Religion." Rush later reflects: "I wish this mode of fortifying the reason of young people in the principles of Christianity were more general. The impressions which are made upon their fears, or their faith, by sermons and creeds soon wear away, but arguments fixed in the understanding are indelible" (*Autobiography*, 31–32).

27. Rush, *Autobiography*, 37.

28. Hartley had published his *Observations on Man* in 1749, applying Lockean physiology to the study of the brain and transforming the field of psychology throughout Europe and especially at Edinburgh.

29. Rush, *Autobiography*, 4.

30. Benjamin Rush, "An Address to the Inhabitants of the British Settlements in America upon Slave-Keeping" (Philadelphia, 1773), 29–30.

31. Benjamin Rush, "A Plan for Establishing Public Schools in Pennsylvania, and for Conducting Education Agreeably to a Republican Form of Government" (1786) in *Essays, Literary, Moral, and Philosophical* (Philadelphia: Thomas and William Bradford, 1806), 2–4.

32. Ibid., 1.

33. Ibid., 8.

34. Rush, "A Plan for Establishing Public Schools in Pennsylvania," 9.

35. Ibid., 10–11.

36. Rush, "An Address to the Inhabitants," 22.

37. Ibid., 28, 13–14.

38. Rush, *Essays, Literary, Moral, and Philosophical* (Philadelphia: Thomas and William Bradford, 1806), 114–124.

39. Rush, "An Address to the Inhabitants," 28.

40. John Adams to Mercy Otis Warren, April 16, 1776, in A. Koch and W. Peden, eds., *The Selected Writings of John and John Quincy Adams* (New York: Knopf, 1946), 57.

41. George Washington to Marquis De Lafayette, February 7, 1788, John C. Fitzpatrick, ed. *The Writings of George Washington* (Washington, DC: U. S. Government Printing Office, 1939), 29:410.

42. James Madison (as "Publius"), *The Federalist*, No. 55 (New York: Signet Classics, 2003), 343.

43. Ralph Lerner, "Commerce and Character: The Anglo-American as New-Model Man," *The William and Mary Quarterly*, Vol. 36 No. 1 (1979), 8–9.

44. Keteltas, 594–596.

45. Samuel Cooper, "A Sermon Preached Before His Excellency, John Hancock, Governor, the Honorable Senate, and House of Representatives of the Commonwealth of Massachusetts, October 25, 1780, Being the Day of the Commencement of the Constitution and Inauguration of the New Government," printed in Sandoz, I:635–636.

46. Henry Cumings, "A Sermon Preached at Lexington on the 19th of April, 1781," printed in Sandoz, I: 677.

47. See Joseph A. Conforti, "Samuel Hopkins and the New Divinity: Theology, Ethics, and Social Reform in Eighteenth-Century New England," *William and Mary Quarterly*, Vol. 34, No. 4, 1977, 576–580. Writes Conforti on page 577: "In Hopkins' view, the quietistic emphasis of *True Virtue* made Edwards vulnerable to the charge that he had involved practical religion in a cloud. Edwards's detailed descriptions of the subjective nature of regeneration, when combined with the mystical quality of his concept of Being in general, encouraged passive contemplation and rapt otherworldliness."

48. See Mark Valeri, "The New Divinity and the American Revolution," *William and Mary Quarterly*, Vol. 46, No. 4, 1989, 751–752. Joseph Bellamy, in *True Religion Delineated* (1750), wrote that "The moral image of God does radically consist in a temper of mind or frame of heart perfectly answerable to the moral law; the moral law being, as it were, a transcript of the moral perfections of God" (*The Works of The Rev. Joseph Bellamy*, New York: Stephen Dodge, 1811, 197–198). Samuel Hopkins' approach to making true virtue more realistic is to limit its horizon. In *An Inquiry into the Nature of Holiness* (1773), for instance, Hopkins writes, "The law of God is the standard of all moral rectitude or holiness. Holiness consists in conformity to this, and in nothing else . . . All obedience to the law of God is reduced to one thing: love; love to God and our neighbor, including ourselves" (*The Works of Samuel Hopkins*, Boston: Doctrinal Tract and Book Society, 1854, 13–14).

49. Jonathan Edwards Jr., *The Works of Jonathan Edwards, D.D., Late President of Union College* (Boston: John P. Jewett & Co., 1854), 185.

50. See, for example, Timothy Dwight, *The Nature and Danger of Infidel Philosophy, Exhibited in Two Discourses, Addressed to the Candidates for the Baccalaureate in Yale College* (New Haven: Printed by George Bunce, 1798).

51. Cf. Richard M. Gamble, "The Last and Brightest Empire of Time: Timothy Dwight and America as Voeglin's Authoritative Present, 1771–1787," in *Humanitas*, Vol. 20 (2007), pp. 13–14; see *The Anarchiad* (*New Haven Gazette*, 1786–1787), *The Political Greenhouse* (*Connecticut Courant*, 1799), and *The Echo* (*American Mercury*, 1791–1805) for examples of their joint publications. See also Timothy Dwight, *The Conquest of Canaan* (Hartford: Printed by Elisha Babcock, 1785); *The Triumph of Infidelity* (1788); and *American Poems* (Litchfield: Collier & Buel, 1793).

52. Timothy Dwight, *Greenfield Hill: A Poem* (New York: Childs and Swaine, 1794), 111.

53. Ibid., 153.

54. Ibid., 111.

55. Benjamin Rush, *Letters*, Ed. L. H. Butterfield (Princeton University Press, 1951), II:919.

56. Ibid., 1189.

57. Robert H. Abzug, *Cosmos Crumbling: American Reform and the Religious Imagination* (New York: Oxford University Press, 1994), 29.

Chapter 5

1. Alexis de Tocqueville, *Democracy in America*, tr. George Lawrence (New York: Harper Collins, 1969), 293.

2. Timothy Dwight, *Greenfield Hill: A Poem* (New York: Childs and Swaine, 1794), 151.

3. Lyman Beecher, "A Sermon Containing a General History of the Town of East Hampton," September 21, 1803 (New London, 1804), 27.

4. Charles Roy Keller, *The Second Great Awakening in Connecticut* (New Haven: Yale University Press, 1942), 148–151.

5. Quoted in James W. Fraser, *Pedagogue for God's Kingdom: Lyman Beecher and the Second Great Awakening* (Lanham, MD: University Press of America, 1985), 57.

6. Ibid., 53–56.

7. Ibid., 37–38.

8. See J. F. Thornbury, *God Sent Revival: The Story of Asahel Nettleton and the Second Great Awakening* (Grand Rapids, MI: Evangelical Press, 1977); Christine Leigh Heyrman, *Southern Cross: The Beginnings of the Bible Belt* (New York: Knopf, 1997); Charles E. Hambrick-Stowe, *Charles G. Finney and the Spirit of American Evangelicalism* (Grand Rapids, MI: Eerdmans, 1996); David W. Kling, *A Field of Divine Wonders: The New Divinity and Village Revivals in Northwestern Connecticut, 1792–1822* (University Park: Pennsylvania State University Press, 1993); and John H. Wigger, *Taking Heaven By Storm: Methodism and the Rise of Popular Christianity in America* (New York: Oxford University Press, 1998).

9. Cf. *The Religious Intelligencer* (New Haven), 1818–1837; *The Christian Herald* (New Hampshire: Portsmouth), 1818–1835; *The Christian Watchman* (Boston), 1819–1848; *The Christian Observer* (Louisville: Kentucky), 1840–1850; and Dickson D. Bruce, *And they All Sang Hallelujah: Plain-Fold Camp-Meeting Religion, 1800–1845* (Knoxville: University of Tennessee Press, 1974).

10. Nathan O. Hatch, *The Democratization of American Christianity* (New Haven: Yale University Press, 1989), 4.

11. Robert T. Handy, *A History of the Churches in the United States and Canada* (New York: Oxford University Press, 1977), 175.

12. Andrew R. Murphy, *Prodigal Nation: Moral Decline and Divine Punishment from New England to 9/11* (New York: Oxford University Press, 2009), 52.

13. Charles I. Foster, *An Errand of Mercy: The Evangelical United Front, 1790–1837* (Chapel Hill: University of North Carolina Press, 1960), 278.

14. Tocqueville, 513.

15. Handy, 175.

16. Gordon S. Wood, "The Democratization of Mind in the American Revolution," in Robert H. Horwitz, ed. *The Moral Foundations of the American Republic* (Charlottesville: University Press of Virginia, 1979), 102.

17. William G. McLoughlin, "Religious Freedom and Popular Sovereignty: A Change in the Flow of God's Power, 1730–1830," in Joseph D. Ban and Paul R. Dekar, eds. *In the Great Tradition: Essays on Pluralism, Voluntarism, and Revivalism* (Valley Forge, PA: Judson Press, 1982), 174.

18. Lyman Beecher, "A Reformation of Morals Practicable and Indispensable," October 27, 1812 in New Haven, in *Sermons Delivered on Various Occasions* (Boston: Jewett & Co., 1852), 97–98.

19. Lyman Beecher, *The Memory of Our Fathers*, 1827, printed in *Sermons Delivered on Various Occasions* (Boston: T.R. Marvin, 1828), 296–297.

20. Beecher, *Memory of Our Fathers*, 302–303.

21. Cf. Cotton Mather, *The Negro Christianized: An Essay to Excite and Assist that Good Work, the Instruction of Negro-Servants in Christianity* (Boston: B. Green, 1706); John Woolman, *Some Considerations on the Keeping of Negroes* (1746, 1760), printed in *The Journal and Essays of John Woolman*, Amelia Mott Gummere, ed. (New York: Macmillan Company, 1922); George Whitefield, "Letter to the Inhabitants of Maryland, Virginia, North and South–Carolina" (January 23, 1740), printed in *Three Letters from the Reverend Mr. G. Whitefield* (Philadelphia: Benjamin Franklin, 1745); Samuel Davies, *Virginia's Danger and Remedy: Two Discourses Occasioned by the Severe Drought in Sundry Parts of the Country, and the Defeat of General Braddock* (Glasgow: J. Bryce and D. Paterson, 1756); Anthony Benezet, *A Caution and Warning to Great-Britain and Her Colonies in a Short Representation of the Calamitous State of the Enslaved Negroes in the British Dominions* (Philadelphia: D. Hall, 1767); John Wesley, *Thoughts on Slavery* (London: R. Hawes, 1774); Samuel Hopkins, *A Dialogue Concerning the Slavery of the Africans* (Norwich: Judah P. Spooner, 1776); Jonathan Edwards Jr., "Some Observations Upon the Slavery of Negroes," printed under the name Antidoulios in *The Connecticut Journal and the New-Haven Post-Boy* (October 1773).

22. Theodore Dwight Weld, *The Bible Against Slavery: An Inquiry into the Patriarchal and Mosaic Systems on the Subject of Human Rights* (New York: Antislavery Society, 1838), 10–11.

23. Jonathan Blanchard and N. L. Rice, *A Debate on Slavery Held in the City of Cincinnati, on the First, Second, Third, and Sixth Days of October, 1845, Upon the Question: Is Slaveholding in Itself Sinful, and the Relation Between Master and Slave, a Sinful Relation?* (Cincinnati: Wm. H. Moore & Co., 1846), 12.

24. Heman Humphrey, *Parallel Between Intemperance and the Slave Trade: An Address Delivered at Amherst College, July 4, 1828* (Amherst: J.S. and C. Adams, 1828), 4.

25. Charles Grandison Finney, "The Sinner's Natural Power and Moral Weakness," preached in Oberlin, OH, August 13, 1856, printed in Finney, *Sermons on Gospel Themes* (New York: Dodd, Mead, & Co., 1876), 192–193.

26. Finney, "The Sinner's Natural Power," 197.

27. Charles Grandison Finney, "Fast Day Sermon," May 14, 1841 (*The Oberlin Evangelist*, June 9, 1841).

28. Ibid.

29. Murphy, 10.

30. Beecher, "A Reformation of Morals," 79.

31. Robert L. Dabney, "The Christian's Best Motive for Patriotism," printed in *Fast Day Sermons: The Pulpit on the State of the Country* (New York: Rudd & Carleton, 1861), 82, 88–89.

32. Henry Ward Beecher, "Peace Be Still," printed in *Fast Day Sermons: The Pulpit on the State of the Country* (New York: Rudd & Carleton, 1861), 270.

33. Finney, "Fast Day Sermon," 1.

34. Beecher, "A Reformation of Morals," 93–94.

35. Lyman Beecher, "The Remedy of Intemperance," printed in *Six Sermons on Intemperance, Delineating Its Nature, Occasions, Signs, Evils, and Remedy* (Edinburgh: J. Dickson, 1846), 18–19.

36. Handy, 175.

37. Charles Grandison Finney, "Hindrances to Revivals" (1835), printed in Finney, *Lectures on Revivals of Religion* (Cambridge, MA: Harvard University Press, 1960), 308.

38. Beecher, *The Memory of Our Fathers*, 294–295.

39. Benjamin Lundy, "Address to the Public," *The Genius of Universal Emancipation*, July 1821.

40. Finney, "Hindrances to Revivals," 293, 306.

41. Ibid., 288.

42. Ibid., 306.

43. Lyman Beecher, "A Reformation of Morals Practicable and Indispensable," 98–99.

44. William Lloyd Garrison, *The Liberator*, July 23, 1836, in Truman Nelson, *Documents of Upheaval: Selections from William Lloyd Garrison's The Liberator, 1831–1865* (New York: Hill and Wang, 1966), 99.

45. Robert H. Abzug, *Cosmos Crumbling: American Reform and the Religious Imagination* (New York: Oxford University Press, 1994), 160.

46. Humphrey, "Parallel Between Intemperance and the Slave Trade," 4.

47. Garrison, *The Liberator*, December 15, 1837, in Nelson, *Documents of Upheaval*, 141.

48. C.C. Goen, *Broken Churches, Broken Nation: Denominational Schisms and the Coming of the American Civil War* (Macon, GA: Mercer University Press, 1985), 77.

49. Henry J. Van Dyke, "The Character and Influence of Abolitionism," printed in *Fast Day Sermons: The Pulpit on the State of the Country* (New York: Rudd & Carleton, 1861), 163.

50. Goen, 82–83.

51. Peter Cartwright, *Autobiography*, quoted in Goen, 89.

52. Abraham Lincoln, *Second Inaugural Address*, March 4, 1865.

53. See Jonathan Edwards, *A Faithful Narrative of the Surprising Work of God in the Conversion of Many Hundred Souls in Northampton* (Boston: S. Kneeland, 1738) and *The Great Christian Doctrine of Original Sin Defended* (Boston: S. Kneeland, 1758).

54. Nathaniel W. Taylor, "Concio ad Clerum," A Sermon Delivered in the Chapel of Yale College, September 10, 1828 (New Haven: Maltsby & Hallock, 1842), 37.

55. J. F. Thornbury, *God Sent Revival: The Story of Asahel Nettleton and Second Great Awakening* (Grand Rapids: Evangelical Press, 1977), 161.

56. The Arminian wing of the First Great Awakening, led by Methodist missionaries John and Charles Wesley, remained a relatively small faction, confined to Southern colonies.

57. Finney outlines and defends the new measures in his Oberlin lecture, "Measures to Promote Revivals" (1835), printed in Charles Grandison Finney, *Lectures on Revivals of Religion* (Cambridge, MA: Harvard University Press, 1960).

58. Asahel Nettleton, "Total Depravity," in Bennet Tyler, ed. *Remains of the Late Rev. Asahel Nettleton, D.D.* (Hartford: Robins and Smith, 1845), 315.

59. Nettleton, "True Repentance Not Antecedent to Regeneration," in Tyler, 63.

60. Quoted in Thornbury, 170–172.

61. Charles Grandison Finney, *Sermons on Important Subjects* (New York, 1836), 191.

62. Nettleton, Letter to Gardiner Spring, May 4, 1827, printed in Lyman Beecher, *Letters of Rev. Dr. Beecher and Rev. Nettleton on the "New Measures" in Conducting Revivals of Religion* (New York: G. & C. Carvill, 1828), 30.

63. Thornbury, 178.

64. Lyman Beecher, *Autobiography*, Vol. I (Cambridge: The Belknap Press of Harvard University Press, 1961), 472.

65. Thornbury, 195.

66. William Lloyd Garrison, "*The Liberator* and Slavery: Introductory Remarks," *The Liberator*, January 7, 1832, printed in Nelson, 42.

67. Garrison, *The Liberator*, November 1845.

68. Mark A. Noll, *The Civil War as a Theological Crisis* (Chapel Hill: University of North Carolina Press, 2006), 31.

69. Richard Fuller and Francis Wayland, *Domestic Slavery Considered as a Scriptural Institution* (New York: Sheldon &. Co., 1860), 170.

70. Fuller and Wayland, 246–248.

71. Henry J. Van Dyke, "The Character and Influence of Abolitionism," preached on December 9, 1860, in the First Presbyterian Church of Brooklyn, printed in *Fast Day Sermons: The Pulpit on the State of the Country* (New York: Rudd & Carleton, 1861), 137, 163–164.

72. Henry Ward Beecher, "Peace Be Still," printed in *Fast Day Sermons*, 271–291.

73. Julia Ward Howe, "The Battle Hymn of the Republic," *The Atlantic Monthly*, February 1862.

74. William Adams, *Christian Patriotism* (New York: Anson D. F. Randolph, 1863), 10.

75. J. Henry Smith, "A Sermon Delivered at Greensboro" (Greensboro, NC, 1862), 11.

76. J. P. Philpott, *The Kingdom of Israel* (Fairfield, TX, 1864), 45.

77. Stephen Elliott, "New Wine Not to Be Put into Old Bottles" (Savannah, GA, 1862), 9.

78. B. M. Palmer, "National Responsibility Before God: A Discourse Delivered at the Day of Fasting" (New Orleans, 1861), 18.

79. Drew Gilpin Faust, *The Creation of Confederate Nationalism: Ideology and Identity in the Civil War South* (Baton Rouge: Louisiana State University Press, 1988), 30.

80. Absalom Jones, "Thanksgiving Sermon," in Dorothy Porter, *Early Negro Writing, 1760–1837* (Boston: Beacon, 1971), 338.

81. L. C. Lockwood, "The Song of the Contrabands: O Let My People Go" (New York: Horace Waters, 1862).

82. Eddie S. Glaude, Jr. *Exodus! Religion, Race, and Nation in Early Nineteenth-Century Black America* (Chicago: University of Chicago Press, 2000), 9, 12.

Chapter 6

1. Henry Ward Beecher, "The Strike and Its Lessons," in *Christian Union*, August 8, 1877.

2. Henry George, *Progress and Poverty: An Inquiry into the Cause of Industrial Depressions and of Increase of Want with Increase of Wealth . . . The Remedy*, 1879 (New York: Robert Schalkenbach Foundation, 1955), 347.

3. Beecher, "The Strike and Its Lessons."

4. Walter Rauschenbusch, *Christianity and the Social Crisis* (Louisville, KY: Westminster/ John Knox Press, 1991), 60–61.

5. George Marsden, *Fundamentalism and American Culture*, 2nd ed. (New York: Oxford University Press, 2006), 11.

6. Sydney E. Ahlstrom, *A Religious History of the American People* (New Haven: Yale University Press, 1972), 842.

7. Philip D. Jordan, *The Evangelical Alliance for the United States of America, 1847–1900: Ecumenism, Identity and the Religion of the Republic* (New York: Edwin Mellen Press, 1982), 11.

8. Josiah Strong, *Our Country: Its Possible Future and Its Present Crisis* (Cambridge, MA: Harvard University Press, 1963), 202.

9. Paul Starr, *The Creation of the Media: Political Origins of Modern Communication* (New York: Basic Books, 2004), 242–244.

10. The most effective temperance group, however, was the Anti-Saloon League (est. 1893), which focused exclusively on electing "dry" candidates to state and national office, a strategy that paid off with the 1919 passage of the Eighteenth Amendment, and the subsequent Volstead Act to ban the sale of liquor (Ahlstrom, 867–871).

11. Ian Tyrrell, *Reforming the World: The Creation of America's Moral Empire* (Princeton University Press, 2010), 67.

12. Due to legal restrictions, far fewer people (not more than double-digit thousands) emigrated across the Pacific from Asia during this period.

13. Ahlstrom separates Protestant immigrants of this period into five subgroups: (1) nominal members of state churches who dropped all religious affiliations in the New World; (2) dissenters (such as the Mennonites) who, like the Puritans of the seventeenth century, came to America in order to form disciplined communities of fellowship; (3) those who joined preexisting American churches; (4) those who extended the reach of European state churches into American neighborhoods (this was the largest group); and (5) those, like the Christian Reformed Church from the Netherlands, who maintained their former confession but under new denominational leadership in America (Ahlstrom, 752–754).

14. See Michael O. Emerson and Christian Smith, *Divided By Faith: Evangelical Religion and the Problem of Race in America* (New York: Oxford University Press, 2000).

15. Charles R. Erdman, "The Coming of Christ," in *The Fundamentals*, Volume IV, 87.

16. Marsden, 51.

17. Charles Darwin, *On the Origin of Species By Means of Natural Selection* (Ontario: Broadview Press, 2003), 132.

18. Ibid., 134.

19. Ibid., 144.

20. Francis Bowen, "The Latest Form of the Development Theory" (1860), in *Gleanings from A Literary Life* (New York: Scribners, 1880), 216.

21. Newman Smyth, *Through Science to Faith* (New York: Charles Scribner's Sons, 1904), 39.

22. Smyth, 95–104.

23. Henry Ward Beecher, "Evolution in Human Consciousness of the Idea of God," preached in Brooklyn on May 24, 1885, printed in Beecher, *Evolution and Religion* (New York: Fords, Howard, and Hulbert, 1886), 30.

24. Ibid., 26.

25. Ibid., 29.

26. Beecher specifically highlights the serial character of the scriptures: "The Bible is not a book written as John Milton wrote 'Paradise Lost,' nor is it a book written as a man writes history. It is not a book; it is a series of books, with intervals of hundreds of years between. It is the record of the progress of the human race in their development into the divine ideas through the medium of right-living. It is the serial history of the construction of the noblest elements that belong to human consciousness" (Beecher, 37).

27. Beecher, 41.

28. Lester Frank Ward, "Neo-Darwinism and Neo-Lamarckism," Annual Address of the President of the Biological Society of Washington, January 24, 1891 (Washington, D.C.: Gedney & Roberts, 1891), 71.

29. William Jennings Bryan, "Supplementary Address in the Scopes Case," printed in *The World's Most Famous Court Trial: Tennessee Evolution Case* (Cincinnati: National Book Company, 1925), 335.

30. Sumner, "The Absurd Effort to Make the World Over," in *On Liberty, Society, and Politics*, 260–261.

31. Smyth, 160.

32. Alexis de Tocqueville, *Democracy in America*, tr. George Lawrence (New York: Harper Collins, 1969), 531.

33. George, 353.

34. "The People's Party Platform," printed in *The Omaha Morning World-Herald*, July 5, 1892.

35. William Jennings Bryan, Address to the Democratic Convention in Chicago, IL, July 9, 1896.

36. William Graham Sumner, "The Forgotten Man," in Robert C. Bannister, ed., *On Liberty, Society, and Politics: The Essential Essays of William Graham Sumner* (Indianapolis: Liberty Fund, 1992), 206.

37. Sumner, "The Forgotten Man," in Bannister, 207.

38. See Sumner, "The Concentration of Wealth: Its Economic Justification" (1902) in Bannister, 149–153.

39. Sumner, "The Forgotten Man," in Bannister, 209.

40. Kathryn J. Oberdeck, *The Evangelist and the Impresario: Religion, Entertainment, and Cultural Politics in America, 1884–1914* (Baltimore: Johns Hopkins University Press, 1999), 156.

41. Thomas Winter, "Contested Spaces: The YMCA and Workingmen on the Railroads, 1877–1917," in Nina Mjagij and Margaret Spratt, eds., *Men and Women Adrift: The YMCA and the YWCA in the City* (New York: New York University Press, 1997), 65.

42. Ibid., 66–67.

43. Ibid., 69–71.

44. Ibid., 70.

45. Irvine turned to muckraking journalism and novel-writing after only a couple of decades in ministry. Kathryn J. Oberdeck's *The Evangelist and the Impresario* offers the most detailed account of Irvine's ministry, drawing on reproductions of his sermons in New Haven newspapers, as well as his personal archives.

46. Oberdeck, 141–142.

47. Alexander Irvine, *From the Bottom Up: The Life Story of Alexander Irvine* (New York: Gusset & Dunlap, 1909), 207–208.

48. Quoted in Oberdeck, 161.

49. From Irvine's first sermon at the People's Church, May 10, 1903, quoted in Oberdeck, 166.

50. Irvine, *From the Bottom Up*, 240.

51. Ibid., 245–246.

52. Oberdeck, 173.

53. Ahlstrom, 801.

54. Walter Rauschenbusch, *Christianity and the Social Crisis* (Louisville, KY: Westminster/John Knox Press, 1991), xxxviii.

55. Rauschenbusch, 1.

56. Ibid., 13.

57. Ibid., 13, 19.

58. Ibid., 67, 60.

59. Ibid., 67, 60, 48.

60. Ibid., 210, 360, 372.

61. Theodore T. Munger, "Education and Social Progress," in *Century Illustrated Magazine*, June 1887.

62. Henry Ward Beecher, "The Strike and Its Lessons," in *Christian Union*, August 8, 1877.

63. Ibid.

64. Henry Ward Beecher, "Industry and Idleness," in *Wellman's Miscellany*, January 1873.

65. Henry Ward Beecher, "The Administration of Wealth," in *Herald of Health*, November 1867.

66. Ibid.

67. Henry Ward Beecher, "The Tendencies of American Progress: Thanksgiving Sermon," in *Christian Union*, December 3, 1870.

68. Beecher, "The Strike and Its Lessons."

69. Newman Smyth, "Social Problems in the Pulpit, Sermon I: The Claims of Labor," in *The Andover Review: A Religious and Theological Monthly*, April 1885.

70. Newman Smyth, "Social Problems in the Pulpit, Sermon II: Use and Abuse of Capital," in *The Andover Review: A Religious and Theological Monthly*, May 1885.

71. William Graham Sumner, "The Concentration of Wealth: Its Economic Justification" (1902), in Robert C. Bannister, ed., *On Liberty, Society, and Politics: The Essential Essays of William Graham Sumner* (Indianapolis: Liberty Fund, 1992), 151.

72. Newman Smyth, "Social Problems in the Pulpit, Sermon III: Social Helps," in *The Andover Review: A Religious and Theological Monthly*, June 1885.

73. Smyth, "Sermon II: Use and Abuse of Capital."

74. Charles Erdman, "The Church and Socialism," in *The Fundamentals: A Testimony to the Truth*, Volume IV (New York: Garland Publishing, 1988), 110.

75. Ibid., 111–116.

76. Ibid., 111.

Chapter 7

1. "Text of Eisenhower's Address at the Republican Party Dinner Held at the Boston Garden," *New York Times*, September 22, 1952, 22.

2. "Text of Nixon's Statement Rejecting the Report of Obscenity Panel," *New York Times*, October 25, 1970; Francis X. Clines, "Reagan Plays the Issues in More than a Single Key," *New York Times*, May 13, 1983; also see John J. Pitney, "Tocqueville Fraud," *The Weekly Standard*, November 13, 1995.

3. George Marsden, *Fundamentalism and American Culture*, 2nd 3d. (New York: Oxford University Press, 2006), 67.

4. John A. Hutchison, *We Are Not Divided: A Critical and Historical Study of the Federal Council of the Churches of Christ in America* (New York: Round Table Press, 1941), 20.

5. Preamble to the "Plan for Federation" (1905), in Hutchison, 35.

6. Alva W. Taylor, "The Moral Aftermath of War—Part III," *Christian Century*, 36:2 (January 9, 1919), 14–15.

7. Woodrow Wilson, "The Present Task of the Ministry," *Christian Century*, 36:28 (July 10, 1919), 15.

8. As Ruotsila puts it, "it was on the League of Nations issue that the battle between the fundamentalists and the liberal Christians was first joined in the political arena." Markku Ruotsila, "Conservative American Protestantism in the League of Nations Controversy," in *Church History*, 72:3 (September 2003), 593.

9. Arno C. Gaebelein, *The League of Nations in the Light of the Bible* (New York: Our Hope Press, 1919), 3–4.

10. Ruotsila, 595.

11. See Thomas H. Nelson, "The Real Issue in Tennessee," *Moody Monthly*, 26: 1 (September 1925), 11, and H. L. Mencken, *A Religious Orgy in Tennessee: A Reporter's Account of the Scopes Monkey Trial* (Hoboken: Melville House Publishing, 2006), 4.

12. "Amateur Dramatics at Dayton," Editorial, *Christian Century*, 42:31 (July 30, 1925), 969.

13. "Editorial Notes," *Moody Monthly*, 26:1 (September 1925), 3.

14. Acts 4:32–37 (English Standard Version).

15. "Editorial Book Review of *Our Economic Life in the Light of Christian Ideals,*" *Moody Monthly*, July 1933 (Vol. 33 No. 11), 482–483.

16. Joseph T. Larsen, "America's Sin in Forgetting God," *Moody Monthly*, July 1933 (Vol. 33, No. 11), 486.

17. Timothy Dwight, "Greenfield Hill" (New York: Childs and Swaine, 1794), 151.

18. George McCready Price, "World Civilization Nearing Its Climax," *Moody Monthly*, July 1933 (Vol. 33, No. 11), 483.

19. Tona J. Hangen, *Redeeming the Dial: Radio, Religion, and Popular Culture in America* (Chapel Hill: The University of North Carolina Press, 2002), 6, 53, 17.

20. Ibid., 17.

21. Ibid., 112–125.

22. Charles Crowe, "Religion on the Air," *Christian Century* 61:34 (August 23, 1944), 973. Fundamentalists formed the National Religious Broadcasters later that year in part in order to self-impose a code of conduct concerning donations (Hagen, 113).

23. Harold John Ockenga, "The Unvoiced Multitudes," in *Evangelical Action! A Report of the Organization of the National Association of Evangelicals for United Action* (Boston: United Action Press, 1942), 26–27.

24. Ibid., 28.

25. Ibid., 31.

26. Mel Larson, "Tasting Revival," in *Revival in Our Time: The Story of the Billy Graham Evangelistic Campaigns, Including Six of His Sermons* (Wheaton, IL: Van Kampen Press, 1950), 11–13.

27. Billy Graham, "The Home God Honors," in *Revival in Our Time*, 104.

28. Billy Graham, "We Need Revival," in *Revival in Our Time*, 71.

29. Ibid., 72.

30. Ibid., 72–73.

31. Ibid., 79.

32. "Billy Graham Answers! A Transcript of the Interview Broadcast," *Moody Monthly*, 51:6 (February 1951), 374.

33. See Fred Mitchell, "Is There Hope for China?" *Moody Monthly*, 50:12 (August 1950), 816, and James R. Graham, "Chiang Kai-shek, Communism's Consistent Foe," *Moody Monthly*, 51:10 (June 1951), 650–651.

34. Wilbur M. Smith, "The New Stamp," and The Editors, "Nation Under God," *Moody Monthly*, 54:11 (July 1954), 25, 9.

35. I Corinthians 6:14 specifically warns against comingling with nonbelievers; see Williams, 71.

36. See Noel Smith, *Baptist Bible Tribune*, June 1963.

37. Charles R. Bell, Jr. "A Southern Approach to the Color Issue," *Christian Century*, 61:32 (August 9, 1944), 923–924.

38. S. Jonathan Bass, *Blessed Are the Peacemakers: Martin Luther King Jr., Eight White Religious Leaders, and the "Letter from the Birmingham Jail"* (Baton Rouge: Louisiana State University Press, 2001), 41.

39. Ibid., 233.

40. Ibid., 95–96.

41. Ibid., 104–110.

42. Ibid., 235–236.

43. Ibid., 239, 244.

44. Ibid., 241.

45. Ibid., 33–35.

46. Ibid., 77, 84.

47. Ibid., 214–224.

48. Ibid., 252–253.

49. The only *Moody Monthly* article on race relations lengthier than a paragraph in all of 1963 and 1964, in fact, is two-page effort, "Are We Reaching the American Negro?" (December 1963, Vol. 64, No. 4), by B. M. Nottage, who advocated more aggressive evangelism to blacks, lest they "become the most godless element in the nation."

50. Quoted in Williams, *God's Own Party*, 76.

51. Darren Dochuk, *From Bible Belt to Sunbelt: Plain-Folk Religion, Grassroots Politics, and the Rise of Evangelical Conservatism* (New York: W. W. Norton, 2011), xviii.

52. Walton, 35.

53. Governor John Winthrop invoked this image, from the Gospel of Matthew, in his sermon aboard the *Arabella* in 1630, to exhort the forthcoming settlers of the Massachusetts Bay Colony to observe a covenant of grace with each other, providing a "model of Christian charity" for the world to observe. Reagan quoted the Winthrop sermon at length in 1974, in a speech to the Conservative Political Action Conference, as he advanced the contention that "our heritage does set us apart." He deployed the imagery sporadically throughout his career, including in his farewell address as president, in which he declared that the city "still stands strong and true on the granite ridge, and her glow has held steady no matter what storm. And she's still a beacon, still a magnet for all who must have freedom, for all the pilgrims from all the lost places who are hurtling through the darkness, toward home" (Ronald Reagan, Farewell Address, January 11, 1989).

54. Jerry Falwell, *Strength for the Journey*, 360.

55. A 1971 resolution from the Convention urged "Southern Baptists to work for legislation that will allow the possibility of abortion under such conditions as rape, incest, clear evidence of severe fetal deformity, and carefully ascertained evidence of the likelihood of damage to the emotional, mental, or physical health of the mother" (Williams, 115). "Debates on the timing of the entry of the soul into the fetus," wrote one doctor for *Christianity Today* in 1970, "have kept philosophers happy since before the Christian era; they seem irrelevant to the gynecologist who sees a large number of spontaneous miscarriages. The sanctity of life is a useful concept, but its biblical basis proves singularly elusive. Psychiatric opinions on the aftermath of therapeutic abortion are so divergent as to prove useless. The gynecologist can only pray that the decision in this case would be that which the Lord would have taken had he been sitting in the same chair." R. F. R. Gardner, "Christian Choices in a Liberal Abortion Climate," *Christianity Today* (Vol. XIV, No. 17, May 22, 1970), 8.

56. "Abortion and the Court" (Editorial), *Christianity Today* (Vol. XVII, No. 10, February 16, 1973).

57. Francis A. Schaeffer, *How Should We Then Live? The Rise and Decline of Western Thought and Culture* (Wheaton, IL: Crossway Books, 1976), 256.

58. Williams, 171.

59. Bill Bright, *Your Five Duties as a Christian Citizen* (Peachtree City, GA: New Life Resources, 1976).

60. Schaeffer, 105.

61. Ibid., 246.

62. Ibid., 218–219.

63. Rus Walton, *One Nation under God* (Old Tappan, NJ: Fleming H. Revell Co., 1976), 50–51.

64. Ibid., 33.

65. Williams, 133.

66. Tim LaHaye, *The Battle for the Mind* (Old Tappan, NJ: Fleming H. Revell Co., 1979), 211.

67. Williams, 164–169.

68. Ibid., 170–172.

69. Ibid., 174.

70. Ibid., 189–190.

71. Ronald Reagan, "Announcement for Presidential Candidacy," November 13, 1979, http://www.reagan.utexas.edu/archives/reference/11.13.79.html, accessed on February 25, 2013.

72. Ronald Reagan, "Address to the National Association of Evangelicals," March 8, 1983, http://voicesofdemocracy.umd.edu/reagan-evil-empire-speech-text/ accessed on February 25, 2013.

73. "About the Faith and Freedom Coalition," http://ffcoalition.com/about/, accessed on January 25, 2012.

74. Sarah A. Soule, "Going to the Chapel? Same-Sex Marriage Bans in the United States, 1973–2000," *Social Problems* (Vol. 51, No. 4, 2004), 453.

75. Alan Ehrenhalt, "A Tent Divided," *New York Times* (November 13, 2005).

76. Ryan Lizza's 2011 profile of Rep. Bachmann, a member of the Tea Party Caucus in the House of Representatives, during her run for the presidency cites the influence of Francis Schaeffer in shaping her political values. Her ideological positions consistently merge conservative Christianity to a small-government ethos, opposing federal (and even state) influence over local schools and supporting the rights of schools to display the Ten Commandments (Ryan Lizza, "Leap of Faith: The Making of a Republican Frontrunner," *The New Yorker*, August 15, 2011).

77. Robert Costa, "Ryan Shrugged," *The National Review*, April 26, 2012; Jennifer Burns, "Atlas Spurned," *New York Times*, August 14, 2012.

78. Sarah A. Soule, "Going to the Chapel? Same-Sex Marriage Bans in the United States, 1973–2000," *Social Problems* (Vol. 51, No. 4, 2004), 453.

79. Peter Sprigg, "The Top Ten Harms of Same-Sex 'Marriage,'" Issue Brief for the Family Research Council, April 2011.

80. Robert Levy, Cato's chairman, decried "an irrational and unjust system that provides significant benefits to just-married heterosexuals while denying benefits to a male or female couple who have enjoyed a loving, committed, faithful, and mutually reinforcing relationship over several decades." While a complete privatization of marriage would be preferable, he argued, equality of state benefits is the only acceptable alternative. "Gay couples are entitled to the same legal rights and the same respect and dignity accorded to all Americans" (Robert A. Levy, "The Moral and Constitutional Case for a Right to Gay Marriage," *New York Daily News*, January 7, 2010).

81. Ashley Parker, "When Opposites Influence," *New York Times*, August 18, 2010; Ken Mehlman, "Making the Same-Sex Case," *Wall Street Journal*, November 20, 2012; Sam Stein, "Cheney Offers Support for Gay Marriage," *Huffington Post*, July 2, 2009.

82. David R. Swartz, *Moral Minority: The Evangelical Left in an Age of Conservatism* (Philadelphia: University of Pennsylvania Press, 2012), 53–56.

83. Ibid., 57.

84. Ibid., 56.

85. John R. W. Stott, "Imitating the Incarnation," *Post-American*, Vol. 3, No. 9 (December 1974), 3.

86. Jim Wallis and Wes Michaelson, "The Plan to Save America: A Disclosure of an Alarming Political Initiative by the Evangelical Far Right," *Sojourners*, Vol. 5, No. 4 (April 1976).

87. Angela M. Lahr, *Millennial Dreams and Apocalyptic Nightmares: The Cold War Origins of Political Evangelicalism* (New York: Oxford University Press, 2007), 6.

88. See "Text of Barack Obama's Keynote at the Call to Renewal's Building a Covenant for a New America Conference in Washington, D.C.," *New York Times*, June 28, 2006.

89. Robert D. Putnam and David E. Campbell, *American Grace: How Religion Divides and Unites Us* (New York: Simon & Schuster, 2010), 127–128.

90. Ibid., 123.

91. Ibid., 4, 130.

92. Corwin E. Smidt, *American Evangelicals Today* (Lanham, MD: Rowman & Littlefield, 2013), 226.

93. Cal Thomas and Ed Dobson, *Blinded by Might: Can the Religious Right Save America?* (Grand Rapids: Zondervan, 1999), 21–22.

94. Ibid., 23.

Epilogue

1. Alasdair MacIntyre, *After Virtue: A Study in Moral Theory* (Notre Dame: University of Notre Dame Press, 2007), 69.

2. Stanley Hauerwas, *After Christendom? How the Church Is to Behave If Freedom, Justice, and a Christian Nation Are Bad Ideas* (Nashville: Abingdon Press, 1991), 46, 72.

3. Stanley Hauerwas, *The Peaceable Kingdom: A Primer in Christian Ethics* (Notre Dame: University of Notre Dame Press, 1983), 96–97.

4. Ibid., 100.

5. Oliver O'Donovan, *Resurrection and Moral Order: An Outline for Evangelical Ethics* (Grand Rapids: Eerdmans, 1986), 25.

6. Ibid., 228–229; Oliver O'Donovan, *The Desire of the Nations: Recovering the Roots of Political Theology* (Cambridge: Cambridge University Press, 1996), 249.

7. Joan Lockwood O'Donovan, "Natural Law and Perfect Community: Contributions of Christian Platonism to Political Theory," *Modern Theology*, V. 14, No. 1 (January 1998), 20.

8. Oliver O'Donovan, *The Desire of the Nations*, 247–248.

9. Nicholas Wolterstorff, *Justice: Rights and Wrongs* (Princeton University Press, 2008), 225.

10. Ibid., 236.

11. Ibid., 76.

12. Ibid., 225.

13. Nicholas Wolterstorff, *Hearing the Call: Liturgy, Justice, Church and World* (Grand Rapids: Eerdmans, 2011), 357.

14. Wolterstorff, *Hearing the Call*, 193.

15. David Platt, *Radical: Taking Back Your Faith from the American Dream* (Colorado Springs: Multnomah Books, 2010), 111.

16. Ronald J. Sider, *The Scandal of the Evangelical Conscience: Why Are Christians Living Just Like the Rest of the World?* (Grand Rapids: Baker Books, 2005), 22.

17. http://www.newevangelicalpartnership.org/?q=node/25, accessed on January 24, 2014.

18. Marcia Pally, *The New Evangelicals: Expanding the Vision of the Common Good* (Grand Rapids: Eerdmans Publishing Company, 2011), 13.

19. Michael Gerson, "Ron Paul's Land of Second-Rate Values," *The Washington Post*, May 9, 2011; Gerson, "Ayn Rand's Adult-Onset Adolescence," *The Washington Post*, April 21, 2011.

20. Michael Gerson, "Pope Francis the Troublemaker," *The Washington Post*, September 23, 2013.

21. Michael Gerson and Peter Wehner, *City of Man: Religion and Politics in a New Era* (Chicago: Moody Publishers, 2010), 65, 19.

22. Gerson and Wehner, 67.

23. Gerson and Wehner, 70.

INDEX